REBEL CORK'S
Fighting Story
1916 — 21

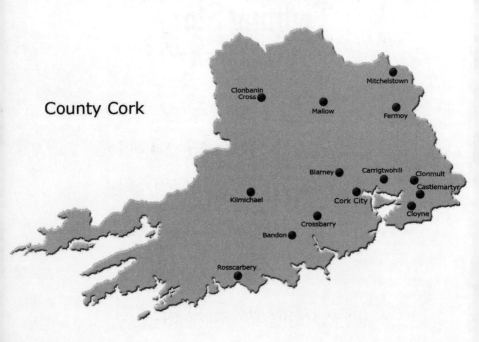

County Cork

Clonbanin Cross

Mitchelstown

Mallow

Fermoy

Blarney

Carrigtwohill

Clonmult

Castlemartyr

Kilmichael

Cork City

Cloyne

Crossbarry

Bandon

Rosscarbery

REBEL CORK'S
Fighting Story
1916 — 21

Told By The
Men Who Made It

With a Unique Pictorial Record of the Period

INTRODUCTION BY PETER HART

SERIES EDITOR: BRIAN Ó CONCHUBHAIR

MERCIER PRESS
IRISH PUBLISHER – IRISH STORY

MERCIER PRESS

Cork

www.mercierpress.ie

Originally published by *The Kerryman*, 1947

This edition published by Mercier Press, 2009

© Preface: Brian Ó Conchubhair, 2009

© Introduction: Peter Hart, 2009

© Text: Mercier Press, 2009

ISBN: 978 1 85635 644 2

10 9 8 7 6 5 4 3 2

A CIP record for this title is available from the British Library

Printed and bound in the EU.

CONTENTS

PREFACE (2009)

As we approach the centenary of the 1916 Easter Rising and the Irish War of Independence/Anglo-Irish War (1919–1921), interest among scholars and the general public in these historic events gathers unrelenting pace. Recent years have witnessed a slew of books, articles, documentaries and films, emerge at home and abroad all dealing with the events and controversies involved in the struggle for political independence in the period 1916–1922. While many of these projects have re-evaluated and challenged the standard nationalist narrative that dominated for so long, and indeed have contributed to a more nuanced and complex appreciation of the events in question, the absence of the famous *Fighting Story* series – initially published by *The Kerryman* newspaper and subsequently republished by Anvil Books – is a notable and regrettable absence. First published in Christmas and special editions of *The Kerryman* newspaper in the years before the Second World War, the articles subsequently appeared in four independent collections entitled *Rebel Cork's Fighting Story, Kerry's Fighting Story, Limerick's Fighting Story* and *Dublin's Fighting Story* between 1947–49. The choice of counties reflects the geographical intensity of the campaign as Dr Peter Hart explains in his new introduction to *Rebel Cork's Fighting Story*: 'The Munster IRA … was much more active than anywhere else except Longford, Roscommon and Dublin city.' Marketed as authentic accounts and as 'gripping episodes' by 'the men who made it', the series was dramatically described as 'more graphic than anything written of late war zones', with 'astonishing pictures'

9

and sold 'at the very moderate price of two shillings'. Benefiting from *The Kerryman*'s wide distribution network and a competitive price, the books proved immediately popular at home and abroad, so much so that many, if not most, of the books were purchased by, and for, the Irish Diaspora. This competitive price resulted in part from the fact that 'the producers were content to reduce their own profit and to produce the booklet at little above the mere cost of production'. Consequently, however, the volumes quickly disappeared from general circulation. Dr Ruán O'Donnell explains in the new introduction to *Limerick's Fighting Story*, 'The shelf life … was reduced by the poor production values they shared. This was a by-product of the stringent economies of their day when pricing, paper quality, binding and distribution costs had to be considered [which] rendered copies vulnerable to deterioration and unsuited to library utilisation.'

The books targeted not only the younger generation, who knew about those times by hearsay only, but also the older generation who 'will recall vividly a memorable era and the men who made it'. Professor Diarmaid Ferriter notes in the new introduction to *Dublin's Fighting Story* that these volumes answered the perceived need for Volunteers to record their stories in their own words, in addition to ensuring the proper education and appreciation of a new generation for their predecessors' sacrifices. The narrative, he writes 'captures the excitement and the immediacy of the Irish War of Independence and the belief that the leaders of the revolution did not urge people to take dangerous courses they were not themselves prepared to take'. These four books deserve reprinting, therefore, not only for the important factual information they contain, and the resource they offer scholars of various disciplines, but also because of the valuable window they open on the mentality of the period. As Professor J.J. Lee observes in the introduction to *Kerry's Fighting Story*, for anyone 'trying to reconstruct in very different times the historical reality of what it felt like at the time, there is no substitute for contemporary accounts, however many questions these accounts may raise. We know what was to come. Contemporaries did not.' The insight these books offer on IRA organisation at local level suggest to Dr Peter Hart 'why IRA units were so resilient under pressure, and how untrained, inexperienced men could be such formidable soldiers ... Irish guerrillas fought alongside their brothers, cousins, school and teammates, and childhood friends – often in the very lanes, fields and streets where they had spent their lives together'. In addition these texts reveal the vital roles, both active and passive, women played in the struggle of Irish independence.

The establishment of Anvil Books in 1962 saw a reissuing of certain volumes, Cork and Limerick in particular. The link between *The Kerryman* and Anvil Books was Dan Nolan (1910–1989). Son of Thomas Nolan, and nephew of Daniel Nolan and Maurice Griffin, he was related to all three founders of *The Kerryman* newspaper that commenced publishing in 1904. His obituary in that newspaper describes how he 'was only a nipper when he looked down the barrels of British guns as His Majesty's soldiers tried to arrest the proprietors of *The Kerryman* for refusing to publish recruitment advertisements. And he saw the paper and its employees being harassed by the Black and Tans.' On graduating from Castleknock College, he joined the paper's staff in 1928 replacing his recently deceased uncle, Maurice Griffin. His father's death in 1939 saw Dan Nolan become the paper's managing director and his tenure would, in due course, see a marked improvement in its commercial performance: circulation increased and ultimately exceeded 40,000 copies per week, and advertisement revenue also increased significantly. Under his stewardship *The Kerryman*, according to

Séamus McConville in an obituary in the paper, 'became solidly established as the unchallenged leader in sales and stature among provincial newspapers'. Recognising his talent, the Provincial Newspaper Association elected him president in 1951. Among his projects were the Rose of Tralee Festival, Tralee Racecourse and Anvil Books. Founded in 1962 with Nolan and Rena Dardis as co-directors, Anvil Books established itself as the pre-eminent publisher of memoirs and accounts dealing with the Irish War of Independence. Indeed the first book published by Anvil Books was a 1962 reprint of *Rebel Cork's Fighting Story* in a print run of 10,000 copies.

Conscious, no doubt, of the potential for controversy, the original foreword was careful not to present the *Fighting Stories* as 'a detailed or chronological history of the fight for independence', and acknowledged 'that in the collection of data about such a period errors and omissions can easily occur and so they will welcome the help of readers who may be able to throw more light upon the various episodes related in the series. Such additional information will be incorporated into the second edition of the booklets which the present rate of orders would seem to indicate will be called for in the very near future.' Subsequent editions of *Rebel Cork's Fighting Story* and *Limerick's Fighting Story* did appear in print with additional material as O'Donnell discusses in his enlightening introduction to *Limerick's Fighting Story*, but the proposed *Tipperary's Fighting Story*, as advertised in the Limerick volume with a suggested publication date of 1948 and a plea for relevant information or pictures, never materialised. This 2009 edition adheres to the original texts as first published by *The Kerryman* rather than the later editions by Anvil Books. A new preface, introduction and index frame the original texts that remain as first presented other than the silent correction of obvious typographical errors.

The preface to the final book, *Dublin's Fighting Story*, concluded by noting that the publishers 'would be satisfied if the series serves to preserve in the hearts of the younger generation that love of country and devotion to its interests which distinguished the men whose doings are related therein'. The overall story narrated in these four books is neither provincial nor insular, nor indeed limited to Ireland, but as Lee remarks in *Kerry's Fighting Story*, it is rather 'like that of kindred spirits elsewhere, at home and abroad, an example of the refusal of the human spirit to submit to arbitrary power'. The hasty and almost premature endings of several chapters may be attributed to the legacy of the Irish Civil War whose shadow constantly hovers at the edges, threatening to break into the narrative, and in fact does intrude in a few instances. Lee opines that writers avoided the Civil War as it 'was still too divisive, still too harrowing, a nightmare to be recalled into public memory. Hence the somewhat abrupt ending of several chapters at a moment when hopes were still high and the horrors to come yet unimagined.'

Ireland at the start of the twenty-first century is a very different place than it was when these books were first published. Irish historiography has undergone no less a transformation and to bridge the gap four eminent historians have written new introductions that set the four *Fighting Stories* in the context of recent research and shifts in Irish historiography. Yet Lee's assessment in reference to Kerry holds true for each of the four volumes: 'Whatever would happen subsequently, and however perspectives would inevitably be affected by hindsight, for better and for worse, *Kerry's Fighting Story* lays the foundation for all subsequent studies of these foundation years of an independent Irish state.' As we move toward the centenary of 1916, the War of Independence, the Anglo-Irish Treaty and the Civil War, it is appropriate and fitting that these key texts be once again part of the public debate of those events and it is sincerely hoped that as Ruán O'Donnell states: 'This new life of a classic of its genre will facilitate a fresh evaluation of its unique perspectives on the genesis of the modern Irish state.'

Dr Brian Ó Conchubhair
Series Editor
University of Notre Dame
Easter 2009

ACKNOWLEDGEMENTS

I AM GRATEFUL not only to these scholars who penned the new introductions for their time and expertise, but also to the following who assisted in numerous ways: Beth Bland, Angela Carothers, Aedín Ní Bhroithe-Clements (Hesburgh Library), Rena Dardis, Ken Garcia, Dr Peter Hart, Alan Hayes, Dyann Mawhorr, Don and Patrica Nolan, Tara MacLeod, Seán Seosamh Ó Conchubhair, Professor Diarmuid Ó Giolláin, Professor Nollaig Ó Muraile, Interlibrary Loans at the Hesburgh Library, University of Notre Dame, and Eoin Purcell, Wendy Logue and the staff at Mercier Press. Táim an-bhuíoch do gach éinne atá luaite thuas, m'athair ach go háirithe as a chuid foighne agus as a chuid saineolais a roinnt liom go fial agus do Thara uair amháin eile a d'fhulaing go foighneach agus an obair seo ar bun agam.

DR BRIAN Ó CONCHUBHAIR

INTRODUCTION (2009)

IN THE YEARS before 1916, Cork saw a lot of political violence, but it was fighting between rival nationalist parties – 'Mollies' versus 'All For Irelanders' – not against the government. When a rebellion did take place, in 1916, Cork's Easter Rising was confined to a single family and home, the Kents of Bawnard House. The year ended with a by-election in West Cork in December, more faction-fighting and a victory by the Irish Parliamentary Party (IPP). With its leaders in jail and most of its arms surrendered, the story of the Irish Volunteers in the rebel city and county might well have ended there, in a crippling failure of organisation and nerve. But Tomás MacCurtain and Terence MacSwiney are not remembered as the men who gave up without a shot while Dublin burned, and West Cork is not known to history as a hotbed of moderation. Instead, Cork emerged in the years after 1916 as the heartland of the republican revolution, and its Irish Republican Army (IRA) brigades gained a reputation as the most powerful and deadly guerrilla force in Ireland. So, what accounts for this extraordinary change? Who was the Cork IRA? What made them such an effective force? What sort of war did they fight? And what were the consequences of their violence?

WHY CORK?

BETWEEN THE EASTER Rising and 11 July 1921 Truce, over five hundred people were killed in Cork by bullets or bombs, and another five hundred-plus were wounded. These numbers make the county by far the most violent place in Ireland in this period. And, since the IRA was responsible for about 60 per cent of these casualties, Cork's guerrillas were by a wide margin the most violent in Ireland, accounting for nearly one in three of all IRA victims. Bandon district alone – the Fallujah of the Irish resistance – produced over ten times as many casualties as the whole of County Antrim, and was well over a hundred times as violent per capita. Moreover, it was the boys of the whole of County Cork who did the fighting. Contrary to some local beliefs, the West Cork brigade was not much more successful than their comrades in Mid- or North Cork, or in the city, nor did they suffer more. Each brigade – and often each battalion – had its strong and weak points, victories and defeats. It was not just the boys of Cork, either. The Munster IRA as a whole was much more active than anywhere else except Longford, Roscommon and Dublin city. So to ask 'why Cork?' is also to ask: why Munster? One answer is that the Volunteers in the south started taking on the Royal Irish Constabulary (RIC) much earlier than anywhere else. By the autumn of 1918 and the winter of 1919, militants throughout the province were gearing up for war. The famous Soloheadbeg ambush in Tipperary in January 1919 was just one episode in this process: as early as March 1918, the Eyeries RIC barracks was raided for arms, and in July 1918, the Ballyvourney Volunteers ambushed two constables, shooting one and beating the other senseless according to the police report. In other words, the south had a head start.

What also set Cork and its neighbours apart was that it wasn't just armed Volunteers doing the fighting. They were also backed by an enthusiastic (and angry) popular movement. Through 1916, 1917, 1918 and 1919, policemen and soldiers in Munster faced far more confrontational crowds than elsewhere, and riots became commonplace. There were also fights between Irish Parliamentary Party supporters and the zealous young converts to Sinn Féin. Militancy was not just found in the ranks of the IRA, and not just among men either, as many Sinn Féiners and rioters were women. One of the first republicans to be arrested in Cork city was Teresa O'Donovan, who broke her umbrella over a policeman's head in April 1917. Where did this militancy come from? In part, it drew on a heritage of struggle over rents and the ownership of land between farmers and landlords (backed by the government), particularly in the Land War and Plan of Campaign in the 1880s. This struggle had been the previous generation's rebellion, and nowhere were these battles fought harder than in Cork. Also important in determining whether a community would produce strong IRA units was its support for patriotic education. If we map Christian Brothers' schools and Irish classes taught in national schools across Ireland, we find that both were good predictors of revolutionary violence – and both were relatively plentiful in Cork.

WHO WERE THE IRA?

To UNDERSTAND THE IRA, however, we must also ask who they were. All Cork Volunteers were men, almost all (at least 99 per cent) were Catholic and most were young (over three-quarters under thirty). They came from a broad range of backgrounds. About a third or so in units outside Cork city worked on farms, most as sons assisting their parents, the rest as labourers or servants. The majority had other trades and occupations, in offices, shops, mills, creameries, garages and elsewhere. Skilled apprentices and journeymen played a large role in the movement, just as they had with the Fenians fifty years before, and this was particularly true in the city. In general, IRA men tended to be better employed, more skilled and more upwardly mobile than both their peers and their fathers, and this lent a hard-working, self-improving, aspirational spirit to grass-roots republicanism. In this sense, they embodied the New Ireland they were fighting for.

As many as 20,000 men (out of a total population of nearly 400,000 people) may have joined the Cork IRA prior to the July 1921 Truce – or at least claimed to have done so afterwards. Many were purely nominal or very temporary members who at most attended a few drills during the 1918 conscription crisis. IRA records distinguished between these paper soldiers, 'reliable' men who would at least show up for company parades, and 'active' men who could be counted on for actual operations. Of the over one thousand men on the official rolls of the Bandon battalion, for example, fewer than five hundred were on the books in July 1919, of whom less than three hundred were deemed 'active'. By the spring of 1921, at the height of the guerrilla war, only two hundred and thirty of these were even considered 'reliable'. Some of this attrition was due to imprisonment or death, but the majority of inactivists just dropped out or faded away, at least until the Truce. They shouldn't be branded cowardly or unpatriotic, though. Some – especially farmers' sons – had to support a family and others had real moral objections to the kind of war the IRA was fighting. They hadn't signed up to ambush policemen or raid people's houses.

Why did they join? It wasn't political or cultural indoctrination: for most young men the Volunteers was the first organisation they had joined. In fact, they often embraced the whole movement all at once, with Sinn Féin and the Gaelic League as part of the package. Nor were any new ideas required, as combative nationalism and suspicion of the British state were deeply ingrained parts of Irish political culture. Most veterans don't seem to recall the decision to join as being all that memorable or difficult: it was the obvious thing to do at the time, in much the same way as young patriots all over Europe had flocked to their nation's colours in 1914. For those who were committed to both the ends and the means of armed struggle, though, that commitment could assume an often mystical intensity, and the movement became a way of life. This quasi-religious identification with the cause often drew on the example of the Easter Rising, and on the experience of attending Requiem Masses for its martyrs in the summer of 1916. One such convert was Liam Lynch, at the time a hardware clerk in Fermoy. He saw the Kents of Bawnard House being brought as prisoners through the streets in May 1916, and thereafter dropped his allegiance to the Irish Parliamentary Party and many of his former friends, and fervently embraced republicanism. Never a natural leader or fighter, he made himself both by sheer force of will and ended up commanding the North Cork brigade, the 1st Southern Division, and ultimately the whole (anti-Treaty) IRA. Such people gave the movement its evangelical edge, but they weren't typical. Perhaps the most important factor in determining who joined or who would fight was not what you believed but who you knew. Volunteer companies were self-created on local initiative and officers were elected. Inevitably, they were formed around already existing social networks, in workplaces, neighbourhoods, on sports teams and among friends and family. Strong bands of republican co-workers could be found in the Haulbowline shipyards, the Passage dockyards, the Clondulane and Blarney mills, and most numerously, in the new Ford tractor and car plant.

Neighbourhood and family were inextricably bound together. Of the members of the Macroom battalion who can be traced in the 1911 census, half had at least one brother in the same company, and much the same result can be found in other rural units. Even in

Cork city, where young men were less likely to live with parents, well over a third of those whose names and exact addresses are known were family or next-door neighbours. In other words, people didn't usually join the Volunteers as individuals, they joined as part of a tightly-knit group who already knew each other well. If you weren't part of such an in-group, however, you probably found yourself on the fringes, or on the outside. This also helps explain why IRA units were so resilient under pressure, and how untrained, inexperienced men could be such formidable soldiers. Just as men in conventional armies might fight for their comrades rather than their country, Irish guerrillas fought alongside their brothers, cousins, school- and team-mates, and childhood friends – often in the very lanes, fields and streets where they had spent their lives together. For the most part, then, people didn't join the Volunteers because they were radicals. They became radicalised (or republicanised) because they joined the Volunteers.

In 1917 and 1918, drilling, marching, attending meetings, electioneering, collecting money or flying the tri-colour were all potentially illegal activities, leading to numerous clashes with the police, arrests and imprisonment. This in turn led to prison protests, including hunger strikes, which often led in turn to early releases, a heightened sense of revolutionary momentum and further confrontations with the authorities. Young men were taken away from home, often for the first time, and brought together with other activists from all over the country. Many spent more than one stretch in prison: some were in and out three or four times before the Truce.

In many ways, going back to the months after the Easter Rising, the IRA as it emerged in 1919 and 1920 was forged in British and Irish prisons. Corkmen were to the fore in the greatest of the hunger strikes, in the spring of 1920 and again that autumn. The former, which lasted twenty-three days, ended in a stunning victory over Dublin Castle, as hundreds of men were released on parole, over a hundred of whom came from Cork. These were the backbone of the flying columns formed later that year: nine of the men at the Kilmichael ambush were veterans of this strike. The reorganised British administration would not be so weak again, however. When Cork Volunteers started a new protest in August, the government refused to give in. Mick Fitzgerald and Joseph Murphy and, most famously, Terence MacSwiney, died from starvation in October 1920 before the strike was called off, thereby saving the lives of the remaining protesters in Cork jail.

THE IRA'S WAR

THE IRISH VOLUNTEERS didn't start out as an underground army and they weren't designed to fight a revolutionary war. Their original purpose was defensive: to uphold the Irish claim to self-government and protect national rights against unionist (both British and Irish) belligerence and Liberal backsliding. This held true after the 1914 split over participation in the Great War, and it still remained the case after the Easter Rising, as many (most?) of the new recruits in 1917 and 1918 joined to protest British policy, to support Sinn Féin, and – perhaps most important of all – to avoid or resist conscription. The latter threat doubled the size of most units almost overnight: the Clonakilty company, for example, went from forty to one hundred and fifty members in the spring of 1918. The Volunteers were initially neither armed nor illegal, and most of their early campaigns were designed to confront restrictions on assembly and display and to attract publicity. New companies were still announcing their formation in the *Cork Examiner* as late as March

1918. When conscription did finally become an imminent threat, in April 1918, Volunteer planning envisioned a second rising, only this time on a truly national scale. In each parish and town, local companies would seize public buildings, block roads and rail lines, and attack local police barracks: quite the opposite of a clandestine guerrilla war. The prospect of such an onslaught terrified the RIC, forced the government to stay its hand and ultimately proved that the strategy of using the Volunteers as a deterrent, and as a tool for mobilising public opinion, was at least as effective as that of 1916-style open war. Nevertheless, war was what a militant minority within the Volunteers wanted, and many of them were organised as a secret revolutionary force, in the form of the Irish Republican Brotherhood (IRB). The IRB had used the movement as its vehicle to launch the 1916 Easter Rising, and it too had reorganised, and was once again in a dominant position within the Volunteers by the end of 1918. The 'IRA' as it emerged in 1919 – a leaner, tougher, secret army – represented a kind of fusion between the two.

Of course, people didn't need to belong to a secret society to be republicans or revolutionaries, and many who were, such as Tomás MacCurtain and Terence MacSwiney, didn't necessarily like the idea of a secret war. However, 1916 – both its triumphs and its embarrassments – helped produce an aggressive new mindset among a network of key activists. Weapons must never again be surrendered; the authorities must always be resisted; revolution was too important to be left to the politicians. British repression also had a radicalising impact, as people who faced truncheons and guns, or raids on their homes, or the prospect of prison, often lost initial scruples. The fear of conscription created a demand for arms, which led to widespread arms raids on private homes and on policemen and soldiers. As a result, between 1917 and 1919, the IRA shot thirteen policemen, seven soldiers and four civilians, while losing six dead and seven wounded themselves. Many of these casualties were unintended, the result of raids or ambushes gone wrong. The police also shot another twelve non-Volunteers, and beat up many, many others, mostly during riots (where IRA guns also began to appear in 1918 and 1919). It would be hard to say when a 'war' as such broke out in Cork, but one killing stands out: that of Constable Edward Bolger on Sunday 14 December, 1919, in the IRA stronghold of Kilbrittain. This was the first deliberate assassination of a policeman in the county, and it was a determined one: the gunmen shot him several times after he had fallen to make sure he was dead. Bolger had been a zealous enemy of the local Volunteers, seven of whom had been released from prison that Friday.

This is a book of 'fighting stories', and there were plenty of fights to follow in 1920 and 1921. Most people who were killed in Cork in those years, however, did not die in combat. A third were civilians: more than one hundred killed by the IRA, mostly as suspected spies or informers, and over fifty by the RIC (now including Black and Tans and Auxiliaries) and army, mostly as suspected rebels. In thirty-odd cases, we don't know who killed them, and there are other people who just disappeared. Even when guerrillas, soldiers and policemen shot one another, it wasn't usually a fight as such. If we define 'combat' as what happens when armed groups encounter one another, then most of the war's combatants who died, did so unarmed, helpless or alone. In this regard, British forces were much more murderous than the IRA, as less than half of the nearly two hundred Volunteers casualties in 1920–21 occurred in battle. The rest were shot 'attempting to escape', 'resisting arrest' or the like. Through 1920, the IRA were far more chivalrous, and only one in four of their targets were gunned down like Constable Bolger. That summer and autumn were the heyday of the flying columns, culminating in the devastating ambush at Kilmichael in

November 1920 that knocked a whole Auxiliary company out of action.

After Kilmichael came martial law, however, and a new British military offensive. The flying columns went from being the hunters to the hunted, and February 1921 brought Kilmichael in reverse: the destruction of the previously unbeatable East Cork column at Clonmult. Ambushes continued, but grew more dangerous and less successful, with fewer arms captured and fewer policemen and soldiers killed. In 1921, the IRA and British forces had exactly the same record when it came to killing each other outside combat, while violence as a whole continued to escalate. It was terror and counter-terror, tit-for-tat, with ordinary people bearing an increasing share of the suffering.

British officers would look back on the Truce of 11 July 1921 as a missed opportunity, claiming that they had the IRA on the run. This was not true. The secret army had regrouped after its winter setbacks and was capable of waging a long war yet. Nevertheless, the kind of war it was becoming was only a foretaste of what might have happened if no truce had been declared, as both sides intended to unleash violence far beyond anything previously employed. As it was, though, the IRA had survived intact and was able to re-emerge from the shadows more popular and powerful than ever, victorious in the eyes of their supporters. For a few months that summer, anything seemed possible and the Republic appeared to have been won.

Dr Peter Hart
Memorial University
Newfoundland
March 2009

FOREWORD

ALMOST THIRTY YEARS ago a small body of men engaged in combat with the armed forces of an empire. Militarily they were weak. Their strength lay in their faith in their cause and in the unflinching support of a civilian population which refused to be cowed by threats or by violence.

For almost two years these men successfully maintained the unequal struggle and finally compelled their powerful adversary to seek a truce. The battles in which they fought were neither large nor spectacular: they were the little clashes of guerrilla warfare – the sudden meeting, the flash of guns, a getaway, or the long wait of an ambush, then the explosive action, and death or a successful decision. And the stake at issue was the destiny of an ancient people.

Before the war years imposed a restriction upon newsprint, as upon other commodities, *The Kerryman*, in its various Christmas and other special numbers, told much of the story of these men, the men of the flying columns, the active service units of the Irish Republican Army. It now gathers these stories into book form together with others hitherto unpublished.

All the stories in these *Fighting Series* booklets are either told by the men who took part in the actions described, or else they are written from the personal narrative of survivors. The booklets do not purport to be a detailed or chronological history of the fight for independence, but every effort has been made to obtain the fullest and most accurate information about the incidents described. The publishers are conscious, however, that in the collection of data about such a period errors and omissions can easily occur and so they will welcome the help of readers who may be able to throw more light upon the various episodes related in the series. Such additional information will be incorporated into the second edition of the booklets which the present rate of orders would seem to indicate will be called for in the very near future. It is also pointed out that *Rebel Cork's Fighting Story* deals exclusively with events which took place inside the county boundary. It would require another volume to recount the part taken in the fight for freedom by Cork men operating in other sectors of the country.

The publishers believe that the younger generation who know about those times by hearsay only will find these survivors' tales of the fight of absorbing interest, while to the older generation they will recall vividly a memorable era and the men who made it. In short, they feel that *Fighting Story* series, the story of the Anglo-Irish War county by county, is a series that will be welcomed by Irish people everywhere. For that reason, so that the booklets may have the widest possible circulation, they are being sold at a price within the reach of everyone. To sell these booklets, with their lavish collection of illustrations of unique historical interest, at the very moderate price of two shillings, the publishers were content to reduce their own profit and to produce the booklet at little above the mere cost of production. They will be satisfied if the series serves to preserve in the hearts of the younger generation that love of country and devotion to its interests which distinguished the men whose doings are related therein.

The Editor

THE CORK CITY VOLUNTEERS

by SHANDON

THE ORGANISATION AND activities of the Irish Volunteers and the IRA in Cork city were so intimately related to the general development of these bodies in the county that it is difficult to treat them separately. From the very earliest days of the movement the Cork leaders visualised and worked for the outspreading of the organisation to every part of the county. In this they were successful, and to this work they devoted much time and energy, so that when the final stages of the struggle were reached, Cork city was represented in Cork No. 1 brigade by two battalions, an active service unit operating in the city and a special intelligence section. These units operated as an integral part of the brigade and, except for the fact that brigade headquarters was in the city and that enemy disposition and tactics imposed the necessity for a different type of warfare, the city battalions were not very different to the other eight battalions in the brigade. There was close co-operation between city and county; the city battalions contributed their quota of men and arms to the brigade column when it was established. The position was very different to that in Dublin where the whole city area formed a brigade.

Pearse said in 1915 that there was nothing more terrible in Irish history than the failure of the last generation. The United Irishmen had failed in 1798, Emmet in 1803, the Young Irelanders in 1848 and the Fenians in 1867. But they had failed nobly and had left a tradition of armed resistance which appeared to be submerged and forgotten by the generation of which Pearse spoke. For the first time in the long history of our struggle for freedom a recognised Irish leader was prepared to accept on behalf of the nation, and as a final settlement of our claims, something far less than that complete separation from England which had been the historic claim of previous generations.

That a movement in the historic tradition for the achievement of freedom by force of arms emerged at all is due primarily to the unobtrusive existence in these dead years of the Irish Republican Brotherhood. They believed that freedom could not be achieved or defended without the ability to vindicate it in arms, and they kept their purpose steadily in mind while they nursed their numerically weak organisation and waited for conditions which would make possible the development of a widespread physical force movement. The IRB was a secret oath-bound society, pledged to the achievement of an Irish Republic by force of arms. Though small in numbers it was selective, widespread and circumspect; it had men in many other organisations and its influence, though never open, was far greater than its numbers would appear to indicate. It watched, it advised through its members, but it took no active lead anywhere openly. The secret of its strength lay in the fact that in a time of confused vision and decadent leadership in national affairs it knew its own mind and it had a definite policy. The IRB had a small number in Cork city, and when the opportunity of arming Irishmen for national defence came in 1913, they took a leading and decisive part in the foundation of the Volunteers and in the development of their policy. The essential non-party basis of the movement was something entirely new and novel in the Ireland of that day. Cork, because of the bitter partisan rivalry between the Redmondite and

O'Brienite factions, presented the Volunteer leaders with a problem more difficult of solution than the same one elsewhere, and it is a tribute to the patriotic and prudent leadership of men like Tomás MacCurtain, Terence MacSwiney and Seán O'Hegarty that their own higher conception of national service impressed itself on the general body and laid the firm foundations of the steadfast organisation that withstood the battle ordeal of the active years.

When the split came in 1914, Cork city had 2,000 men organised in two battalions. All except a handful – fewer than fifty – elected to follow Redmond, and the work of the previous ten months was in ruins. But, in striking contrast to their opponents, the minority had a clear-cut policy. They had faith in themselves and in their cause, and they set to work again undaunted. In time Cork came to see that they were right, and public opinion swung slowly back in their favour. In a year, so much progress had been made that the two city battalions were reorganised, weaker than before but steadily developing; control by company, battalion and brigade councils had been established in contrast to the committee system of earlier days, and a large hall had been taken over in Sheares Street.

The Cork men, like most of the rest of the country, were confused and misled by the number of contradictory orders in 1916, and their planned contribution to the insurrection did not materialise. It is a complicated story, all the facts of which have not yet been published. A subsequent inquiry absolved the Cork leaders from any blame. They were arrested and interned until the Christmas of 1916. The insurrection had brought a great awakening, an imperative call to the Irish people to rally again to the cause. Francis Ledwidge, writing his haunting elegy for Thomas MacDonagh in the mud and misery of a Flanders' trench, is but one example of its wide appeal. When the leaders began to reorganise in 1917, a new spirit was stirring in the people, and amongst the Volunteers its keynote was a determination to renew the conflict which had gone down in fire and death in Dublin. In a loose but effective way in this and the following year the whole of nationalist Cork organised itself for the struggle. The Volunteers, Fianna Éireann, Cumann na mBan, Sinn Féin, the Prisoner's Dependants' fund and the National Aid Association provided scope for the activities of all, young and old, men and women. Leadership, by right and of necessity, was in the hands of the Volunteers, and with them the other bodies worked in close and generally amicable co-operation.

During 1917 organisation was steadily improved, public feeling hardened; there were frequent arrests and hunger strikes, and occasional clashes with armed police in the streets. Raids by police and military on halls and houses used by the various national organisations, and the forcible closing of the Volunteer Hall in Sheares Street by the military authorities, gave an indication of the reactions of the crown forces to the growing strength of republicanism. Public parades in uniform of the two city battalions were held in November and were followed by more arrests. The main efforts of the city battalions were concentrated on training and on procuring arms. A very successful raid, one of the first of its kind in Ireland, was carried out by the 1st battalion on the Cork grammar school, which was being used by the British military for training purposes. A number of rifles and some equipment were secured. In September, a Royal Irish Constabulary sergeant who attempted to hold up and question an armed Volunteer officer was fired on and wounded.

The year 1918 brought an intensification of the clashes between police and military and civilians in the streets. Rarely were Volunteers involved in these clashes; they were steadily and in a disciplined way perfecting their training and adding to their store of arms. Arms were purchased from soldiers or anywhere they could be procured, and there were a few cases of soldiers being disarmed. In November, a Cork Volunteer officer set a fine example to the whole force by his spirited action in defence of his arms in a police raid. Donncadh MacNeilus opened fire on the police who attempted to search his lodgings for arms, and a head constable was seriously wounded. After a fierce struggle with five other policemen, MacNeilus was overpowered and taken to Cork jail. His rescue from under the noses of the military guard in that fortress on 11 November created a sensation at the time. It was planned by the brigade staff and carried out brilliantly by men of the 1st and 2nd battalions. In 1918 also the brigade devised an elaborate and safe communications system by cyclist dispatch riders to every battalion headquarters in the county. Eight routes radiated from the city, one of them reaching to Castletownbere, and the first stages of all these routes were operated by officers and men of a special cyclist company attached to brigade headquarters. They had been drawn from the two city battalions.

During 1919 there took place considerable progress in training, an intensified effort to get arms, and the development of special services. Halls were no longer available for training, which consequently was carried out mainly in the country districts immediately outside the city most convenient to the various companies. It was a better type of training than could have been done indoors by way of close order drill and lectures, and, as every parade was open to the possibility of a raid by the enemy, the training developed alertness and a sense of the need for security measures.

The special services organised included, in addition to communications mentioned above, engineering, intelligence, signals, transport and medical.

The effort to get arms led to the planning of what would have been the largest operation undertaken by the city battalions up to that time if it had come off. An aerodrome in the course of construction for American forces at Ballyquirk, near Killeagh, eighteen miles from Cork, was guarded by a party of British troops. It was planned to raid it early in July and seize the arms. It was realised that the operation would probably involve fighting, and the 4th battalion, in whose area Ballyquirk was situated, had not sufficient arms to undertake the job single-handed. The two city battalions co-operated by sending out men and arms. The operation was under the control of Terence MacSwiney, brigade vice-commandant. The time of the attack had been set for midnight, and he and other city officers set out from the city in a car, taking with them all the available rifles in the city battalions. Other officers and men had gone ahead on bicycles. Unfortunately the car broke down, and MacSwiney and his party did not reach Ballyquirk until 4 a.m., by which time most of the city and local men had dispersed.

Towards the end of 1919, the demand for action was coming more and more insistently from the companies and battalions. There was a high standard of discipline, and sanction was sought from GHQ, first for the carrying out of simultaneous attacks on police patrols in the city, and later for attacks on police barracks. The proposal for the city operation was turned down flat by GHQ, although it could certainly have been carried out and would have netted the city battalions about a hundred .45 revolvers and a fair quantity of ammunition. It was only at the end the year, and after the brigade commandant, Tomás MacCurtain, had spent a considerable time in Dublin pressing it, that sanction was given for attacks on a limited number of police barracks.

Early in 1920 the active campaign became, in a limited way, a matter of GHQ policy. The brigade felt it could go ahead without referring every specific proposal for GHQ sanction, and the greatly increased activity of 1920 and 1921 was a reflection of the situation that operations were limited only by available arms and opportunities. There never was any shortage of men; the two city battalions could muster 2,000 men at this time; but it was of course impossible either to arm all of them or to utilise any substantial number of them in operations. The intelligence service had become well organised, and its activities resulted in the execution in February of the spy, Quinlisk, who had got some distance with his plan to betray Michael Collins. Attacks on police patrols became frequent. There were two in March, in one of which a policeman was killed. In May two policemen were killed and another wounded in an attack on the Lower Road. Evacuated Royal Irish Constabulary barracks and income tax offices were burned, sniping and bomb attacks were maintained on the occupied barracks and military cars, motor-cycles and mails were seized.

The murder by the crown forces of the brigade commandant, Tomás MacCurtain, in March, was a severe blow, but it steeled the determination of every Volunteer to destroy or drive out forever the ruthless instruments of that foul policy. Terence MacSwiney became commandant, Seán O'Hegarty vice-commandant and Dan Donovan O/C 1st battalion. Mick Murphy was O/C 2nd battalion. In June the two city battalions were turned out in strength to co-operate with the 6th battalion in the attack on Blarney Royal Irish Constabulary barracks. In July King Street Royal Irish Constabulary barracks was attacked and destroyed in daylight, and in August city men carried out an ambush on military lorries at White's Cross, near the city. In July, also, Divisional Commissioner Smyth, who had shortly before made his infamous proposals to the Royal Irish Constabulary at Listowel, was shot dead in the County Club. In the following month DI Swanzy, who had been in charge of the police district in which Tomás MacCurtain was murdered, and who had been hurriedly and secretly transferred after it, was traced to Lisburn and there executed by men from the city battalions. In October Terence MacSwiney died on hunger strike in Brixton. At the end of the previous month an attempt had been made to capture General Strickland, commanding the British 6th division with headquarters at Cork, but the attempt failed. It was intended to hold him as hostage for MacSwiney. A very tense atmosphere had developed in the city; attacks on crown forces were almost continuous, both in daylight and during curfew hours. Three British intelligence officers were captured and shot at Waterfall, near the city; a number of civilians organised into a spy ring by the British military authorities were executed. In December, the 1st battalion carried out an attack on two lorries of Auxiliaries at Dillon's Cross and, on the same night, these forces, assisted by the military, fired and destroyed the centre of the city.

A city active service unit and a special intelligence section, both composed of whole-time men from the city battalions, had been organised, and in 1921, they developed a whole series of attacks on enemy police and military. As well as the daylight attacks, curfew patrols came in for a good deal of attention at night, so that the enemy was given no rest, and these attacks were continued right down to the Truce. In the face of great difficulties and dangers, with limited armament and opposed to forces far superior in numbers and equipment, the city men had settled down in grim determination to wage the conflict to the bitter end. They had suffered losses through death and wounds and arrests; they were fighting under conditions even more searching than those under which their fellow soldiers in the country columns fought. It is a tribute to their patriotic fighting spirit that, when the end came, their morale was never higher. They had played a worthy part in the historic fight for freedom.

In a short article it is not possible to do justice to all the varied aspects of that conflict, even in one city, and the foregoing falls short of an exhaustive list of the activities of the Cork City battalions. It is hoped that some day it will be recorded with the completeness it has so well deserved.

RESCUE OF MacNEILUS FROM CORK JAIL

by F. O'DONOGHUE

THE ESCAPES OF the Irish political prisoners from English jails in this country and abroad are a part of the thrilling story of the nation's long struggle for freedom. Some, like the rescue of the 1848 prisoners from English convict settlements, were accomplished after long and careful preparations and with the co-operation and assistance of the prisoners themselves; others, like the rescue of Colonel Tom Kelly and Captain T. Deasy at Manchester, were successful and tragic for the rescuers, but called forth that noble spirit of self-sacrifice in the interests of a comrade which caused the names of the Manchester martyrs to be remembered forever in song and story. In the more recent phase of the nation's struggle from 1916 onwards, there is scarcely a jail or fortress in the country from which some Irishman, held there for his part in the fight for liberty, has not escaped or been rescued. Among these, one of the earliest and most successful was the rescue of Donncadh MacNeilus from Cork jail on 11 November 1918. It was, perhaps, unique in this, that it was planned and carried out entirely from outside, and without any assistance from inside the prison.

Donncadh MacNeilus was a Volunteer officer who was attached

to the Cork brigade since he had come from his native Donegal. On the morning of 4 November 1918, five men of the Royal Irish Constabulary, one of them armed with a .38 Webley revolver, raided his lodgings and attempted to arrest him. He was armed and resisted arrest. In the desperate struggle which followed, Head Constable Clarke was very seriously wounded and it was only on the arrival of reinforcements with carbines and in charge of a district inspector that MacNeilus was finally overpowered. When the news spread it was realised, not alone by his comrades in Cork, but in every part of Ireland where Volunteers were armed, that a lead had been given in armed resistance to capture at a time when such a lead was needed. The armed might of the British army of occupation was then in search of evidence everywhere that many doubted the wisdom or feasibility of challenging it in arms. Nevertheless, the militant spirit of the Volunteers was growing steadily with the growth of their organisation and their proficiency in the use of arms; and this valiant defence of his liberty and his arms by one man, alone and against superior numbers, set a standard for his comrades, and put the respective positions of the Volunteers and the British army of occupation again in their proper perspective. The wounded head constable was in danger of death, and if he died the fate of MacNeilus was inevitable – unless a rescue could be effected.

The prisoner had been taken to Cork jail, unhurt except for some minor scratches. With him was arrested Denis Kelliher, in whose house at 28 Leitrim Street the fight took place and who had gone to the assistance of MacNeilus in resisting the raiding party.

One thought was uppermost in the minds of his comrades from the moment of his arrest – he should be rescued! But when they came to consider how the attempt was to be made they were faced with the situation that they knew practically nothing of the position inside the prison, except that there was an armed military guard always on duty; they knew nothing about the supervision of visits to prisoners or the internal organisation of prison. The Volunteers had no contact with any person in or employed in Cork jail. They started from scratch, and in six days completed their arrangements and brought them to a successful issue. The operation was a good example of that careful attention to detail in planning and audacity in action which were features of so many subsequent Volunteer operations and which contributed largely to their success. On the night of 4 November, a hastily summoned meeting of the available members of the brigade council was held at the house of the acting brigade commandant, who was in charge of the operation. The available information amounted only to this: that the wounded head constable was in danger of death, and that untried prisoners were allowed one visit of ten minutes duration each day between 10 a.m. and 11 a.m. or between 3 p.m. and 4 p.m. Two visitors were allowed in together, and no visits were allowed on Sundays. It was decided to send Florrie O'Donoghue on a visit to MacNeilus on the following morning, in the course of which he was to observe the disposition of the guards, the method of supervising the admission of visitors and interviews, the nature of the gates and locks, and any other details that might be useful. He was, if possible, to suggest a plan for the rescue, and convey to MacNeilus that the effort would be made. Owing to the vigilance of the warders on duty he was unable to convey the message at the first visit, but he did so on the following day, when he again visited the prisoner accompanied by Rev. Fr MacNeilus – the prisoner's brother.

The prison is surrounded by a high wall, standing clear of the buildings within. The entrance is closed on the outside by a pair of heavy iron-bound doors, in one of which is a small wicket. The outer doors give access to a small space closed on the inner side by a pair of heavy wrought-iron gates, extending the full height of the archway. Opening off the space between the two gates, and to the left, is the visitors' waiting-room, in which a warder is always on duty. Not more than six persons were allowed in the waiting-room at the same time. The visiting cell was situated near the centre of the prison and was approached from the main gate by a path running inside the outer wall, and past the main gate into the prison buildings at which the military sentry was on duty. These circumstances governed the decision as to the choice of plan for the rescue, and when the council had considered them the plan was quickly decided upon.

Then began a systematic consideration of every minute detail, a close examination of every point at which the plan might break down or miscarry. A time schedule was decided upon, because the success of the plan depended to a great extent upon synchronising the movements and the actions of two, and possibly three, pairs of ostensible visitors and a group of Volunteers acting outside the prison without any means of knowing what was happening inside. MacNeilus himself should receive two visitors on the afternoon of the day decided upon; any proposed visits by friends of his on that day should be prevented without occasioning comment, and two other prisoners had to be got to reserve visits for the afternoon of the same day. Seán Scanlan visited MacNeilus on the Wednesday, and in shaking hands with him across the barrier managed to pass a small note – 'Be prepared for anything' – and said 'Friday'. The rescue was first planned for Friday 9 November, but owing to arrangements not being complete it was postponed to Monday 11 November [sic]. O'Donoghue made another visit on Thursday to convey the change of date, and check up the proposed plan against the prison routine.

Then came the afternoon of Monday 11 November. At 3.25 p.m. two Volunteers, Joe Murphy and Martin Donovan, presented themselves at the prison gate and asked to see MacNeilus. They were admitted through the wicket to the waiting-room and the gate locked behind them. Their request was telephoned to the main prison buildings by the warder on duty, and they sat down to wait. Five minutes after the first pair had been admitted a second pair of Volunteers, Christy MacSweeney and Paddy Healy, presented themselves at the main gate and asked to visit a prisoner from Tipperary whose name they had. They were admitted to the waiting-room. Three minutes later a third pair of Volunteers, Frank McCarthy and Jerome Donovan, walked up to the main gate, asked for another prisoner and were admitted. So far all was well and according to plan – there were no other visitors. If four only out of the six had succeeded in getting in, the plan would have gone on. It was all the better that the whole six had got inside. One of the Volunteers was in clerical attire in order to allay possible suspicion.

Meanwhile the remainder of the rescue party took up their allotted positions in the neighbourhood of the prison, watching carefully for the time when, in accordance with their instructions, they should hold up all persons approaching the prison. The last pair had been five minutes inside the prison when the outside party came into action. Paddy Varien cut the telephone wires leading into the prison, and the isolation of the building was completed. The late Fr Dominic, brigade chaplain, arrived in the vicinity and remained until the end. Just at the moment when the outside party was coming into action the first unexpected incident happened. A party of military with a horse and cart drove up to the prison gate. The outside party was in a terrible predicament. If their comrades inside had not gone into action and they on the outside held up this party, the whole job might be ruined. Varien was actually at the top of the pole cutting the wires when the military arrived. On the other hand, if our men inside had come into action and the soldiers were admitted, there was a chance of dealing with them at the gate before the alarm could spread to the main buildings. It was decided to let them pass. This was a usual time for police to arrive with prisoners; they would be armed and that contingency had been provided against.

Inside the prison a warder had just come from the main buildings to take Joe Murphy and Martin Donovan to the visiting cell when the soldiers knocked at the main gate. They had actually been taken through the inside gates and these were being locked behind them, when the warder stopped on hearing the knock to see who it was at the outer gate. The other warder opened it and the six Volunteers inside the prison saw the soldiers. Was it a trap? Had someone dropped an incautious word, and was the whole plan known to the enemy? Had they waited only until the six men were inside the prison to swoop on them? Six men waited tensely, guns ready for instant action, while the soldiers filed in. Would they turn into the waiting-room? No. They continued into the prison grounds, and the warder taking Joe Murphy and Martin Donovan to the visiting cell admitted them through the main gate on the path to the prison buildings. He then continued with his two visitors to the visiting cell, and locked them in. MacNeilus was brought in on the other side of the cell and locked in. The visiting cell had a double barrier between the prisoner and his visitors, and between the two barriers the warder walked up and down during the interviews. The visitors spoke to the prisoners across the barriers. MacNeilus' visitors this evening appeared to be in a hurry to get away (they knew their four companions were inside the prison). After chatting with him for a few minutes they said they had to catch a train and bade him goodbye. MacNeilus, bewildered, tried to prolong the interview. They were insistent. The warder inserted the key in the lock to let them out. And then MacNeilus saw the point of their actions. They were waiting for the right key to be inserted in the lock. In a flash they were upon the warder, sandbags in hand; he was down and unconscious without more than a groan. The key turned in the lock; the door opened. 'Jump Mac', and MacNeilus was over the barrier into the visitors' side of the cell and through the gate into the prison grounds. A revolver was passed to him, and all three started to walk at an easy pace towards the main gate by the path inside the prison wall. They had to pass the sentry. Just then they remembered they had left the door unlocked behind them. Joe Murphy went back and locked it. This was fortunate, because just as they arrived at the gate opening into the centre of the prison the sentry was at the end of his beat and within a few yards. If the three of them were together his suspicions might have been aroused, as only two visitors were allowed up together. He had turned and was facing the other way on his beat when Joe Murphy passed behind him. Once past the sentry all three ran towards the main gate.

In the waiting-room below the four Volunteers waited until five minutes had elapsed after the first pair were taken up to the visiting cell. Then they suddenly closed with the warder, felled him and disconnected the telephone. They tied the warder securely and took his keys. With these they unlocked the outer wicket gate, but though they found the right key on the bunch they could not open the inner wrought-iron gate. If that key failed to turn the whole job was a failure, and neither the two men who were inside nor MacNeilus could get out. They took turns at wrestling with it but the gate would not open. Every second was of importance; if all had gone according to plan in the visitors' cell MacNeilus and his two companions should appear at any moment round the bend of the path. Another effort; suddenly the lock shot back! Round the bend came MacNeilus and his two companions at the double; in a second they were through the inside gate and it was locked behind them. Through the wicket filed the whole party, and that, too, was locked. All the prison gates were locked: no one could get in or out; the rescue party had all the keys – and MacNeilus was again outside the prison walls.

And here the plan broke down! Elaborate arrangements had been made for getting the rescued man safely away. They collapsed because in the tense and rapid sequence of events from the moment of the attack on the warder in the visitors' cell until the whole party was outside the gates, it had not been possible to convey to MacNeilus the arrangements made for his getaway from the vicinity of the jail. The natural jubilation and congratulations of his comrades caused some slight confusion, and a Volunteer had left a bicycle standing outside the prison gate. MacNeilus asked somebody: 'Is this for me?' This particular Volunteer was uncertain, he not being one of those detailed to cover the getaway. MacNeilus mounted the bicycle and rode away in the direction of Thomas Davis Bridge.

From that moment until after seven o'clock he was completely lost; he had eluded not only his captors but his rescuers! Later he sent in word to brigade headquarters that he had arrived at Walsh's at Clogheen, outside the city. What happened was that he had gone some distance before he realised, not seeing any Volunteers, that he was not on the road it was intended he should take. He turned back and cycled almost to the prison entrance again, only to find that everybody had left. He decided to make for Ballingeary, thirty miles away. However, after going a short distance, his bicycle punctured; he put it inside a fence and started across the fields for Walsh's. He ran into a Volunteer funeral going to Currikippane graveyard and escorted by a body of armed police. When they passed he got to Walsh's and sent a message into town.

That night he left Walsh's with Dan Sullivan and F. O'Donoghue about 11.30 and, travelling on foot and avoiding the roads as much as possible, arrived next morning at Berings, where the 6th battalion took over his protection. As he said that night, that little journey illustrated the spirit and national character of the Volunteer movement, for this Donegal man had for his companions, a Corkman and a Kerryman.

THE GREATNESS OF TOMÁS MacCURTAIN

by F. O'DONOGHUE

IN MANY WAYS Tomás MacCurtain was an extraordinary and remarkable man. Except to a small group of workers in the national revival movement he was unknown before 1916; in 1920, when his enemies found it necessary to ensure his removal by murder, he had honourably attained both of the highest offices in the gift of his people – the command of Cork No. 1 brigade of the IRA and the lord mayoralty of the city. The passing of time has but served to confirm the judgment of his own day that, amongst the group of competent and earnest local officers who were his contemporaries, his pre-eminence in leadership was unquestioned and acknowledged. He was a man of plain, unaffected patriotism, devoid of personal vanity; vital, dynamic, self-confident; but withal diplomatic, kindly and musical. He had an enormous capacity for work, apparently inexhaustible energy and driving force, and a deep natural insight and understanding of men. His great fortitude scorned defeat or deviation from any course of action dictated by his principles. His mind had qualities of greatness which were coming to maturity only at his death. In all the years of his manhood these gifts and talents of his were devoted almost exclusively and with persistent intensity to a single purpose. It was the destruction or ejection by armed force of the foreign army of occupation in Ireland. He had, as early as 1911, determined the ultimate issue for himself, and gladly accepted the inevitable principle of physical conflict as the only road to freedom; thereafter all his efforts were concentrated on the acquisition of the means and the force necessary for the task. He did not agree with the view that patriotism was dead; or that all that could be done was to pass on the Fenian tradition of republicanism in secret to a more worthy generation. He believed that his generation, like every other, had a duty to the nation, and that no personal considerations should take precedence over that duty. He believed that the young men who were separatists should come out openly and say so, that however few they were they should preach the gospel of separate nationhood; that they should be self-reliant, that they should arm. And he believed they should set the highest standard, not alone in national service, but in personal integrity and good citizenship.

But he was a realist who took a broad view of civic and national duty. He saw Ireland as a whole, and he saw, as Mitchel did, that any successful plan for undoing a long-standing conquest would have to combine efforts in many fields and embrace many kinds of activity. He was prepared to use, and did use with efficiency and vigour, every honourable means he could create or which came into his hands for the undoing of any part of the conquest. The Gaelic League, the Fianna, the IRB, the Volunteers, and later the control of civic administration, were all weapons to be used in their appropriate time and sphere against the enemy.

Tomás MacCurtain's main preoccupation and most important work from 1913 onwards was the Volunteer organisation. On this he lavished the love and devotion of his generous nature. In it he saw the sword of deliverance and the guarantee of freedom. Death came to him just at the moment when the creative labour of the previous years had given Cork city and county an armed force, well disciplined, trained and animated by a high morale, beginning to strike its first damaging blows against the enemy. On that brigade Tomás MacCurtain had left the imperishable impress of his personality, and the mould of his genius as an organiser and administrator. To it he imparted the fire and spirit of his soldierly zeal, and through it his inspiration lives and will live. The history of the brigade after his death was powerfully influenced by the ideals he had inculcated, and all the practical hard-headed ideas for grappling with the realities of a complex problem which he had contributed. Under his leadership a weapon almost perfect for its purpose had been forged. Even if he had lived to fight with his brigade through the fifteen months of bitter struggle which intervened between his death and the Truce, a most important part of his service would still be represented by his work in the preceding years. There could not have been a successful fight in 1920 and 1921 if that work had not been done, and well done. In the years before and after 1916 there was enacted what Pearse called 'one of the miracles of God, who ripens in the hearts of young men the seeds sown by the young men of a former generation.'

Among those who laboured mightily to reap the harvest of the Fenian sowing none was more successful than Tomás MacCurtain. His sturdy patriotism was of the kind that naturally expresses itself in work and deeds rather than in words, and his whole life was an unbroken record of hard work and faithful service to an ideal. He did not drink or smoke at any period of his life. The Fenian faith was an inspiration to him from childhood. Within a few hundred yards of the farmhouse where he was born at Ballyknockane, Mourne Abbey, was a house which had once been a police barracks, and was captured by the redoubtable Captain Mackey Lomasney in 1867. The youngest of a family of six boys and six girls, Tomás was born on 22 March 1882, and until he was thirteen years of age lived here where the story of that winter's night adventure was current in the countryside. In 1895 he came to live with an elder sister in Cork and attended the Christian Brothers' schools at the North Monastery. Here he laid the foundations of the great proficiency which he subsequently attained by self study in the Irish language.

MacCurtain's first introduction to commercial life was as a clerk in the offices of the City of Cork Steampacket company. After a time he left this to take up a similar post with the carrying firm of Nat Ross. But in these years between 1905 and 1909 his real work began after office hours. There was a hall in Queen Street, rented by the Gaelic League, and known as An Dún. Under its roof was gathered all that was vigorously militant in the national and cultural life of Cork. For the Dramatic Society there Terence MacSwiney wrote his plays; Daniel Corkery, D.L. Kelleher, P.S. O'Hegarty and many others were regular visitors. In the group whose activities were centred here, MacCurtain found young men whose faith was akin to his own, young men of vision and intellect, anxious to find their places in the pitifully weak ranks of those who accepted the full implications of national service.

Here, too, was formed that unbroken friendship and comradeship between MacCurtain and MacSwiney which only death interrupted; MacSwiney was by far the ablest writer and debater in the group; MacCurtain was its most active and resourceful executive. He was foremost in all the anti-recruiting and anti-imperialist activities of the time. He became so successful as a teacher of Irish that the Gaelic League prevailed upon him to devote much of his time to teaching. After periods in Croom and Midleton on this work, he returned to Cork and in 1911 organised a sluagh of Fianna Éireann in the city. They were to be the future officers and leaders of an army. Out of this grew the idea of training some of the older men in drill and military exercises. MacCurtain had a group which drilled and trained as best it could before the organisation of the Volunteers on a national basis.

On the establishment of the Volunteers in November 1913, Cork took immediate action to organise, and in December the inaugural meeting was held in the City Hall. It was a stormy meeting; the Redmondite following took exception to a reference to the Ulster Volunteers made by Eoin MacNeill, the platform was rushed and some of the promoters injured. A Provisional Committee was elected, MacCurtain became its secretary, and the work of organisation began. He represented Cork at the first convention of the Volunteers on 25 October 1914, and was elected a member of the general council.

The split which resulted from Mr Redmond's offer of the Volunteers for service under the British war office, had disastrous effects in Cork as elsewhere. Of the 2,000 men who were present at the Cornmarket, where the issue was put for their decision, fewer than fifty elected to follow MacCurtain and MacSwiney. It was a heavy defeat, but they were not discouraged. Immediately and with vigour they set to work again. Now they had to combat not alone the confusion in the public mind, but also a campaign of vilification, felon setting and victimisation set going against them in the press and elsewhere. Public hostility was intense, sources of finance dried up and officers and men were victimised in their employment. The following quotation from a document issued by the executive committee of the Cork corps in 1914, and probably written by MacCurtain, is an indication of their principles and of the difficulties with which they had to contend:

> It was difficult work to build up an organisation that, while open to Irishmen of all section and parties and classes, was independent of

all; more difficult in Cork than in other parts of Ireland owing to the deplorable political cleavages in our city and county. The leaders of the Volunteers in Cork were determined, however, that, as long as they could, the Volunteer organisation would provide a place where men of all parties may meet in friendship, and band themselves together for military service to our Motherland. Party political questions were rigorously excluded. It was fully recognised and conceded that every individual Volunteer was entitled to hold any opinions he wished on political, social, or religious subjects, and to act and vote outside the Volunteer organisation as he pleased. In the Volunteers he was to recognise that he was a soldier of Ireland, and his only business was how to become an efficient one.

But the work went on. The executive committee was replaced by a brigade council, with MacCurtain as brigade commandant. The work of organising the county was undertaken and prospered. Cork was congratulated by headquarters for its initiative in this regard, and by the end of 1915 the organisation had spread to almost all parts of the county. An older and more worthy ideal had emerged above the pettiness of political wrangling, and the whole energies of MacCurtain and his fellow officers were devoted to rebuilding an army of liberation. They sought to forge the only weapon with which they could confidently strike for freedom, and they never deviated from that purpose. With every passing month the stature of MacCurtain in wise and prudent leadership became more evident. In 1915 Volunteer headquarters in Cork was moved from Fish Street to a large hall in Sheares Street, and here it continued to operate until closed by the enemy in 1918. In 1915 also, MacCurtain relinquished his post with Messrs Suttons and opened a farmers' supply store at 40 Thomas Davis Street, where he went to reside with his wife and family. Here his family continued to live and carry on the business during the long periods of his enforced absence after 1916, and in this house he was brutally murdered by crown forces in the presence of his wife in the early hours of 20 March 1920.

The story of the events of Holy Week and Easter Week, 1916, so far as they influenced the actions of the Volunteers in Cork and in the south of Ireland generally, still remains a matter for full investigation. It may safely be said that all the facts have not been published, and it would take far too much space to relate here the circumstances even so far as they are known. It must suffice to say that a confusion of orders resulted in Cork and the south generally remaining inactive. It is of interest to note, however, that in the autumn of 1917, the executive of the supreme council, IRB, ordered an investigation of all the facts pertaining to the Cork brigade during Holy Week and Easter Week. The report of Diarmuid Lynch, who conducted the investigation, held that no blame rested on Commandant MacCurtain, Vice-Commandant MacSwiney or their fellow officers. The report was later approved by the executive.

In the round-up of republicans which followed Easter Week, MacCurtain was arrested and detained in Richmond barracks, pending court martial. The court martial did not, however, take place and he was deported and interned in Frongoch. Release came at Christmas, and in the new year he had no more than begun to gather up again the broken threads of his brigade organisation when he was re-arrested. On the 27 February 1917, he was deported and, though not interned, was confined to an area in Bromyard, Herefordshire, on a kind of 'ticket-of-leave' existence. This deportation order was cancelled at the general release of prisoners in June. Back in his brigade area once more he took up with renewed energy the work of reorganisation. He planned the establishment of Volunteer companies in every district, covering the entire county, and the development of battalion staffs with territorially defined areas for the proper control and training of these companies. But now he worked under conditions vastly different to those of the pre-1916 period. A new spirit was awakening in the people. It was the springtime of awareness to fundamental things for the young men to whom the sacrifice of 1916 has been an inescapable clarion call to service. Many experienced the exhilaration of discovering a hitherto latent allegiance to an ideal that had almost perished. The spirit of the times was exuberant but uncontrolled; had it lacked direction and concentration it would have spent itself in futility. Young men, eager to serve and ready for sacrifice, flooded into the Volunteers, clothing the bare bones of organisation with vigorous flesh and blood. But flesh and blood and high spirits raise tough problems for the commander. This was fiery material, malleable but without discipline. And while he was delighted to see many winning for themselves a faith which had long been for him a settled conviction, he was too wise not to know that undisciplined men do not win battles; too far-seeing to have any delusions about the problems of discipline, training and armament, which this influx of high-spirited raw material represented. He gave thought to the problem of keeping the new vision unspoiled, the noble ideals untarnished, during the necessarily prosaic process of converting groups of civilians into disciplined military units. His own fine combination of patriotic idealism and practical energy in action was an example and a standard for all. As part of a policy of strengthening national morale, to encourage recruiting for the Volunteers, and in defiance of a British order prohibiting the wearing of uniforms, he ordered public parades of the two city battalions in late September and October 1917. He was arrested, with a number of his officers, after the first Sunday parade. They went on hunger strike in Cork jail, and were released on 25 October.

The conscription threat in 1918 accelerated the influx of recruits into the Volunteers, but many who joined them fell away again when the danger passed. But all the time the brigade was growing in strength and cohesion. In these two years MacCurtain devoted himself to its three vital needs – discipline, training, arms. He had an instinctively right attitude to discipline and his control of the brigade was at all times firm, though never harsh. As a people we do not take kindly to discipline or regimentation; the high standard that he attained was reached by teaching men intelligently the paramount need for it. He set that high standard in the certain conviction that it was essential. The most enduring victories of the time were those won over men's minds and the unshaken morale of the brigade in the following years of intense strain had its firm base on the standard set in the quieter days. He believed, I think, that we did not look closely enough in ourselves for the causes of our failures; he believed there were no reasons which could not be eliminated to make a foreign observer wonder why the Irish 'always fought badly at home'. With a wide experience of the local personal or party animosities which sometimes militated against the progress of a company or a battalion, he was patient in pointing out the road of national service, but ruthless and downright in dealing with anybody who persisted in permitting any personal or party prejudice to take precedence over the welfare of the Volunteer organisation. He took a realistic view of training. There were many difficulties. Time available was limited, enemy interference had to be evaded, competent instructors were scarce, suitable manuals even scarcer. He did not wail about the deficiencies, or permit any-body else to wail about them; his policy was: think, improvise, find ways and means, get on with the job. There was one over-riding consideration – high principles and ardent patriotism would not prevail against the bayonets of our enemies. Even the threat of armed force would win no concessions, much less liberty. The Declaration of the Republic lived; bloody, physical conflict had to be faced and endured before it could be established, men should be fitted and should fit themselves for that ordeal. He did not permit men who were evading arrest merely to go 'on the run'. Very early and very decisively he rounded them up, put them under brigade control, set them training tasks in country battalions, and required weekly reports from them and from the battalion commandants in whose area they were operating, of the training carried out. Monthly reports on training from all battalions were insisted upon. An instruction he prepared for quartermasters at this time has survived. It is a remarkable visualisation of active service conditions as they developed two years later. It is a practical and detailed directive to quartermasters of brigade, battalions and companies on the problems with which they would have to cope.

Tours of inspection through the brigade were a regular feature of Tomás MacCurtain's activities. Those who know the hilly by-roads of County Cork can appreciate the endurance required to inspect twenty-one battalions from Mitchelstown to Castletownbere, from Youghal to Newmarket, while evading police attention, and with a bicycle as a mode of conveyance. He did all his travelling on a bicycle and most of his work of necessity at night. And wherever he went, orders, suggestions, ideas, flowed back from him in a continuous stream to brigade headquarters in the city. He had the ability to grasp the essential in the worst tangle; the diplomatic persuasiveness and clarity of expression to make others see it. He was impatient of slovenliness or lack of method. He had little use for the man who would not or could not get things done. He worked hard himself, and had no hesitation in making his officers work equally hard. And yet there was nothing he liked better than the occasional breaks from work afforded by the gathering of a group of neighbours at the farmhouse where he might happen to be. Here he would sing Irish songs or play the violin for the dancers with a dash and exuberance that were infectious; merriment and laughter would dance in his blue eyes, he would joke and gossip as light-heartedly as the most irresponsible. He had a good voice, a natural talent for music, and a great love of it. He had taught himself to play several instruments, and knew all the houses in which there were good violins. One, at T.J. Golden's, Donoughmore, he had a special liking for, and would look forward eagerly to his visit there. He loved the rich abounding life of the countryside; he took a keen interest in archaeology and local history.

The end of 1918 marked the closing of the preparatory phase in the development of the Volunteer organisation, and a turning point in the direction of the whole national effort for freedom. The brigade was still growing in strength and cohesion, training was progressive, and the right men were emerging as leaders in most of the battalions and companies, even though the system of election for all officers was retained. MacCurtain had now the largest brigade in Ireland territorially, the strongest numerically. It consisted of twenty-one battalions and three attached companies. Its strength was not less than 8,000 all ranks. Its most urgent need was arms; and more and more that paramount need was taking a foremost place in the thoughts and activities of practical leaders like MacCurtain, in whose minds there was no doubt about the ultimate destiny of the force. Special services were being built up as the need for them became evident: engineers, signals, communications, medical, intelligence, transport. In these two years also the gradual change-over was made from a semi-civilian type of control, first by committees and later by brigade and battalion councils, to the accepted military system wherein the commander alone is vested with supreme authority and control over his forces, and the chain of command is clearly recognised and accepted. At the end of 1918 the decision was made by GHQ to divide the county into three brigade areas. MacCurtain presided at the conference of battalions concerned, which elected Liam Lynch as O/C, Cork No. 2 brigade. Michael Collins presided, and MacCurtain attended a similar conference for the West Cork area, which elected Tom Hales as O/C, Cork No. 3 brigade. MacCurtain's brigade still consisted of ten battalions, comprising seventy-seven companies, and over it he exercised control up to his death. The other event which made the end of 1918 a turning-point was the general election in December, which set the seal of the people's approval on the Declaration of the Republic, and immensely strengthened the moral position of the army. MacCurtain was not a candidate, though had he wished it he could have been elected for any constituency in Cork city or county. But his heart was in the Volunteers, where he had found his true vocation, and he had no desire to give it anything but undivided attention. Its problems and difficulties were no more than a gladly accepted challenge to his keen intellect and native shrewdness.

Of the two main requirements for developing a successful fight against the enemy, one, that of trained men, had been in some measure attained. The training was not comprehensive or even sufficient, but it had undoubtedly produced a magnificent fighting spirit, good discipline and an aptitude for acting in combination. The second requirement, arms, had not been reached at all in this brigade. Rifles, shotguns and revolvers were the weapons available, and these were so limited in number and ammunition so scarce, that the whole armament of the brigade would be required to tackle a few police barracks. There were no machine-guns, grenades or explosives, with the exception of small quantities of gelignite of doubtful quality.

With the first phase of his policy in a fair way to completion, MacCurtain gave increasing attention to the question of remedying this deficiency. Importation of arms, except in infinitesimal qualities, was out of the question. But there were 43,000 regular

troops and 16,000 police in Ireland – all armed. The obvious course
was to capture some of the arms; and for many reasons the police
barracks dotted all over the brigade area were the most suitable
objectives. Plans were therefore prepared for a simultaneous attack
on as many of these posts as the very limited equipment permitted,
and the proposal was submitted to GHQ for sanction in the
summer of 1919. No definite policy for the development of the
fight appears to have been laid down by GHQ at this time. The
Volunteer executive still controlled the organisation, and its official
organ *An t-Óglach*, went no further than saying Volunteers had a
right and duty to resist disarmament. Some hopes appeared to be
based on the possibility that Ireland's case would be heard at the
Peace Conference. These hopes faded with Wilson's announcement
in June, and in August 1919, Cathal Brugha, minister for defence,
proposed that the Volunteers swear allegiance to the Dáil as the
government of the Republic. Thereafter the Dáil took governmental
responsibility for the actions of the army. Meantime the proposals
made by MacCurtain's brigade for attacks on police barracks were
not sanctioned and he went to Dublin to press for action. It is an
indication of his own sense of responsibility and of the discipline of
the brigade, that although feeling in favour of action was very strong
and insistent, he would not order or permit any operation without
GHQ sanction. Reporting to the chief-of-staff on 1 November
1919, he said:

> Some action must be taken which will give *all* the men a chance of doing
> something, otherwise the men will fall away and the companies die out.
> We cannot allow this to happen. A meeting of all commandants of the
> brigade, together with the brigade staff, was held last night, and arising
> out of the remarks column of the monthly report of the 8th battalion
> (which I attach herewith) the question of action was again raised and
> discussed. All officers present were unanimous in requesting GHQ to

reconsider the position, and allow us to carry out the work for which we were making arrangements at the time you summoned me to Dublin and called it off in favour of the other idea* … Further that permission be given us to consult and arrange with the other two brigades in the county, for simultaneous action throughout the whole county. I feel that your sanction to this is essential …

The IRB position created a problem also. Members of it who were active Volunteer officers worked through that organisation to procure arms, and there was a danger of the uncoordinated development of the fight. Such a possibility appeared to MacCurtain to contain the seeds of disaster; he felt that the responsible officers of the Volunteers should alone direct and control all operations. With great tact and understanding he handled this thorny problem, and secured an amicable arrangement satisfactory to all concerned. While in Dublin endeavouring to get sanction for his proposed operations he took part in one of the abortive attacks on Lord French. This attack ultimately took place on 19 December, and its greater importance was given as one of the reasons for deferring sanction to the Cork proposals.

MacCurtain returned with sanction for a simultaneous attack on three police barracks, which was as much as it was estimated the equipment of the brigade would enable it to undertake at one time. Carrigtwohill and Kilmurry barracks were attacked on 1 January 1920; the attack on the third barracks did not take place. Carrigtwohill was captured after a fight lasting several hours; Kilmurry successfully resisted the attack. The campaign had opened for the brigade, the policy of guerrilla warfare was accepted, and all the energies of keen and active minds were turned towards its development and intensification.

*   The proposed attack on Lord French.

Tomás MacCurtain was nominated for election to the Cork Corporation in the municipal elections in the opening weeks of 1920. He was the unanimous choice of the newly elected City Council for the lord mayoralty. Though he would have preferred to devote his whole attention to the army, once elected he took up his new duties with the same vigour and ability he had displayed in the Volunteers, and in a short time Cork discovered that it had the most popular, as well as the most efficient, lord mayor in its stormy history.

Commandant M. Leahy, O/C of the 4th battalion, which had captured Carrigtwohill barracks, came to make a personal report to him a few days after he was elected lord mayor. He congratulated the brigade O/C on his election and in reply MacCurtain said: 'I would rather be congratulated on having captured Carrigtwohill barracks.' With characteristic energy he tackled and mastered the new problem of municipal government. He laid it down as a principle that members of public boards should conduct public business as honestly and efficiently as if it were their own; he put a decisive stop to the corruption and jobbery which had disgraced the administration of local government in the city. He was the first to suggest management by commissioners. His public duties made a new call upon his courage. He considered it beneath the dignity due to his office that he should evade arrest. He received anonymous warnings and threats. He knew he carried his life in his hands. He knew that he must be prepared to meet death at any moment, but he was not deflected in the smallest degree from the course of duty which he saw before him. No man in his position ever had fewer personal enemies; but because he would not bend the knee to any tyranny, because he loved his people and served them fearlessly, his people's enemies struck him down. It is indicative of his sincere religious feeling, and of a deep fundamental trait in his character that, both as a prisoner in Frongoch and a leader beset by grave responsibilities and personal dangers, he turned frequently for spiritual refreshment to the profound wisdom and simple sanctity of Thomas à Kempis; and that he found that refreshment in its most acceptable form in Canon Peter O'Leary's translation of *The Imitation of Christ*.

Pearse said: 'We are the voice of an idea which is older than any empire and will outlast every empire.' Tomás MacCurtain was a personification of the idea itself, in that he was so finely representative of the plain people who, outlawed and submerged, had endured the terrific seven hundred years journey through the Valley of Death, and emerged at the end of it all with their faith unshaken, still passionately attached to their own way of life, ready to fight and die for it, and still preserving enough of its characteristic individuality to enable a new nation to be built on historic foundations. He saw with great clarity the service demanded of him and of his generation; with a full knowledge of the sacrifices it would impose on him and on the men he led, he accepted it fearlessly. He believed in the nation's inalienable right to freedom, in the duty of her young men to achieve and defend it in arms; believing these things, he lived to give them expression in action and, bearing witness to their immutable truth, he died.

ARREST AND MARTYRDOM OF TERENCE MacSWINEY

by C. HARRINGTON

ONE IS NECESSARILY diffident in venturing to write on any event or incident of the life of Terence MacSwiney, the second republican lord mayor of Cork, for the reason that Terry enacted within his comparatively short career an individual drama which personified the nation's struggle for independence – strong in his faith in the success of that struggle within his own time. My purpose here, however, is to describe the scene of the lord mayor's arrest, so I shall not intrude into those other phases of his extraordinary active life, upon which eminent authors will find ample scope and material for their literary capabilities.

Cork city on the night of Thursday, 12 August 1920, was to all appearances as peaceable a place as there was on the face of the earth. At least the citizens followed their usual pursuits or patronised their favourite forms of amusement in spite of the fact that the War of Independence was then at its height. It would, however, have been foolish for one to misconstrue the apparent quiet even for the briefest period in the warlike activities to which the citizens had daily grown accustomed; but no one suspected the imminence of an event which in its tragic yet glorious consequences was destined to be of vast and, in fact, decisive influence in the course of our national struggle. At approximately seven o'clock on that evening a small army of British soldiery emerged from the military headquarters, then known as the Victoria barracks, in the city. Their strength was estimated at between two and three hundred men, all armed in complete fighting equipment. They were in lorries, accompanied by armoured cars, and proceeded to the City Hall, which they reached about seven-thirty. On arrival at their destination, it was not long until they were investing the building. The spectacle they presented was not unfamiliar to the citizens, but their descent on the municipal headquarters, particularly at this hour, had an ominous meaning and crowds gathered at all vantage points, eager to witness something sensational. The attitude of the crowd was naturally critical and found vent in jeering the soldiers.

In my narrative my readers will perceive that, besides timing their raid with remarkable judgment, the raiding party showed a peculiar knowledge of the lay-out of the City Hall. They didn't waste time or formality or send word to the caretaker, who resided on the premises; they merely took possession and relied on their own devices to gain access to the various offices and rooms. The building, a fine limestone pile, lay along Albert Quay, facing north. On the western side and at right angles the Free Library jutted out, fronting on Anglesea Street. Between the two buildings was a curved grass plot. On the eastern side of the City Hall was a yard, and outside this ran Eglington Street, parallel to Anglesea Street, leading to the swimming baths. To the rear of the building, within the corporation yard, were situated the corporation workshops, to which I shall refer again later. When it reached the City Hall the military column, headed by an armoured car, proceeded into Anglesea Street and halted, so that its constituents, snakelike, extended along the front and sides of the buildings. I was engaged in my office on the ground floor facing Anglesea Street, having been recalled from my holidays to take the place of my colleagues who had been arrested two days previously. (I might explain that on the advent to office of the first republican corporation of Cork in January 1920, I was chosen from the staff to act as private secretary to the lord mayor.) My recall now was at the request of the chief of my former department, as I was familiar with the work. I would return to the lord mayor's room in a day or two. In order to have the wages books ready by Friday, I and another official of the department were obliged to work after the usual office hours. Hence my presence in the building on this Thursday night, 12 August 1920. I left the office at seven o'clock to get a hurried cup of tea at a nearby shop. On my way out I met the lord mayor. He was also O/C Cork No. 1 brigade, Irish Republican Army, and was on his way in to an important brigade council meeting in his room. It was attended by all but one of the officers of the brigade staff and the city battalion commandants, as well as the late General Liam Lynch, who had come to consult with the brigade council on army matters. The brigade officer who was absent from that meeting, owing to army work in the country, normally had custody of the secret code used by the Royal Irish Constabulary. This code came into the hands of the IRA through their intelligence department, and proved very useful. In case it would be required that night, the copy of the code for that particular week was left with the lord mayor by this officer, who was not returning to Cork until next day. The prosecution attempted to attribute particular importance to this document, and made it the basis of one of the charges against the lord mayor when he was court-martialled. The lord mayor's reply to this charge illustrated the position between the army of occupation and the Irish people at the time. He maintained that he, as lord mayor, was the only person in Cork legally entitled to hold the secret code.

When I met the lord mayor on my way to tea on the night of 12 August, we had a brief conversation, in the course of which he reminded me of a direction he had given me the previous day to the effect that I was to resume duty with him on the following morning. I then went on to tea and returned about seven-thirty. Just as I was resuming my work I saw military armoured cars and lorries full of soldiers come round from the quay into Anglesea Street and stop in a line outside the boundary railing of the City Hall. The soldiers at once dismounted and, climbing over the railings, came across the green towards our offices. Seeing what was afoot, I immediately rushed upstairs to warn the lord mayor. Between the top of the stairs on my side of the building and the lord mayor's suite on the other side was an open corridor, about sixty yards long. I raced along this corridor, at the end of which I met the lord mayor coming from his room. In the circumstances of the moment one might, perhaps, expect to find him showing signs of nervousness. But those who knew Terence MacSwiney will appreciate that even in circumstances of risk or danger to himself he was capable of maintaining those qualities of calm and nonchalance which were his outstanding characteristics. His attitude during his trial and the nobility of his unflinching perseverance in his subsequent hunger strike protest, bear ample testimony to this.

When I met him he was rolling a piece of twine. He knew what was going on. Fearing that he had in his possession documents of value to the enemy, I asked him if he had anything on him that I could take. He said he had not. Meanwhile the military had taken possession of the ground floor. The lord mayor and I proceeded together down the back stairs on that eastern side of the building. At the foot of the stairs was the main back door of the City Hall. As we reached the foot of the stairs we were confronted by a soldier armed with rifle and fixed bayonet. He called on us to halt, but it was evident that he did not yet recognise the lord mayor. I was aware that the lord mayor had, some time previously, been provided with the keys of specially camouflaged doors, made on the instructions of his colleagues of the corporation, by which in such an emergency he could make his escape into the corporation workshops. As the lord mayor went towards the back door I saw an opportunity of diverting the soldier's attention, and I proceeded to walk towards the vestibule. The soldier followed me, calling on me to halt. As I kept walking, I heard the lord mayor endeavouring to open the latch of the back door. On reaching the vestibule, followed by the soldier, I was stopped by the officer in charge of the military, who directed me under escort to the night entrance passageway to await search. The lord mayor had meanwhile gained the corporation yard by a roundabout way, having gone out through a window, and was at least clear of the building, which the military were scouring. But, unfortunately, he was without the keys which would have given him access to the workshops and probable escape. He had, it appears, left the keys wherever he had stayed the previous night. It will be understood that at this period, for obvious reasons, Terry did not always stay at his own house. The fates were against him that night. Soldiers of the raiding party who had traversed Eglington Street had wandered in through the swimming baths and come out in the corporation yard. Here they found the lord mayor with a group of men, some of his army colleagues, who had all made the yard their objective as the only means of escape open when the raid commenced. They were in a hut, but in no way immune from observation. This was about nine o'clock.

Meanwhile, the officer in charge of the military conducted a most thorough search at the night entrance to the building, of those who had been apprehended during the raid, and who included justices, lawyers, litigants, and the large body of people who were interested in the proceeding of a court, referred to later on. The search over, the military prepared to return to the barracks, taking with them the lord mayor and ten other captives. The fact that members of the brigade staff were let go is probably due to the ignorance of the military, who did not realise the importance of their big capture. Had they been more alert, they would have struck a more severe blow against the IRA in Cork.

To me, it is to this day, something of a mystery why the British raided the City Hall on that particular night. In the ordinary course the City Hall was closed up each evening immediately after the staff had left at six o'clock. It is inconceivable that the army council meeting was known to anybody outside those participating in the meeting. The British plans, however, appeared to have been well laid, whether as a result of superior intelligence, or by some strange stroke of fortune. On that fateful night a session of the Dáil court for the city was held in the Council Chamber in the City Hall, and an important action down for hearing was that in which a prominent English Assurance Company was plaintiff. Whether that particular case was known to the powers that were, I cannot say, but there is a strange coincidence in the fact that the raid took place at an hour in which, in the ordinary way, the building would have been locked up and, except for the night watchman and the resident caretaker, devoid of life.

On 30 March 1920, Terence MacSwiney was unanimously elected lord mayor of Cork by the corporation, composed of representatives of Sinn Féin, the Redmondite, O'Brienite and unionist parties. Because of his exceptional capabilities, of the important offices he held and of the dangerous circumstances of the time, he was earnestly advised by his colleagues to have care for himself and, as it were, to make his public appearances as few as his duties allowed. His answer was an emphatic, 'No: I know my responsibilities, here I will stay, come what will.' In fact, his new duties found him redoubling his enthusiasm for and devotion to the cause which he ever held sacred. No official was more constant or regular in attendance at the City Hall than Lord Mayor MacSwiney. He performed his mayoral duties without fee or monetary reward, because he had with characteristic unselfishness, assigned his salary elsewhere. It must be borne in mind, so as to appreciate the calibre of the man, that at this period Terence MacSwiney had achieved the most signal honours in the gift of his native city and county. All carried heavy responsibilities. He had represented the mid-Cork constituency in the Dáil since the memorable election of 1918, and since March 1920, following the murder of his soldier-comrade, Tomás MacCurtain, he had been made lord mayor of Cork and brigadier of the army No. 1 brigade, Cork. But no one found greater pleasure in hard work.

I think it appropriate to quote here in full his speech on his acceptance of the office of lord mayor. The speech must rank amongst the most remarkable of patriotic addresses. It can be accepted as expressing as completely as time and the occasion permitted, the extraordinary spiritual quality and depth of Terry's political creed. It will be remembered that the period was full of danger for anybody who dared to give expression publicly to patriotic sentiments and, considering the circumstances, it was relatively easier at the time to speak defiance from the dock than from such a place as the Civic Council Chamber. That speech, made to the full corporation and in the presence of a crowded gallery, for the occasion was an historic one, is as follows (taken from the *Cork Examiner* report):

I shall be as brief as possible. This is not an occasion for many words, least of all, a conventional exchange of compliments and thanks. The circumstances of the vacancy in the office of lord mayor governed inevitably the filling of it. And I come here more as a soldier stepping into the breach, than as an administrator to fill the first post in the municipality. At a normal time it would be your duty to find for this post the councillor most practised and experienced in public affairs. But the time is not normal. We see in the manner in which our late lord mayor was murdered an attempt to terrify us all. Our first duty is to answer that threat in the only fitting manner, by showing ourselves unterrified, cool and inflexible for the fulfilment of our chief purpose – the establishment of the independence and integrity of our country – the peace and happiness of our country. To that end I am here. I was more closely associated than any other here with our late murdered friend and colleague, both before and since the events of Easter Week, in prison and out of it, in a common work of love for Ireland, down to the hour of his death. For that reason I take his place. It is, I think, though I say it, the only fitting answer to those who struck him down (applause).

Following from that there is a further matter of importance only less great – it touches the efficient continuance of our civic administration. If this recent unbearable aggravation of our persecution by our enemies should cause us to suspend voluntarily the normal discharge of our duties, it would help them very materially in their campaign to overthrow our cause. I feel the question of the future conduct of our affairs is in all our minds. And I think I am voicing the general view when I say that the normal functions of our corporate body must proceed, as far as in our power lies, uninterrupted with that efficiency and integrity of which our late civic head gave such brilliant promise. I don't wish to sound a personal note, but this much may be permitted under the circumstances – I made myself active in the selection of our late colleague for the office of lord mayor. He did not seek the honour and would not accept it as such, but when put to him as a duty he stepped to his place like a soldier. Before his election we discussed together in the intimate way we discussed everything touching our common work since Easter Week [*sic*]. We debated together what ought to be done, and what could be done, keeping in mind as in duty bound not only the ideal line of action, but the practical line at the moment as well. That line he followed with an ability and success all his own. Gentlemen, you have paid tribute to him on all sides. It will be my duty and steady purpose to follow that line as faithfully as in my power, though no man in this council could hope to discharge its functions with his ability and his perfect grasp of public business in all its details and as one harmonious whole (applause).

I have thought it necessary to touch on this normal duty of ours, though – and it may seem strange to say it – I feel at the moment it is even a digression. For the menace of our enemies hangs over us, and the essential immediate purpose is to show the spirit that animates us and how we face the future. Our spirit is but to be a more lively manifestation of the spirit in which we began the year – to work for the city in a new zeal, inspired by our initial act when we dedicated it and formally attested our allegiance, to bring by our administration of the city, glory to our allegiance, and by working for our city's advancement with constancy in all honourable ways, in her new dignity as one of the first cities in Ireland to work for and, if need be, to die for. I would recall some words of mine on that day of first meeting after the election of lord mayor. I realised that most of you in the minority here would be loyal to us, if doing so did not threaten your lives, but that you lacked the spirit and the hope to join with us to complete the work of liberation so well begun. I allude to it here again, because I wish to point out again the secret of our strength and the assurance of our final victory. This contest of ours is not on our side a rivalry of vengeance, but one of endurance – it is not they who can inflict most, but they who can suffer most, will conquer – though we do not abrogate our function to demand and see that evil-doers and murderers are punished for their crimes. But it is conceivable that they could interrupt our course for a time; then it becomes a question simply of trust in God and endurance. Those whose faith is strong will endure to the end, and triumph. The shining hope of our time is that the great majority of our people are now strong in that faith. To you, gentlemen of the minority here, I would address a word. I ask you again to take courage and hope. To me it seems – and I don't say it to hurt you – that you have a lively faith in the power of the devil, and but little faith in God. But God is over us, and in His divine intervention we have perfect trust. Anyone surveying the events in Ireland for the past five years must see that it is approaching a miracle how our country has been preserved. God has permitted this to be, to try our spirits, to prove us worthy of a noble line, to prepare us for a great and noble destiny. You amongst us who have yet no vision of the future have been led astray by false prophets. The liberty for which we today strive is a sacred thing – inseparably entwined as body and soul with that spiritual liberty for which the Saviour of men died, and which is the inspiration and foundation of all just government. Because it is sacred, and death for it is akin to the sacrifice on Calvary, following far off but constant to that Divine example in every generation our best and bravest have died. Sometimes in our grief we cry out foolish and unthinking words. 'The sacrifice is too great.' But it is because they were our best and bravest that they had to die. No lesser sacrifice could save us. Because of it our struggle is holy – our battle is sanctified by their blood and our victory is assured by their martyrdom. We, taking up the work they left incomplete, confident in God, offer in turn sacrifice from ourselves. It is not we who take innocent blood, but we offer it, sustained by the example of our immortal dead and that Divine example which inspires us all for the redemption of our country. Facing our enemies we must declare our attitude simply. We ask for no mercy, and we will make no compromise. But to the Divine author of mercy we appeal for strength to sustain us, whatever the persecution, that we may bring our people victory in the end. The civilised world dare not continue to look on indifferent. But if the rulers of earth fail us we have yet sure succour in the Ruler of Heaven; and though to some impatient hearts His judgments seem slow, they never fail, and when they fall they are overwhelming and final.

A copy of the speech was found in the course of the raids on the night of the lord mayor's arrest, and was the subject of a major charge at his court martial.

It was not generally known that Lord Mayor MacSwiney worked in his room in City Hall almost every night up to ten or eleven o'clock. I was privileged to be with him as his clerical assistant. He attached particular importance to working thus at night because, as he put it, his work could be better carried out without the risk of interruption by the numerous callers on so many errands, desirable and otherwise, to public offices at the time.

Thus it was that, in the midst of his public activity, at an hour when most people would be enjoying a respite after their day's labour, he was taken prisoner by the British, and it was very soon to appear that they were determined that such a formidable opponent should be rendered as impotent as they could make him. Within an hour-and-a-half after his arrest and conveyance to the barracks, the military again raided the lord mayor's room in the City Hall, and it was in this second raid that they captured the documents on which they formulated the charges against him. Some of these documents are mentioned by the lord mayor in his speech at the court martial which I will quote.

The lord mayor lost no time in making the only form of protest against his arrest which was in his power to adopt. He refused to take food and had endured over three days of fasting when he was court-martialled on the following Monday, 16 August. His comrades, who had been arrested with him, joined him in this protest, but they were released on 15 August. The court martial proceedings were chiefly marked by the proud and dignified manner maintained by the lord mayor – despite the ordeal he was going through and of which he showed physical signs. I give here quotations from the *Cork Examiner* of the trial:

When asked if he was represented by council, the lord mayor said: I would like to say a word about your proceedings here. The position is that I am Lord Mayor of Cork and Chief Magistrate of the City. And I declare this court illegal, and that those who take part in it are liable to arrest under the laws of the Irish Republic.

He was then asked if he objected to the personnel of the court, and replied: What I have said covers that.

When asked to plead, his Lordship said to the President: Without wishing in any way to be personal to you, I want to point out that you are guilty of an act of presumption to question me.

President: Any statement that you wish to make later on will be taken down.

The lord mayor: It is not necessary. It is only attaching importance to the proceedings.

The Prosecutor then outlined the case for the prosecution, in the course of which he described the raids on the City Hall and the arrest of the lord mayor and his companions who were brought to the barracks, arriving there about ten o'clock. He stated that it was in the second raid – at eleven-thirty p.m. (during the curfew hours) – on the night of the lord mayor's arrest that the papers which were the subject of the charges were found. In spite of the absence of direct evidence these papers were held to belong to his Lordship.

The sergeant-major who was in charge of the detention barracks that night gave evidence that when asked to take off his chain of office the lord mayor said: 'I would rather die than part with it.' He added that he took everything from the lord mayor except the chain.

At the close of the prosecution, the lord mayor, in response to the president's request if he had anything to say, rose from his seat.

The president: You may remain seated, Mr MacSwiney.

The lord mayor: I believe I will be able to hold on my feet until after the close of the proceedings and then it is immaterial. These proceedings, as I have said, are quite illegal. Anything I have to say is not in defence and it is in the written statement, parts of which are made the subjects of charges here in this illegal court. You have got to realise, and will have to realise it before very long, that the Irish Republic is really existing. I want to remind you of the fact that the gravest offence that can be committed by any individual is an offence against the head of the state. The offence is only relatively less great when committed against the head of a city, and the illegality is very much more grave when in addition to seizing that person, his building and private room are violated and his papers taken. I wish to reverse the position and for the moment put you, gentlemen, in the dock.

One of the documents seized is a resolution relating to our allegiance to the government of the Republic. There was quite a similar document there too. It was a resolution drawing attention to the verdict and inquest on my predecessor, in which a jury found a unanimous verdict that the British government and its police were guilty of his murder. And now it must be obvious to you that if that were an invention, it would be so grave a matter that it would be the chief charge here today, even in this illegal court. But that document is put aside, and I am gratified to be here today, notwithstanding all its inconveniences and other annoyances, to have that brought out, because this action in putting that document aside is an admission, an assent to a plea of guilty on behalf of those who committed the murder. That being the position, you must know that holding the office I do is absolutely grave for me, in view of the way my predecessor was sent to his death. I cannot say that but the same will happen myself at any moment. We always regard soldiers as other than policemen, and though misguided in coming to this country, they are still men of honour.

I knew where the code was, but did not know who separated it from other documents; but it must have been done to make two charges against two individuals. No one is responsible but me. I know where that paper was and where it was sworn to be. My respect for your army, little though it was, owing to happenings in this country of late, has now disappeared. It is a document that ought to be only in my possession. No one else could have it without my consent without committing an offence. Anyone who used such cypher to transmit messages about the Irish people is guilty of a crime against the Irish Republic. If he were a private citizen he would not consent to address the court, but by virtue of his position he wanted to point out and make it clear to the court that acting on directions from higher quarters could not absolve them from the consequences of the actions of their court. My entire answer to this court, or any court, is the document the original of which you have seized. But I would draw your attention to the fact that there were seized amongst my papers a copy of a letter I addressed to His Holiness the Pope on the occasion of the Beatification of Oliver Plunkett. His Holiness has read that letter by now, and it will be of interest to him to learn that it is a seditious document when found in my possession. Another letter taken was one I received from the President of the Municipal Council, Paris, asking for information relative to the port. I supplied that information and kept a copy of my reply. It will be of interest to the French government to know that it is an offence for the President of the Municipal Council of Paris to address letters to me, and that when found in my pockets they are seditious documents.

Another matter to which I wish to refer is to the number of visiting cards found. These were cards of distinguished foreign journalists from America, France and other parts of Europe; when linked with my name they are taken as evidence of seditious conspiracy!

He added that documents which were found in one place should not have been stated to have been found in another place for the purpose of implicating other people. I am the one person responsible. The officer and private had committed perjury in this regard. I must frankly say that I am sorry for it, because as a soldier of the Irish Republic I like to respect soldiers of every kind.

His attitude was expressed in the speech he delivered when elected lord mayor, and which they cited in part as sedition. They were brave words. They asked no mercy and sought no compromise. 'That is my position,' his Lordship concluded, 'I ask for no mercy.'

The president having announced that the court found him guilty on certain charges, the lord mayor said that he had decided the terms of his detention whatever their government may do. His Lordship was then sentenced to two years' imprisonment. On the following morning, between 3 and 4 a.m. he was placed on board a British naval sloop and landed that night at Pembroke Dock in South Wales, and immediately entrained for London, where he arrived on Wednesday morning, 18 August. About 4 a.m. he was handed over to the governor of Brixton jail. The long agony had begun. The lord mayor's hunger strike lasted seventy-four days. The details of that heroic episode are familiar to the Irish people. He died on 25 October 1920.

Terence MacSwiney personified the national cause and resolved to sustain his challenge, as that of the nation, to the Empire. He had stood to his word. The English government, however, maintained their spiteful attitude to the end, and to deprive the Irish capital of its eagerly awaited opportunity to pay respect to the mortal remains of the martyred lord mayor, they intercepted the remains at Holyhead and had them conveyed to Cork on board a naval vessel. The body was received in Cork by the Irish Republican Army and laid in state in the City Hall where, amidst memorable scenes, the citizens thronged to see the last of their beloved leader. On Sunday 31 October, he was buried in the republican plot, Saint Finbarr's cemetery, by the side of his friend and comrade, Tomás MacCurtain. It was the last of Terry, his spirit remains an example and an inspiration for all time.

THE ATTACK ON BLARNEY POLICE BARRACKS

by F. O'DONOGHUE

BLARNEY ROYAL IRISH Constabulary barracks was attacked on the evening of 1 June 1920. In the previous nine months the policy of attacks on barracks had been gradually developed, and had resulted in the capture of a number of these posts in Cork county and the evacuation of a number of others. In some cases, as at Carrigtwohill, the arms and equipment had fallen into the hands of the successful attackers; in other attacks such as that at Carrigadrohid, the capture of the barracks was not effected, but the structure was so badly damaged that it had to be evacuated. These early attacks had two objectives: first the capture of badly needed arms and ammunition to enable larger operations to be undertaken, and, secondly, the driving in of these small outposts, which were potential sources of information for the enemy, manned as they were in many cases by men with considerable local knowledge. The continued occupation of these barracks by enemy forces acted as a restriction on the movements and actives of local IRA units, and was a constant danger to our lines of communication. Forcing the evacuation of these posts had the effect of clearing large areas of country of all hostile forces; and in conjunction with the destruction of bridges and the trenching of roads, created a position in which the enemy could enter certain areas only in considerable force, and even then had his movements handicapped and slowed down by transport difficulties and the ever-present danger of unexpected attack. He was, moreover, deprived to a large extent of local information and forced to confine his forces more to barracks and certain restricted areas.

To compel the evacuation of Blarney barracks in the state of development of this policy which had been reached in the summer of 1920 was important to Cork No. 1 brigade, because the barracks menaced one of the main lines of communication between brigade headquarters and the 6th, 7th and 8th battalions, with headquarters at Donoughmore, Macroom and Kilnamartyra, respectively. The capture of arms was secondary in this attack, the main purpose of which was the destruction of the post.

Blarney village, in which the barracks stood, is about six miles from Cork and four from Ballincollig. In both places there were stationed some thousands of British soldiers, and in addition there was at Ballincollig a considerable concentration of Royal Irish Constabulary, who had been brought in from evacuated or captured barracks. No transport difficulties in the way of broken bridges or trenched roads intervened between either point and Blarney village. Consequently it was necessary to have a very large protective force for the attacking party, to fell trees and raise obstructions on the maze of roads leading to the village both from Cork and Ballincollig, and to engage the reinforcements which were certain to set out to Blarney the moment the Verey lights of the garrison intimated that an attack on their post was in progress.

In this case, owing to the peculiar circumstances, the number of men engaged was much larger than in the case of barrack attacks generally. The actual attacking party did not exceed thirty-five men, but in the various protective duties associated with the attack there were engaged very considerable numbers of men drawn from the 1st and 6th battalions. The barracks was not in an isolated position: it stood between the courthouse on one side and Smith's Hotel on the other. It was a substantial building, with loop-holed walls and the usual steel shutter and sandbag defences. There were in occupation at the time a sergeant and eight men. There was no possibility of approach to the building from the rear, and attack upon it with rifle fire or bombs from the front being regarded as an ineffective waste of valuable munitions, it was decided that the attack would be made by blowing a breach with explosives through the wall between the public bar in the hotel and the barracks, and if possible rushing the breach thus made and capturing the building. It was realised that, owing to the close proximity of strong enemy forces, probably not more than an hour would be available for sustained attack, and that the only hope of complete success lay in making a breach large enough for the attacking party to get through into the barracks.

The men of the 1st battalion from Cork city, who had been selected for the attacking party, assembled at Killeens, outside the city. They took cover so as not to attract attention from the many who were walking in the neighbourhood on that lovely summer evening. There they waited for the cars from Cork to pick them up and take them to Blarney. The explosive, consisting of a prepared wooden frame enclosing slabs of gun cotton, was brought out there also. About nine o'clock a party of IRA men entered the garage of a motor company at Cornmarket Street and prepared five vans and a large private car for the road. These vehicles were sent out singly at short intervals (the premises were within a hundred yards of the Bridewell barracks), and timed so that the last one would reach Killeens at 9.40 p.m.

Meanwhile on every one of the maze of roads leading into

Blarney, with the exception of the Waterloo road, which was kept open as a line of retreat for our own motor vehicles, armed parties from the 1st and 6th battalion began to take up positions and make preparations for the effective blockading of these roads against motor transport. Trees were partly cut ready for felling, and inquisitive passers-by were detained. At 9.40, the last of the motor vehicles arriving at Killeens, the waiting men climbed in and the cars set off for Blarney. Outside the village the men in the vans dismounted and the vans were taken round the back of the village to the Waterloo road. The private car with its passengers drove up to the hotel door. The party in it entered the hotel, bringing the explosive with them. Already inside were two Volunteers who had walked out from the city earlier so as to be in a position to observe any matter that might affect the plan of attack as originally arranged. Ten o'clock was closing time, and it was a matter of a few minutes to get the remaining customers outside and the occupants of the hotel into a place of comparative safety. The doors were then closed and the explosive placed in position against the wall dividing the public room in the hotel from the barracks. A few men took up positions covering the front of the building; the remainder of the attacking party, other than the eight men already in the hotel, advanced to a position outside, from which they could rush quickly into the hotel as soon as the charge was blown.

At ten o'clock the charge was touched off, and a violent explosion, which was heard clearly in Cork city, shook the barracks and the hotel. The ground rocked with the force of the explosion, bricks, broken glass and plaster fell in all directions, and the hotel was filled with an impenetrable cloud of dust and smoke. For the party outside the explosion was the signal for their rush into the hotel; they were in before the debris ceased to fall, but so thick was the atmosphere that it was impossible to distinguish anybody or to see what effect the explosion had had upon the barrack wall. Firing started outside, both at the barracks and from it, in the interval of waiting for the dust to settle a little. After a while it became possible to see dimly what the effect of the explosion had been. A large area of the wall had been blown down, and in a substantial portion of it, to a depth of a couple of feet, but to our amazement the breach was still backed by solid masonry, and there was no aperture into the barrack. Afterwards it was possible to see the reason for this. The explosive had been placed on our side of the wall, opposite a point in the barrack building where a cross-wall joined the side-wall, and against which two corner fireplaces had been built. We had attacked the most solid block of masonry in the whole building.

It began to grow dusk outside, and in the gathering darkness inside the hotel a thorough investigation was made to find if there was any possible means of effecting an entrance to the barrack. When it was seen that the capture of the building could not be effected with the means and in the time at the disposal of the attacking party, and when it was clear that the post had been so badly damaged that its evacuation was a certainty, it was decided to withdraw. There was the problem of getting approximately four hundred men on protective duty out of the net which the enemy was already drawing around the area. Many of these men were poorly armed and could not be expected to hold off well-equipped enemy forces for more than a short period. The first contact between our men on protective duty and the enemy took place on the road from Carrigrohane Cross to Ballincollig, where a lorry of military ran into an IRA party preparing to cut trees on this road. The exchange of fire delayed the military, and the small IRA party retired in good order and without casualties. At Leemount another slight skirmish occurred, which further delayed the military.

Twenty-five men from the Donoughmore company of the 6th

battalion, armed with rifles and shotguns, had taken up a position at Healy's Bridge. They were supported by a section of twenty men from the Grenagh company in another position close by. At this point, about 10.20 p.m., the Donoughmore men engaged a party of military who were advancing on foot along the road towards Blarney from the Leemount direction. This party of military, about fifty strong, had been forced to leave their lorries further down the road, where trees had been felled. After an engagement lasting nearly half an hour, the military retired towards Leemount and awaited reinforcements. Afterwards the military advanced with great caution, and it was midnight before their advance guards arrived in Blarney. Meanwhile the withdrawal of the whole of the IRA force was taking place. The party engaged in the barrack attack utilised the motor transport to get back to the outskirts of the city, via the Waterloo road, and got their arms into a place of safety. All the men engaged in the whole operation got back to their own areas, and there were no casualties. The barracks was evacuated on the following day, and on the same evening was completely destroyed by the Blarney company.

The result of the operation may be summed up as having removed a dangerous enemy post and cleared a vital communication line, ensuring consequent freedom of movement for our men and greater safety for local units, as well as providing a valuable training exercise on a large scale under conditions very similar to those in which the fight developed in that and in the following year.

THE CAPTURE OF GENERAL LUCAS

by GEORGE POWER

FEW EPISODES IN the War for Independence captured the public imagination as did the capture of General Lucas on the banks of the Blackwater on a summer evening in 1920. For months afterwards the small boys of the neighbouring villages could be heard singing one of those unending ballads of which the introductory line to each verse began – 'Can anybody tell me where did General Lucas go?' The older generation, of course, felt something akin to horror at the temerity of these young people who so singularly lacked the respect and proper appreciation due to red tabs and gold braid. Nevertheless, the capture of General Lucas and his two staff officers was no haphazard incident, but rather the result of careful deliberation and planning on the part of the O/C Liam Lynch, and staff, Cork No. 2 brigade of the IRA.

At this time the O/C of the Fermoy battalion, Michael Fitzgerald, was on hunger strike in Cork jail as a protest against his detention without trial for many weeks. Realising that he would thereby lose an excellent officer, and a valued comrade, Liam Lynch conceived the daring idea of capturing the most senior of the British officers in Fermoy and holding him as a hostage. This appeared a formidable task indeed, but with the efficiency of the IRA Intelligence Service in those days, even the apparently impossible was sometimes achieved. A close, but unobtrusive watch was kept on the movements of the senior officers of the British garrison at Fermoy. Daily and even more frequently, intelligence reports were made to brigade HQ. Eventually an interesting report from the Fermoy battalion stated that General Lucas, with two of his staff, had left the barracks at Fermoy one morning for a day's fishing on the River Blackwater, east of the town. Only the general's personal servant went with the party as escort. The IRA officers were quick to appreciate the opportunity thus offered and plans were immediately made to carry out the capture of the British officers.

It thus happened that on a June evening in 1920, Liam Lynch, with three of his staff officers, Paddy Clancy, Seán Moylan and George Power, proceeded by car to a place called Kilbarry, on the banks of the Blackwater, about three miles east of Fermoy. It had been learned that the British officers had arrived there earlier in the day. The fishing lodge was quietly occupied and the general's personal servant arrested and handed over to a few of the local Volunteers who had been mobilised for the purpose of keeping the place under observation. The IRA officers then proceeded in search of General Lucas and the other two officers who were known to have accompanied him. One of the British officers was encountered a short distance from the fishing lodge; taken completely by surprise he offered no resistance and was led back a prisoner to the lodge. Shortly afterwards the second officer was located, just as he had tied up after the day's sport and was treated likewise. There was yet no trace of General Lucas and, as it was getting late in the afternoon, it was decided that two of the IRA officers should proceed, one up and the other down the river, in search of the missing officer.

It was coming through a small wood that George Power

unexpectedly ran into General Lucas, as he was making his way back towards the lodge. There was a moment's mutual scrutiny and on being given a sharp command to drop his fishing rod and put up his hands, the British general hesitated at first, but finally complied. He allowed himself to be disarmed and marched back to the fishing lodge. On his arrival there he was ordered to join his two brother officers who seemed much relieved to see their CO return unharmed. At that stage the IRA officers were not certain of the identity of their first two prisoners, so it was decided to ask General Lucas if he had any objection to naming his two comrades. To which he replied, 'None', provided he was made aware of the identity of his captors. Whereupon one of the IRA officers introduced Liam Lynch as O/C Cork No. 2 brigade, with three officers of his staff. Lucas then replied by pointing out Colonel Danford of the Royal Artillery, and Colonel Tyrell of the Royal Engineers, adding 'What do you propose to do with us?' He was informed that the three were to be held prisoners pending further instructions from IRA HQ. In the meantime facilities would be accorded them to communicate with their relatives.

The first part of the plan having been brought to such a successful conclusion, it was necessary to remove the captured officers well away from the Fermoy area without delay, as it was fully realised that the reactions to this incident would be swift and far-reaching. Accordingly it was decided to use in addition to the Ford car in which the IRA officers had travelled, the British officers' large touring car, for which a Volunteer driver was quickly found. The arrangement now made was that Seán Moylan and George Power would travel with Colonel Tyrell in the Ford car, and Liam Lynch with Paddy Clancy would accompany Lucas and Danford in the other car. The Ford was to travel fifty to one hundred yards ahead of the touring car, but to keep in touch as far as possible.

Making a detour south of Fermoy, the convoy set off on the hazardous journey west, which carried them virtually through the British lines. For a time all went well, the Ford maintaining its appointed distance ahead with the occupants keeping a watchful eye on the following car. As they approached the main Fermoy–Cork road, the Ford temporarily lost contact with the second car at a wide, sweeping bend in the road. By that time the British officers had begun to realise the gravity of the situation for them. Their instinct and training led them to make a bid for freedom, but the attempt had to be made quickly before they were transported further away from their familiar surroundings, into the mountainous country which they were now approaching. The general and his staff officer held a brief conversation in a strange language – subsequently discovered to be Arabic. Suddenly at a pre-arranged signal, the two prisoners sprang on their captors. The attack was so sudden and the element of surprise so complete that the IRA officers were at first taken at a disadvantage and almost disarmed before they realised what had happened. In the mêlée, the driver lost control and crashed the car into the ditch, being himself rendered unconscious by the impact. It was, therefore, an even fight between the four protagonists. The struggle between Lynch and Lucas was particularly severe, as both were strongly built, well-trained men, about six feet in height. In the first onslaught Lucas got on top of Lynch, making frantic efforts to wrench the gun from him and had all but succeeded when the door of the touring car gave way. They both rolled onto the roadway, still struggling wildly, until finally Lynch wore down his opponent and the general shouted 'I surrender'.

Meanwhile Paddy Clancy and Colonel Danford were fighting desperately, with Colonel Danford on top. He had almost succeeded in throttling the IRA officer when Lynch, turning around, took in the situation at a glance. He shouted to the British officer,

'Surrender or I shoot', but Colonel Danford ignored the command and maintained his savage grip on Clancy's throat. There was now no alternative and, without further hesitation, Lynch fired. Colonel Danford felt the sharp sting of a bullet wound in his jaw and collapsed over his opponent. The fight was then over. In the meantime, the occupants of the Ford car had proceeded on some distance, oblivious to the fact that a life and death struggle was taking place in the other car. Several valuable minutes had passed before they realised that something was amiss and decided to go back on their tracks. Immediately they rounded the wide bend in the road, an extraordinary scene met their gaze. The big touring car lay almost wrecked in the ditch, with the driver still unconscious by the wheel. Nearby on the grass verge lay Colonel Danford, with General Lucas bending over him rendering first aid. Some further distance away Liam Lynch was attending to Paddy Clancy, who still seemed badly shaken.

An entirely new and dangerous situation then confronted the IRA officers. The large touring ear was completely out of action, the Ford car was small and unreliable, and there was no time to arrange for alternative means of transport. After a hurried conference it was decided to allow Colonel Tyrell to remain with his badly wounded comrade, and the Volunteer driver, now fully recovered, was sent to get medical aid for him. George Power was instructed to return east in the Waterford direction and to proceed to Dublin, in order personally to report the whole affair to GHQ. The remainder of the party, including General Lucas, now the only prisoner, packed into the Ford and resumed the interrupted journey toward the Lombardstown area, close to which brigade HQ was located at that time.

It is interesting to recall that General Lucas, having failed in his bid for escape, became quite resigned to his lot and showed no resentment towards his captors. Indeed, Lynch and himself had many interesting discussions on a variety of subjects, but mainly on military matters, during the course of his captivity. On his eventual return to 'civilisation', General Lucas paid warm tribute to the chivalry of his IRA captors.

THE SACKING OF CORK

by F. O'DONOGHUE

THE BURNING OF Cork city by the British army of occupation on the night of 11 December 1920, was the most colossal single act of vandalism committed in the whole period of the national struggle from 1916 to 1921. But it would be a mistake to regard it as an isolated incident, or to accept in explanation of it the conventional excuse that the armed forces of England, drink-sodden and nerve-racked from a contest in which they were being worsted, had run amok and destroyed the city in a fit of frenzy. Indeed, to that ignominious excuse the spokesmen of the British government were ultimately driven; having passed through the successive stages of denying 'that there was any evidence that the fires were started by crown forces', of charging the burning of their own city first upon the IRA, and then upon the citizens themselves, and finally in ignorant and reckless desperation, assuring the world that the fires in the City Hall and Carnegie Library had spread from Patrick Street across the river and several intervening blocks of unburned buildings. It was an excuse, nevertheless, and one that was very far from the truth.

The burning and looting of Cork was not an isolated incident, but rather the large-scale application of a policy initiated and approved, implicitly or explicitly, by the government from which all authority of the British forces in Ireland was alleged to derive. That was a policy of subjugation, by terror, murder and rapine; of government by force of arms; of the deliberate destruction of those industries and resources whose absence would inflict the greatest hardship and loss upon the nation; of ruthless hunting down and extermination of those who stood for national freedom. The policy was, of course, presented to the world in a coat of smooth lies. 'Great Britain has no quarrel with Irishmen; her sole quarrel is with crime, outrage and disorder' – thus General Macready; the 'crime, outrage and disorder' being the acts of war of an Irish army, constitutionally acting under the authority of a national government elected by the vast majority of the Irish people, and engaged in a righteous war to expel the armed forces of an alien government. And that master of the art of mystification, Mr Lloyd George, with his eye on the influence of our people in the United States, had this to add: 'Fundamentally, the issue is the same as that in the war of north and south in the United States; it is an issue of secession and union', forgetting, or hoping that the public would forget, that this was a nation older than England, that had in every generation asserted its claim to independence, that had six times in the past three hundred years asserted it in arms, and that there was no analogy between our relations with England and the relations of north and south in the American Civil War.

A brief glance of the record of British forces in Ireland in the six months before the burning of Cork will be sufficient to indicate how this policy was being put into effect and how well these forces were carrying out their mission of 'preserving law and order'. The records of that time bear witness to the cold-blooded murder of men identified with the republican movement; to the arrest and imprisonment, in jails and internment camps, of thousands of Irishmen; to the deliberate drowning of unarmed men; to the shooting of unarmed prisoners on the pretence that they were attempting to escape; to the killing of untried and unarmed prisoners; to beatings, threats, insults and the whole litany of savage brutality by the forces of a powerful empire striving to extinguish in blood the nationhood of this people. In one month these 'forces of law and order' had burned and partially destroyed twenty-four towns; in one week they had shot up and sacked Balbriggan, Ennistymon, Mallow, Miltown-Malbay, Lahinch and Trim. These armed forces comprised three main groups, i.e. the army, the Royal Irish Constabulary and the Auxiliaries. The Royal Irish Constabulary included the remnant of the original force which had not retired or resigned and a reinforcement of British jail-birds and down-and-outs who had been hastily recruited into the force in England when candidates had ceased to offer themselves in Ireland. These instruments of despicable policy were the origin of the expression 'Black and Tan'. Owing to a shortage of uniforms in the early days of their appearance in Ireland, they wore the khaki trousers of the regular army and the dark green, almost black, tunic of the Royal Irish Constabulary. As fighting material they were of the poorest type, untrained, undisciplined and vicious; as policemen it would have been difficult in any country to assemble a more incongruous set of ruffians for police work; but they were not intended for police work – the Royal Irish Constabulary had ceased to be a police force except in name.

The Auxiliary force was of a different type. About 1,500 strong, they were organised as a separate command and consisted exclusively of ex-officers of the British army and navy, most of whom had seen service in the Great War. The establishment of this force was the last desperate effort of the British government to forge a weapon to defeat the IRA. They had fifteen companies scattered throughout the country; the men were very highly paid, and were a reckless, courageous, desperate force, hard-drinking and unprincipled. They were fitting instruments for the work they were intended to do, and the doubtful honour of leadership in the work of burning, shooting and destruction fell to them. Ultimate responsibility for the acts of all these forces rested on the British cabinet. The Auxiliaries were not uncontrolled soldiers of fortune, acting without authority, which they were sometimes conveniently represented to be; nor were their crimes the unpremeditated reaction of men exposed to the hazards of guerrilla warfare. Their actions had the sanction of a higher authority, although it was the policy first to give an indignant denial to any charge made against these forces, to stigmatise such a suggestion as a base calumny on heroes who fought in the Great War; and later, perhaps, under stress of undeniable proof, to admit grudgingly that a few Auxiliaries did get a trifle excited here and there. Neither were the Auxiliaries an irregular force, as was sometimes suggested. Lloyd George, in his letter to the bishop of Chelmsford on 19 April 1921, states specifically: 'There are no "irregular forces of the crown". The Auxiliary division of the Royal Irish Constabulary is a regular force.' Logically, then, when it is proved that these forces burned Cork, there can be no ambiguity as to where responsibility rests. Notwithstanding that there was a confusion of control and divergence of policy in the British command in Ireland, and possibly in the British cabinet on Irish policy, the burden of responsibility for what happened here is inescapable.

To understand the lack of cohesion that existed between the British forces in Ireland, it must be realised that there were two authorities representing Great Britain in this country, the civil and military. Normally, the civil authority, represented by Dublin Castle, controlled the police force; and when the Auxiliary division was established it was nominally under the control of this department. But the work which this or any other section of the police forces was doing was not police work; they were all armed military forces engaged in savage repression. The control of the regular military forces was in the hands of a military officer. In the martial law area (and Cork was in this area on the night of the burning) the police forces, Black and Tans, and the Auxiliaries were under the control of the military governor; in Dublin the Auxiliaries were subject to the military authorities, but the Royal Irish Constabulary were not. In the remainder of the country, outside the martial law area, the Auxiliaries were alleged to be under the control of the senior Royal Irish Constabulary officers, divisional commissioners and county inspectors. In this confusion of control it is not surprising to find each section acting without the knowledge or co-operation of the other sections, and not infrequently one section solemnly going through the farce of investigating offences committed by members of another section. The one shining example of their unanimity, in desire and action, was their co-operation in the burning of Cork.

A company of the Auxiliaries (K company) had been stationed at Cork military barracks since October 1920, and had indulged in raids on houses, holding up and searching civilians in the streets, robbery and insulting behaviour. In November and December their drunken aggressiveness became so pronounced that no person was safe from their molestations. Age or sex was no protection. Poor women were robbed of their few shillings in the streets by these 'gentlemen' in broad daylight. After their raids on houses articles of value were frequently missing. Whips were taken from shops with which to flog unoffending pedestrians. Drink was demanded at the point of the revolver.

The IRA determined to put an end to this intolerable situation. Ambushes were laid at various points in the city over a period of several weeks, and that at Dillon's Cross on the night of 11 December was the first to come off. The difficulties faced by the

IRA in operating in the city in this period were immense. Enemy forces had barracks in all parts of the city; they were equipped with fast cars, lorries and armoured cars, in which they could swoop on any part of the city at short notice. They were, of course, vastly superior in numbers and armament to the IRA. One thing they lacked which the IRA had in generous measure – the co-operation of the people – and without it they were blind and impotent. That a group of armed men could frequent a particular locality for long periods day after day without their presence being remarked upon was inconceivable. Yet IRA men frequently did duty of this kind, and no word was ever passed to the enemy by the hundreds who must have seen them daily. The ambush at Dillon's Cross took place within a couple of hundred yards of the military barracks. Lorries of Auxiliaries were bombed and raked with revolver fire. At least one Auxiliary was killed and twelve were wounded. The IRA party of six men got away without injury to a single man. An ambush had been laid in the same position two weeks earlier, but did not come off.

Indiscriminate shooting in the main streets of the city commenced shortly after eight o'clock; and it was remarked that it was Black and Tans and not the Auxiliaries who were so engaged. Curfew was at ten o'clock, but long before that hour the streets were almost deserted. An air of impending disaster was evident everywhere; many had been warned to get to their homes, as trouble was expected that night. This was before the ambush took place. It is difficult to say with certainty whether or not Cork would have been burned on that night if there had not been an ambush. What appears more probable is that the ambush provided the excuse for an act which was long premeditated and for which all arrangements had been made. The rapidity with which supplies of petrol and Verey lights were brought from Cork barracks to the centre of the city, and the deliberate manner in which the work of firing the various premises was divided amongst groups under the control of officers, gives evidence of organisation and pre-arrangement. Moreover, the selection of certain premises for destruction and the attempt made by an Auxiliary officer to prevent the looting of one shop by Black and Tans: 'You are in the wrong shop; that man is a loyalist', and the reply, 'We don't give a damn; this is the shop that was pointed out to us', is additional proof that the matter had been carefully planned beforehand.

About ten o'clock, two houses at Dillon's Cross were set on fire by Auxiliaries and Black and Tans. Auxiliaries patrolled the roads in the neighbourhood to prevent any attempt being made to extinguish the fires. One man who attempted to save his furniture from a house next door to one of those on fire was immediately fired upon and assaulted. He was dragged through a neighbour's backyard, put up against a wall and threatened to be shot. Only the intervention of some women saved his life. When these fires were started a call was sent to the fire brigade, and a section of the brigade from Grattan Street started out to go to Dillon's Cross. On arrival in Patrick Street, through which they had to pass on their way, the firemen saw that Grant's drapery warehouse was on fire. They decided, on seeing the immensity of this conflagration, to go to the fire brigade headquarters at Sullivan's Quay for assistance. From there the military authorities at Cork barracks were asked on the phone to send their fire-fighting appliances to the fires at Dillon's Cross. No notice was taken of the request and the fires at Dillon's Cross blazed on until the houses were charred ruins.

Before the curfew hour at ten o'clock motley groups of armed ruffians appeared upon the streets; the emptying city rang to the crack of indiscriminate rifle and revolver fire. Some in these groups wore uniforms, some were in civilian attire; here and there a police greatcoat would be observed over civilian clothes, or ordinary overcoats over police or military uniforms. Auxiliaries, Black and Tans, soldiers – some were half drunk, many were shouting and jeering, all were wild, furious, savage, exultant in the urge to destruction. A tram car going up Summerhill, full of passengers and on its last journey for the night, was set upon by Auxiliaries and Black and Tans; the passengers were dragged or pushed out upon the road, searched, threatened, abused, beaten with rifle butts and fired upon. A priest who was a passenger in the tram was singled out for special attention. He was put up against a wall, his overcoat, jacket and vest and collar were torn off; he was knocked sprawling upon the ground and told to say 'To hell with the Pope'. He refused and was told he would be shot. Another group intervened; he was kicked again and told to run. He was unable to do so after the treatment he had received, and was pushed up the hill with the muzzle of a rifle in his back. His clothes were kicked before him some distance up the hill, and he was fired at while attempting to pick them up. As curfew hour approached the few pedestrians upon the streets became the targets for the shots of the incendiaries. Some were fired at without warning, the moment they appeared round a bend or a street corner. Others were held up, beaten, asked to sing 'God save the King', ordered to run and then fired at. A tram was set on fire near Patrick's Bridge. By ten o'clock the centre of the city was deserted, except for its despoilers.

From their great barracks on the hill above the city, fresh hordes of armed men now issued forth, lorries laden with petrol tins swept through the empty streets and over the river bridges into the main thoroughfares. From the city police barracks other groups emerged, and soon the central streets of the city were overrun by swarming masses of violent men intent upon loot and destruction. All discipline was not quite lost at first; the group that fired Grant's, the first premises in the city to be given to flames, marched up the street in military formation, though most of them were in civilian attire. They were under the command of Auxiliary officers. Later the group setting fire to Cash's was directed by the sharp commands of a military officer. But soon all discipline relaxed and the uncontrolled orgy of burning and looting began. One after another all the principal business houses in Patrick Street were set on fire. At the Munster Arcade, where a number of persons were residing, shots were fired through the doors, the windows were smashed and bombs were thrown into the building. The men and women who were on the premises were ordered out at the point of the revolver, and kept on the street under the guard of two RIC men for several hours. These men and women saw a military officer and an RIC man take tins of petrol and go upstairs into the Munster Arcade; they saw some of the police put masks over their faces; they heard the predominant English accents above the smashing of glass, the crash of bombs and the crack of rifle shots.

Looting was going on all the time. Some of the looted shops were burned, others were not. From many shops groups emerged laden with suitcases; silks and articles of clothing protruding from some of those cases where the looters, in their greed and haste, had failed to pack them properly. The lurid flames rose ever higher into the night sky, and in their ruddy glare the passing lorries of curfew patrols cheered the furious incendiaries. The raging fires were spreading with every passing minute, and soon it seemed as if the whole city must be involved. The fire brigade was doing its heroic best to cope with a situation far beyond the capabilities of its resources. The firemen did marvellous work in confining the fires at some points; but their efforts were hampered; not alone by the inadequacy of the hose lines to deal with an unprecedented conflagration, but by the more serious factor that they were continuously under fire from the incendiaries, and literally took their lives in their hands throughout that awful night. A new line of hose at the General Post Office was got out to assist the quelling of the fires in that locality. It was deliberately cut with bayonets and rendered useless. Firemen were frequently fired at, one at least was hit and the ambulance taking him to the North Infirmary was again fired on. As the night wore on the effects of drink became more and more evident. Hotels and public houses were raided, stocks of spirits were consumed or taken away. The smashing of bottles was added to the all-pervading sounds of destruction. Attempts were made to fire other premises. They failed only because of the drunken exhaustion of sated devils. There was no sleep for the residents in the centre of the city that night. Those who had been driven from their homes, and had seen them given to the flames, sought shelter with friends or in hotels. Residents in houses threatened by spreading fires tried to save their household goods and furniture by removing them to the streets or to houses in a safer position. The awesome roar of raging flames rose like the sound of a great wind above the obscene clamour that marked the flowing tide of destruction. Great pillars of fire produced marvellous combinations of brilliant colour and wreathing form; the crashing of roofs and walls sent up effervescent showers of glowing sparks; over the whole city there hung a dense, dull pall of heavy smoke.

Attempts were made to start fires in shops on the Grand Parade and Washington Street. A fire was actually started in a shop next door to Saint Augustine's church and priory in Washington Street. If this blaze had not been extinguished by some civilians before it had got a firm hold on the premises, it is probable that not alone the shop but the church and priory as well would have been destroyed. The shutters were torn down from a jeweller's shop on the Grand Parade, the windows were smashed and armed bands of looters invaded the shop. Later they were seen emerging with kit bags filled with the contents of the looted shop and making off with their booty in the direction of the Union Quay barracks of the Royal Irish Constabulary. An armed party, led by a military officer, went through Marlboro Street smashing windows on both sides of the street until not a ground floor window was left intact. Boots and shoes were looted from Tyler's shop in Winthrop Street and carried away by the incendiaries.

The City Hall and the Carnegie Library close by it were destined to suffer the same fate as Patrick Street. The City Hall had withstood several previous attempts at burning it; windows that had been broken in an earlier attempt to effect an entrance were now protected by corrugated iron shutters. A few firemen were on duty there every night as a precautionary measure. But this building which had so many historic associations with the national and civil life of Cork was, because of these associations, an object specially marked out for destruction by the British forces. In this hall Tomás MacCurtain had been elected first republican lord mayor of Cork – he who was soon afterwards to make the supreme sacrifice for his faith in that kindly, Gaelic way of life which he himself had personified. Here his body had lain in state, his face serene in death, while his nation mourned for one so well beloved, and the endless crowds, patient in the bleak March wind, waited silently to pass before that guarded bier. And here his successor, Terence MacSwiney, a soldier with calm foreknowledge stepping into the breach of death, had spoken deathless words that called forth a supreme courage in the whole people at a time when it was sought to break their spirit by terror. 'It is not to those who can inflict most but to those who can suffer most that the victory is assured.' This place was forever hallowed by their memory; all their enemies could do was to destroy it. Here the Volunteers had been started; in the shadow of its walls the heartening sound of marching men of an Irish army – the first to be heard in this city for a generation – had carried a measure of hope and encouragement to those who, in patience and obscurity, had laboured through long years for this day. Under its roof those associated with the national movement had passed many a happy night in concert and céilidhe; into it flowed, and there coalesced, in the years 1917 to 1919, all those elements that went to make a great national resurgence, that helped to build up an organisation that withstood the terrific strain of the following years. This place was now marked down for destruction.

About two o'clock on Sunday morning, heavy firing from incendiaries gathered round it drove the firemen on duty in the Hall into the comparative safety of the Bandon railway station behind it. The raiders effected an entrance by getting over the library wall, and with axe and sledge-hammer breaking a door into the back corridor of the Hall. For over two hours they were in possession of the building, while their comrades brought tins of petrol from the Union Quay barracks close by. Deliberate and thorough preparations were made for the total and effective destruction of the building. Explosives were placed in position and the whole contents soaked in petrol. Shortly after four o'clock the 'all clear' was sounded, the raiders emerged, and a terrific explosion was heard. This was followed by about ten lesser explosions in the next half hour and the fire spread with great rapidity to all parts of the building.

Equally thorough and effective preparations were then made for the destruction of the Carnegie Library adjoining the City Hall, and soon this fine building, with its hundreds of thousands of volumes, was a mass of flames. The firemen got a line of hose playing on the Carnegie Library, but a party of police who were on duty close to the hydrant turned the water off as soon as the firemen had turned it on. These parties of policemen were under the control of a head constable and three sergeants, and they deliberately turned off the water at the hydrant every time the firemen turned it on. The firemen protested to the head constable; he said he had no control over these men. After nine or ten attempts to keep the water turned on, the firemen were forced to desist and take their line of hose into Patrick Street. There was then no hope for the City Hall or the Library. The clock on the City Hall tower still rang the quarters above that raging inferno; it struck six for the last time on that tragic Sunday morning, and then clock and tower crashed into the ruins below.

The following extract from the official report of the then superintendent of the Cork fire brigade, Mr Alfred J. Huston, requires no comment:

> I have no hesitation in stating that I believe all the fires were incendiary fires, and that a considerable amount of petrol or some such inflammable spirit was used in one and all of them. In some cases explosives were also used, and persons were seen to go into and come out of the structures and breaking an entrance into same, and in some cases that I have attended the people have been brought out of their houses and detained in by-lanes until the fire had gained great headway. I have some of the petrol tins left behind in my possession.

The most ghastly deed in all that night of horror was the cold-blooded murder of two Volunteers, Con and Jeremiah Delaney, at their home at Dublin Hill, just outside the city. These two brothers had been active Volunteers and their house and farm had been used for safe storage of arms and ammunition. About 2 a.m. on the morning of 12 December loud knocking at their doors awakened members of the family. A party of armed raiders who had arrived in a lorry were outside, and demanded immediate admission –

demanded it loudly and threateningly. Daniel Delaney, father of Con and Jeremiah, admitted them, and was asked his name and if he was a Sinn Féiner. He answered that he was an old man and not interested in politics. He was next asked who was in the house, and he replied that there was no one but his family, who were in bed. Eight men had entered the house, and they demanded to be shown to his sons' room. They entered the room occupied by Con and Jeremiah Delaney, and their uncle, William Dunlea. At the point of the revolver, the raiders ordered them out of bed, and asked if their name was Delaney. Immediately they said 'Yes' they were fired at and mortally wounded. William Dunlea was fired at and wounded in two places. Jeremiah, who was fired at first, died almost immediately, his sister holding a crucifix to his lips. Con survived almost a week, until Saturday 18 December. Their dreadful work accomplished, the murderers went downstairs, but they did not leave the house. The sisters of the wounded boys, terrified and distracted though they were by the stark horror of that awful calamity, were doing what they could for their brothers. One of them on her way downstairs to go for a priest was met by one of the raiders rushing upstairs again, a revolver in one hand, a flash lamp in the other, demanding, 'Is anyone belonging to me up there?' The grief-stricken father answered him, 'Nobody but dead men.' Miss Delaney attempted to get out through the kitchen door to go for a priest and medical assistance. She was prevented from doing so by one of the raiders, who remarked, 'If the house is all right what is the need for a priest?' The murderers remained for about a quarter of an hour before they left in a motor lorry. The members of the family were all in agreement that the raiders wore military uniform, spoke with foreign accents, and that some had handkerchiefs over their faces. A message was sent to the city for the ambulance, but it was too fully engaged to come out. A priest came from the North

Presbytery about 4 a.m., and at eight o'clock the ambulance came and removed Con to the Mercy Hospital.

When the cold dawn broke on that December Sunday morning, revealing the results of the night's madness, what a scene of ruin and desolation the city presented! Many familiar landmarks were gone forever; many a remembered contour and skyline had given place to gaping cavities where whole buildings had collapsed; here and there a solitary wall, windowless and heat-blistered, leaned at some crazy angle from its foundation. The streets ran sooty water, the footpaths were strewn with debris and broken glass, ruins smoked and smouldering, and over everything there was the all-pervading smell of burning. Three million pounds' worth of goods and property had been destroyed.

There was an immediate universal demand for an impartial public inquiry into the burnings. The Cork Corporation, Chamber of Commerce, Harbour Board, and other public bodies joined with the Sinn Féin leaders and local unionists in asking for such an inquiry. The Parliamentary Labour Party offered to prove at such an inquiry 'that the fires were the work of crown forces'. Every party was anxious for the fullest possible investigation, except the British government. The British Labour Commission, which was in Ireland at the time investigating the outrages by British forces, intimated their conviction, after investigation on the spot, that the fires were caused by crown forces, and offered to produce reliable evidence to prove it. Press and public demanded an inquiry. The British government resolutely refused. 'The best inquiry, and the most impartial,' said Hamar Greenwood, 'will be made by the general officer commanding on the spot.'

'In the present condition of Ireland,' declared Bonar Law, 'we are much more likely to get an impartial inquiry in a military court than in any other.' And so the 'impartial investigation' was made by the criminals themselves. And the findings of even that 'inquiry' were never published.

The Cork Corporation sent the following reply to a telegram received by the city engineer from the commanding officer, Cork barracks, asking him to appear before the 'inquiry':

> We have instructed the City Engineer and other corporate officials to take no part in the English military inquiry into the burning of this city, with which we charge the English military and police forces before the whole world. We adhere to the offer made by the City members and the lord mayor to submit evidence already in our possession before an impartial international tribunal, or before a court of fair-minded Englishmen.

The Curfew Report for the night of 11–12 December concocted by the military officer in charge of the curfew patrols, in consultation with the officer in charge of the Auxiliaries, is worth quoting, showing what little reliance can be placed on any official document issued by the army of occupation at that time:

1. Three arrests were made.
2. At 22.00 hours Grant & Co. in Patrick Street, was found to be on fire. Warning was at once sent to all fire brigades.
3. At about 00.30 hours Cash & Co. and the Munster Arcade were reported on fire.
4. At 05.30 hours the majority of the troops were withdrawn, and the remainder at 08.00 hours.
5. Explosions were heard at 00.15 hours, but were not located. No shots were fired by the troops.

F.R. EASTWOOD, Major,
Brigade Major, 17th In. brigade,
Cork, 12/12/20.

To these depths of evasion and lying the campaign in Ireland had reduced the great British army.

There was an implication in the British government's insistence that the inquiry should be held by General Strickland that whatever had happened in Cork that night, the military, as distinct from the Auxiliaries and police forces, had no responsibility for it. The Curfew Report itself is an indication of how far from the truth this contention is. In fact, of the armed forces in occupation of the city, the prime responsibility rested on the military. The area was under martial law. All responsibility for the preservation of public order had been forcibly taken out of the hands of the citizens. A military governor was in control. Curfew commenced at 10 p.m. and no person had authority to be on the streets between that hour and 3 a.m. without a permit from this military governor. Yet it was precisely at the time when the military were in absolute possession and control of the city that the destruction took place. General Strickland and his officers failed utterly to take any steps to prevent the fires, to limit their extent or to stop looting in the area under their command. They had sufficient force to do these things, but the will to do them was absent.

One of the minor mysteries of the night is what became of much of the looted property. General Crozier, who was in charge of the Auxiliary forces in Ireland, put it on record that one member of this force opened up a depot in the north of England for the sale of property looted in Ireland. Whether the Cork loot found its way to this depot or not is still unknown; what is certain is that the military authorities did prevent the sending away of some looted property which had been committed to the post by Auxiliaries. What became of this property ultimately, since it was never returned to the owners?

When it became clear that no impartial inquiry into the burnings would be permitted by the British government, the Sinn Féin organisation took the matter in hand and proceeded to collect evidence in connection with the events of the night of 11 December. Sworn statements were taken from nearly one hundred witnesses, including American citizens and Englishmen, as well as many local persons who were not in sympathy with the national movement. This evidence was detailed and specific, and was so overwhelmingly conclusive that no doubt could remain in the mind of any reasonable person but that the city of Cork had been deliberately burned by the British army of occupation on that night.

THE KENTS AND THEIR FIGHT FOR FREEDOM

by P.J. POWER

Accursed be the false worded tongue of the raider;
Accursed be the sons of the Gael who would aid her;
Let him who feels shame for his ancestor's story
Begone from our pathway – let ours be the glory,
We'll conquer or die, as our fathers of old
Have died for the land of the Green and the Gold.

From a poem written by the late Thomas R. Kent,
Commandant Cork brigade IRA, during Easter Week, 1916

IN THE DAYS when Ireland was fighting desperately against tyran-nical landlordism, the Kent family, of Bawnard House, Castlelyons, four miles from Fermoy, was known throughout the length and breadth of the land for the important part it played in the Land War. For generations the Kents farmed two hundred acres at Bawnard and were models of efficiency as men of the land. The five young Kents, Edmund, Richard, Thomas, David and William, with their respected curate, Rev. Fr O'Dwyer, experienced several long terms of imprisonment during the Land League days. These young men, with their great following of Irish tenant farmers, went a long way towards achieving what their successors succeeded in accomplishing

– the defeat of the tyrannical Landlord and Balfour Coercion Acts. They finally saw the tenant farmers' grievances redressed and their rights vindicated by the Land Acts, which enabled them to purchase their holdings and establish their title to the land, under fair rent and free sale.

In 1889 all members of the Kent family were arrested. Owing to his youth, the younger brother, Richard, was acquitted by the notorious resident magistrates, Colonels Gardiner and Caddel, long since deceased. David received six months' hard labour, and Edmund and William were each sentenced to four months' hard labour for conspiracy with others to evade paying their rents. The sentences were served in Cork County jail. The brothers were also put under rule of bail for refusing to enter into bail for their future good behaviour. They thus gained themselves an additional three months' imprisonment. A short time after their release Thomas, who had been in America, returned and threw his lot into the fight. Both he and William were arrested and brought before the resident magistrate court under the Balfour Coercion Acts. Another trumped-up charge of conspiracy was brought against them. William received six months' hard labour and Thomas was sentenced to two months, these sentences being once again served in Cork jail. A historic scene was witnessed in their native town of Fermoy when they arrived at the station on the expiration of their term of imprisonment. They were warmly received by thousands of their fellow countrymen and escorted all the way home to Bawnard. Subsequently came the Parnell split which created turmoil, confusion and factions in the country. After this sad event, the Kents ceased to take any part in politics, until the Easter Rising in 1916.

The Kents looked upon the passing of Home Rule as a treache-rous act of deception instigated by the British government to 'pull wool over the eyes' of the youth of Ireland, and to persuade them to volunteer for the British army on the pretext of fighting for the freedom of small nations. On the formation of the Ulster Volunteers, organised to defeat Home Rule, the Kents, following discussion amongst themselves, decided that if the Ulster Volunteers were to carry out their threat of marching from Belfast to Cork, means should be devised to prevent them. The march did not take place. The Kents collected rifles and shotguns. Thomas, who was later closely associated with the leaders in Dublin, knew that Ireland's opportunity would arise and would be availed of when England would be engaged in a European war.

In 1914 Thomas and David, with Terence MacSwiney, took an active part in the enrolment of the Irish Volunteers. They called a meeting in Clonmult, and got the famous Clonmult hurlers to march to the village of Dungourney where a British recruiting meeting was being held. Thomas, David and MacSwiney led the men through this meeting and, halting a short distance away from it, addressed the crowd, advising them to join the Volunteers and have nothing whatever to do with the British army. A few weeks afterwards Thomas and MacSwiney were arrested and tried before a bench of magistrates in Cork. Both were remanded, brought up for trial and acquitted. Within a week or two Thomas was again arrested and sentenced to two months' imprisonment, because arms and ammunition were found in the house.

Came the Rising in 1916. Thomas was to be informed by head-quarters in Dublin as to what his position would be in the southern command. He was at that time commandant of the Galtee brigade. No official communication reached him. It was afterwards learned that the man who was entrusted to deliver the dispatch never did so. The first news of the Rising that reached Bawnard was contained in the morning papers. Ammunition was immediately got ready for rifles, revolvers and shotguns, in anticipation of being called up to join their comrades in Dublin. Days passed and no notice came.

Notwithstanding the news that the Rising had been quelled, the Kents did not remain at home by night. They returned to sleep at home for the first time on the night of 1 May, and awoke on the following morning to find the house surrounded by British crown forces. The household was awakened by a loud knocking at the hall door. William, who was sleeping in the eastern portion of the house, jumped out of bed and putting his head out the window, asked 'Who's there?' The answer was 'Police; come down.'

He immediately awakened Tom, who was sleeping in the western side of the house, and said, 'The whole place is surrounded. We're caught like rats in a trap.'

Tom, donning his clothes, armed himself with a rifle, and without showing himself, called out to those below, 'What do you want?' As expected, the answer came, 'We are police and have orders to arrest the whole family.'

The men's mother, over eighty years of age, dressed herself, and the answer of the whole family was flung defiantly to those outside: 'We are soldiers of the Irish Republic and there is no surrender.' The police fired a volley after which a fierce conflict ensued. Armed with three shotguns and a rifle the Kents maintained a strong defence. Head Constable Rowe was shot dead, while others of the Royal Irish Constabulary were wounded during the conflict, which lasted for three hours. Military reinforcements arrived and when the last shot was fired from the house it was seen that David was badly wounded, having lost two fingers and received a gaping wound in his side. Owing to lack of ammunition, the Kents, who had fought so bravely in defence of their home and of the Irish Republic, had no alternative but to surrender.

All during the fight the mother played her part, loading the weapons and assisting with words of encouragement. The house was completely wrecked. Not a pane of glass was left unbroken. The interior was 'tattooed' with the marks of rifle bullets. The altar and statues in the beautiful oratory alone escaped destruction. All round the altar plaster was knocked off the walls, but not one of the statues was struck. This was remarkable. At one period the fire of the attackers was drawn from the men's room to that of their mother, as the British military and Royal Irish Constabulary thought a woman was firing at them through the oratory window.

Following the surrender the Kents were taken through the window, assisted by the military, and were immediately handcuffed. Thomas was not permitted time to put on his boots. Their aged mother was also taken out. David, who was badly wounded, was given aid by a military doctor. Richard, a famous athlete, was not handcuffed and in the confusion he attempted to escape by bounding over a hedge nearby. He was immediately fired on and fell mortally wounded. The Kents were then lined up against a wall of the house by the Royal Irish Constabulary, who prepared to shoot them, when a military medical officer interposed himself between the firing party and the prisoners. Ordering the police to desist, his words to the firing party were: 'I am in command here; enough lives have been lost, and I take these men as prisoners.'

Under heavy military escort the Kents, including their mother, were conveyed to Fermoy military barracks. The mother was subsequently released, while Thomas and William were taken to Cork detention barracks. David and Richard being wounded were taken to the Fermoy military hospital, where Richard died of his wounds two days later. Before his death he received the consolation of the Last Sacrament.

The remains were handed over to the relatives on condition that the funeral would leave the town as quickly as possible. The small cortège wended its way down Barrack Hill and was halted by a barrier on the bridge which was patrolled by military. The general public was not allowed to attend the funeral and a pathetic scene was witnessed when, as it passed Pearse Square, old women with shawls knelt on the sidewalks and told their beads silently, tears streaming down their cheeks. Several young men from Cork Road escorted the remains to Castlelyons, in defiance of the British order.

But for the kindness of Dr Brody, David would have been immediately court-martialled and shot. He kept David under medical treatment in the hospital, and refused to certify him fit for removal until things had calmed down somewhat. Perhaps the British government did not wish to wipe out the whole family. Accordingly, there was a lapse of over two weeks before he was transferred to Cork detention barracks.

Meanwhile, on 4 May, two days after the attack on Bawnard, Thomas and William were court-martialled. William was acquitted, but Thomas was sentenced to death and executed on 9 May by a British firing squad. When asked by the officer in command if he wished to make any last request, Thomas asked that no Irishman would be ordered to shoot him. Another firing squad belonging to the Scottish Borderers was then sent for. Thomas also requested the priest who was in attendance to have his grave consecrated. When offered a stimulant before being led in to his execution, he haughtily refused it, saying that he did not need any, and adding that in a short time he would be before his God. He was buried where he fell, and his remains are still there in the disused detention barracks in Cork city, notwithstanding the fact that William made several requests to have them removed and interred in the family vault at Castlelyons with his brothers Richard and David, who had fought beside him so gallantly at nearby Bawnard.

Arrangements were made for David's trial at Cork detention

barracks, but an order came from the British government that the trial be transferred to Richmond barracks, Dublin. He was subsequently tried there by a military court martial, presided over by Lord Chelesmore, and was ably defended by Mr Patrick Lynch, KC. After a prolonged hearing he was found guilty and sentenced to death, the sentence being subsequently commuted to penal servitude for life. He was transferred to Dartmoor prison and then to Pentonville, from which he was released with other soldiers of the IRA on the general amnesty.

While David was in prison his mother died, and on his return home his health was greatly impaired. At three elections he was elected TD on the Sinn Féin ticket, for the East Cork constituency. He never took his seat in the present Dáil as he refused to take the oath of allegiance. He thus forfeited his deposit, which was never returned. He was sent to America on a mission of propaganda on behalf of the IRA. He returned home after some months, far poorer in health and, after a life of struggle for the freedom of his country, this brave soldier and patriot died at his old home at Bawnard on 16 November 1930. He died as he lived – uncompromised and uncompromising, a faithful soldier of the Irish Republic.

A PATRIOT PRIEST
OF CORK CITY

by F. O'DONOGHUE

A CHARACTERISTIC OF Fr Dominic was his genius for friendship – particularly the friendship of men. After his love of God and his love of Ireland, it was perhaps the most outstanding characteristic of a very lovable personality. He was gifted with qualities of loyalty and sympathetic understanding which made him the ideal friend. It is not only in his native city of Cork, where he was known and loved by everybody connected with the national movement, that this genius of his was evident. It flowered, too, in the wilds of Oregon, where he spent the last years of his life; there his memory is a valued treasure, in shack and mansion, to people in many walks of life, and some not of his own faith. They, with us, mourn the loss of a great priest and a splendid friend.

A picture of him that remains in the mind, recalls that desolate March morning in 1920, when the bullets of official assassins had taken the life of Tomás MacCurtain. Fr Dominic was one of the first to arrive at the stricken home in the grey dawn to offer consolation and sympathy to the widow and little children of the man whose civic chaplain he was. How much the presence of that brown-robed Capuchin must have meant to them in those first hours of stunning tragedy!

Again, in a Brixton prison cell, as chaplain to the second republican lord mayor of Cork, he said Mass twice a week and gave daily Communion to his friend Terence MacSwiney during the long agony of his martyrdom. Afterwards he spoke with enthusiasm of the intense and ardent devotion of the dying patriot, of his desire to join the company of Eoghan Roe O'Neill, Joan of Arc and Tomás MacCurtain in the Third Order. And when death came at last Fr Dominic saw that the spent frame of his friend was robed in the habit of Saint Francis underneath his Volunteer uniform.

Born in Cork in 1883, Fr Dominic was educated at the Christian Brothers' schools and Rochestown monastery, where he entered the Order in 1899. He was ordained on Saint Patrick's Day, 1906. Every phase of the national resurgence found in him an enthusiastic and practical supporter. He took a great interest in the work of the Gaelic League; he was a keen student of the language and a consistent worker for its revival.

After some years of service as chaplain in Greece during the Great War, he returned to Cork in 1917, and from then until 1922 every moment that could be spared from his religious duties was given to the national movement. When the conscription menace was threatening and feverish preparations were being made by the Volunteers for mass resistance to the decree, if the attempt should be made to put it into operation, Tomás MacCurtain appointed Fr Dominic brigade chaplain of Cork brigade. With characteristic energy, he threw himself into the task of making preparation and provision for the spiritual needs of the large bodies of men that would become involved in the conflict. He appointed battalion chaplains, arranged for the celebration of Masses and the giving of the Sacraments under such active service conditions as were anticipated to arise, and generally made admirable provision for the spiritual needs of the Volunteer army.

When the menace of conscription was defeated by the united will of the whole people, and the battle for independence began to develop in the form of guerrilla warfare, Fr Dominic adapted his organisation to the changed conditions, and carried it on up to the time of his arrest by the British forces in 1920. How valuable a factor this silent service was in these years, few outside those directly concerned will ever appreciate. Apart from the physical dangers, sensitive minds were often harassed by the conflicting views on the moral questions involved in the struggle. How many – on both sides of the conflict – sought enlightenment and reassurance on these difficult matters!

He did not think of himself; he sought neither favour nor gratitude; he wanted only to help others in their difficulties, to be the friend to whom all could come in confidence of consolation and advice. He made little of his own troubles and sufferings, and was ever cheerful and unchanging in his views.

With Fr Albert, he was arrested in Church Street Friary, Dublin, in January 1921, and after being first tortured in Dublin Castle by British officers, he was sentenced to five years' penal servitude and deported to an English prison. He was released under a general amnesty in January 1922, and continued in his republican allegiance. When the Civil War broke out he, with Fr Albert, brought spiritual aid to the besieged garrison in the Four Courts, and remained with them until the building was demolished. Afterwards he ministered to both sides in the Wicklow Mountains.

In 1922 he was sent to Bend, Oregon; and when he died there on 17 October 1935, he was pastor of Saint Mary's of the Angels, Hermiston, Oregon, having in the meantime ministered at Lakeview, Bend, Baber and Hermiston.

There, in far away Oregon, his remains lie in a metallic coffin in a non-Catholic cemetery; his last wish – that his bones should rest in Ireland – unfulfilled. He had a premonition of death. In those last years he spoke frequently of his desire to return and die in his own land. He had taken out his first citizenship papers in the United States, but could not go on with it. 'I am a citizen of the Irish Republic,' he said, 'and I can never be anything else.'

Will Irishmen be satisfied to leave the last wish of this patriot priest unfulfilled, be satisfied to leave his remains and those of his fellow-exile, Fr Albert, lie forever in a foreign grave? Surely not.

MICK FITZGERALD, GALLANT SOLDIER OF FERMOY

by P.J. POWER

FIRST OF AN undaunted band of soldiers to follow Tomás Ashe to death by hunger strike was Mick Fitzgerald, gallant hero of Fermoy. Of gentle disposition, strictly temperate and a non-smoker, Mick joined the Irish Volunteers in Fermoy, in March 1914. His outstanding soldierly qualities were soon recognised, and in due course he was appointed O/C of the 4th battalion, Cork 2nd brigade.

To Mick Fitzgerald fell the distinction of being in charge of the small body of men who brought off the capture of one of the first Royal Irish Constabulary barracks to fall to the Volunteers. This took place on Easter Sunday 1919. Having observed Araglen barracks until the constables stationed there had gone to Mass, leaving one policeman in charge, the Volunteers pulled off the capture without a hitch. The remaining constable, not suspecting that there was anything unusual afoot, left the barracks to fetch a bucket of water. On his return he was astonished to see the 'boys' in possession, and before he could recover from the shock, he was pounced upon, securely bound and lodged in a cell. Apart from its daring nature, the episode was not without humour. Having secured the limb of the law, Mick Fitzgerald and his comrades stripped the barracks of rifles, revolvers, ammunition and batons, and in a few minutes decamped with the booty.

About two weeks after the Araglen incident, Mick Fitzgerald was arrested at Clondulane, the authorities having found a quantity of ammunition in the house in which he resided. Brought to Fermoy he was tried and sentenced to two months' imprisonment in Cork jail. This sentence he endured in solitary confinement. Released towards the end of August 1919, he was soon active and was once again a thorn in the side of the British. Notwithstanding an illness due to his recent incarceration, and because of which he was warned by his comrades to desist from his revolutionary activities, he was one of a party of Volunteers who held up a detachment of British military on their way to service at the Wesleyan church, near the Fermoy courthouse. In that daring hold-up, the first of its kind carried out in broad daylight, one British soldier, Private Jones, lost his life, while several other soldiers were wounded. General Liam Lynch directed the action, which had for its objective the capture of the soldiers' rifles. It was entirely successful, the military having been taken completely by surprise.

The British immediately made great preparations for a general round-up in the area, and on the following morning were every-where searching. A large number of Volunteers were arrested, including Mick Fitzgerald, who, as he was rather low-sized, was perhaps identified as having taken part in the Wesleyan incident. He was brought before R.M. Dickson at Fermoy court and charged with the murder of Private Jones. Remanded on the capital charge he was returned to the Assizes but, no jury being forthcoming to try the case, he was put back time and again.

Seeing that there was no other way open to regain his freedom, Mick went on a hunger strike which lasted for sixty-seven excruciating days in Cork jail where, after receiving the Last Sacraments, death came to him as a merciful release from his suffering on 17 October 1920. On Monday night his comrades transferred the remains to the church of SS Peter and Paul in the city, where Mass was said next day for the repose of his soul. As the people were leaving the church when Mass was over, British military in full war equipment, with fixed bayonets and steel helmets, walked over the seats. An officer with drawn revolver handed a notice to the priest who faced the people and informed them that the authorities would only allow a limited number of people to attend the funeral. Meantime, a machine-gun was mounted on the church gates while armoured cars toured the vicinity.

When the funeral, followed by thousands who defied the British order, was on its way by road to Fermoy, armoured cars and Crossley tenders, bearing heavily armed soldiers, followed the cortège to the city boundary. When the remains arrived at Fermoy and were placed in Saint Patrick's church, scenes of the greatest piety and devotion were manifest. The next day the funeral, of huge dimensions, took place to Kilcrumper cemetery. Fearing a demonstration, the military turned out in strength and were posted in various parts of the town. Many persons were searched and questioned, while barbed wire entanglements and machine-guns were mounted on the bridge. At last the mournful procession arrived at the cemetery and Michael Fitzgerald had the honour of being the first soldier of the Irish Republican Army to be interred in its republican plot. Not many hours after the last sod had been laid on his grave, a number of his comrades, evading a strong guard in the town, assembled at the plot and fired a volley as a final tribute and a last farewell to one of the finest soldiers who fought and died for Irish freedom. When fatally wounded on the slopes of Knockmealdown Mountains, some years later, his old chief, the late General Liam Lynch, paid fitting tribute to his memory when, knowing that his last hour was at hand, he said: 'Place me near my loyal and faithful comrade, Mick Fitzgerald.' His wish was granted and today, with others of their comrades, they lie side by side, together in death as in life, those faithful soldiers of the Irish Republic.

SUCCESSFUL RAID ON MALLOW BARRACKS

by PATRICK LYNCH

ON THE MORNING of 28 September 1920, one of the best-planned and most successful coups in the history of the fight in North Cork was brought off in the garrison town of Mallow by the members of the Cork No. 2 brigade. The military barracks in the town were, at the time, occupied by a detachment of the 17th Lancers – a British mounted regiment. The garrison consisted of thirty-eight non-commissioned officers and men who were under the command of a lieutenant.

The extent to which the intelligence grapevine of the IRA had penetrated into the very living quarters of the enemy is illustrated by the fact that for a time before the raid two of the civilian maintenance staff in Mallow barracks were active members of the republican forces. These were Richard Willis and John Bolster, and they worked in the barracks as painter and carpenter respectively. In the course of their normal duties inside the walls they had ample opportunity for the observation of troop movements and the collection of information that was of value to their comrades outside. One morning during the month of September 1920, they were chatting to a young Lancer who had arrived from England only a short time before. Like many young enemy soldiers of his type, he had an exaggerated idea of what a 'Sinn Féiner' looked like. His imagination had developed a picture of wild, bearded, mountainy men and he was, no doubt, encouraged in this belief by the two harmless-looking tradesmen to whom he was speaking. He had never actually seen a 'Sinn Féiner' and he expressed the hope that he would never have to meet them in a fight during his stay in Ireland. It surprised him too, he said, why they did not attack and capture Mallow barracks, as he considered it to be an easy job. The lieutenant in charge he said, and two-thirds of the garrison, went out each morning for a trot to exercise the horses, and while they were away the 'Sinners' could come in and take away all the stuff in the barracks. Impressed by the innocent suggestion of the young Lancer the two IRA men thought over the possibilities of carrying out such an operation and were convinced from what they saw going on in the barracks that it could be successfully embarked on. Messrs Willis and Bolster next broached the matter to the officers of the local IRA company and some time afterwards received instructions to make a sketch-map of the barracks. This they did and on further instructions, proceeded one night to Island Burnfort, where they met the late General Liam Lynch and his staff officers: Owen Harold, Ernie O'Malley, Jack Cunningham and Tadhg Byrnes. With the exception of Ernie O'Malley, who was liaison officer from Dublin, all these officers were Mallowmen. Following consultation and detailed study of the sketch map, Liam Lynch decided to attack the barracks on the following morning. Prior to this one of his staff officers, Owen Harold, had been billeted for some time in a house facing the barracks and from which he was in a position to note the movements of the troops.

Lynch laid his plans and on the following morning all was set for the attempt. Outposts were posted on all the roads leading to the town; a sniping party had been billeted in the Town Hall building on the night before because the Town Hall overlooked the full length of O'Brien Street, in which the Royal Irish Constabulary barracks was situated. The function of the sniping party in the Town Hall was, if the necessity arose, to prevent the police from going to the aid of the military. It will be remembered that the Royal Irish Constabulary was an armed force.

That morning the British followed their well-known routine and about half-past eight the lieutenant in charge went out as usual, to exercise the horses, taking with him the main body of the troops and leaving behind in barracks about fifteen men under the command of his senior NCO, Sergeant Gibbs. Behind in the barracks, too, was left the main bulk of the detachment's armaments as the body exercising the horses only took with them two rifles and five revolvers. Under the watchful eyes of the IRA scouts, the British left the town totally unaware of the dramatic and historic events that were to take place within the hour.

Shortly after nine o'clock the sentry on duty inside the main gate of the barracks noticed Jack Bolster, the barrack carpenter, and Dick Willis, the barrack painter, standing with a 'Contractors' Overseer' at the first entrance to the barrack buildings and, of course, inside the walls. The 'overseer' was in reality an IRA quartermaster who had come in to take part in the attack. He was the late Paddy McCarthy who, a few months afterwards, was shot in a street fight with the Black and Tans in Millstreet. As the sentry watched them Paddy McCarthy pretended to take measurements of doors and windows, while Dick Willis and Jack Bolster worked away as usual. All three had revolvers in their pockets. About twenty yards away and in the centre of the barrack square, the NCO in charge, Sergeant Gibbs, was standing in conversation with the barrack warden, a civilian employee. About half-past nine the sentry answered a knock on the wicket or small door beside the main gate. When he opened the loophole in the door he saw a civilian outside who showed him an envelope which, he said, was for the barrack warden. The sentry opened the door about six inches so as to take the letter, but the civilian, who was Ernie O'Malley, said that he would have to see the barrack warden personally. The sentry attempted to close the door but O'Malley wedged his foot in it and when the soldier turned to beckon the warden to the gate the door was pushed in by two more IRA men and in a matter of seconds the sentry was overpowered and disarmed.

The moment that Sergeant Gibbs noticed the mêlée at the gate he began to run towards the guardroom, where some rifles were stored. On being called on to halt he still continued to double towards the guardroom. Three shots rang out and Gibbs fell mortally wounded on the guardroom steps. The other members of the IRA party waiting outside entered the barracks. In the meantime Jack Bolster, Dick Willis and Paddy McCarthy had posted themselves at strategic points and as soldiers rushed from different parts of the buildings they were calmly held up and marched to the guardroom where they were locked in one of the cells. Three waiting motor cars had, by this time, drawn up at the barrack gate and into these were piled the arms and equipment of the garrison. Petrol and hay were procured from the barrack stores and before departing the Volunteers set fire to the guardroom with the object of burning the barracks. The whole operation was carried out with clockwork precision and in an amazingly short space of time. In all about twenty-seven rifles, two Hotchkiss light machine-guns, boxes of ammunition, a revolver, Verey light pistols and a quantity of bayonets and other military equipment were carried off. The Volunteers stationed in the Town Hall did not have to go into action as the police made no move to come to the assistance of the military.

When the main British body returned to barracks about ten o'clock there was consternation at the success of the raid, and when the news reached their headquarters at Buttevant there was blank amazement. The reaction of the British military command to this courageous IRA operation will remain for long as a blot upon the discipline of the British army and particularly upon that of the officers, non-commissioned officers and men stationed in the area at the time. The night following the raid was one of terror in Mallow. Detachments of armed military from Buttevant and Fermoy entered the town and indulged in an orgy of looting, drinking and burning. Groups of drunken troops moved about the town pitching petrol-filled bottles through any window that showed a light and generally committing acts of blackguardism. The Town Hall, centre of Mallow's civic and social life, was burned to the ground, as was the local creamery, which at that time employed several hundred workers. Many private houses were set alight and so irresponsible was this presumably penal visitation, that even the homes of people not opposed to British rule were attacked.

During the weeks following the raid there was considerable activity all over the area and British raiding parties were night and day at work. The arms taken from the barracks, however, were never recovered and at subsequent engagements throughout the southern area they were used in the hands of dauntless men to strike many telling blows for freedom.

CAUSED MUTINY IN LISTOWEL, SHOT IN CORK

by LEE-SIDER

In June and July 1920, the initiative in the struggle between the Irish and British for dominance in this country was passing to the Irish. British institutions in all departments of national and local government were repudiated and the alternative machinery set up by Dáil Éireann was everywhere being recognised and resorted to by the people. Public bodies declared their allegiance to the government elected by the Irish people; British courts were boycotted and whatever little business came before them was transacted behind barbed wire entanglements, guarded by military and police; the Sinn Féin courts openly dispensed justice and penalised wrongdoers at the instance of the Volunteer police. While the Irish civil populations were freely making use of the new Irish institutions and cheerfully obeying their edicts, the IRA were daily attacking the British crown forces and restricting their movements. Resignations of Justices of the Peace and police were numerous. In six weeks at this period one hundred and seventy-seven resigned. The British judge at the Kerry Summer Assizes told the grand jury that in Kerry twenty-five police barracks, three courthouses and four coastguard stations had been burned and six police patrols attacked. It was always the same as far as the police were concerned, he said; they were unable to obtain a clue and they got no assistance from the people. Railway employees refused to man trains with armed military and police as passengers and were dismissed.

British military and police could only move out from their strongly held barracks in numbers and were everywhere the objects of hostility and resentment, if not of actual attack. Whether they realised it or not they were fighting a native army backed by a united people. The highly efficient Royal Irish Constabulary, on which the British had been wont to rely in every emergency in Ireland for information and loyal co-operation, were proving unequal to the strain. They were in a most unenviable position. Drawn from the homes of the people against whom they were expected to enforce repressive measures, many of them had brothers in the IRA, and many of them, too, had long service and were not prepared to forego generous pensions. If they resigned they lost their pensions and went out among the people who might distrust their motives, and they left behind an organisation from which they could expect hostility and accusations of cowardice.

The infusion of British recruits into the Royal Irish Constabulary was begun and the quartering of British troops in the same barracks with the constabulary did not make harmony within or good relations. The Royal Irish Constabulary man found himself no longer a peace officer. In the rural districts especially he lived behind steel shutters, ostracised by the people from whom he sprang, nightly expecting attack by brother Irishmen. It was a galling situation for spirited men. They had either to lend themselves completely to the designs of their authorities or sullenly await the outcome of events with no stomach for the work on hand.

The British were not content to let the initiative pass from them without a fight. They decided to turn every Royal Irish Constabulary barracks in the country into a fortress from which military would sally forth, guided by the Royal Irish Constabulary with local knowledge, to harass the people night and day, carry out wholesale arrests and kill off the IRA, whom they affected to believe were terrorising the civilian population. This further militarisation of the Royal Irish Constabulary was entrusted to army officers with Great War service who could utilise their knowledge of defensive raiding tactics to the full.

Colonel Gerald Bryce Ferguson Smyth was appointed divisional commissioner for Munster on 3 June 1920. He had entered the British army in 1905, served in the Great War, in which he lost an arm, and was mentioned four times in dispatches. He had commanded a battalion of the King's Own Scottish Borderers and was thirty-five years of age.

On 17 June 1920, the Royal Irish Constabulary in Listowel were ordered to hand over their barracks to the British military and to transfer themselves, with the exception of three who were to remain in Listowel to act as guides for the soldiers, to different stations in the district. The Royal Irish Constabulary men held a meeting and decided not to obey the order. Next morning County Inspector Poer O'Shee visited Listowel and tried to induce the men to obey. Fourteen of them tendered to him their resignations which were not accepted. On the morning of 19 June two motor cars arrived in Listowel conveying Colonel Smyth, General Tudor, County Inspector Poer O'Shee and other military and police officers. The constables were assembled in the barrack day-room, where they were addressed by Colonel Smyth, the divisional commissioner. The only report of this speech is that supplied subsequently for publication by the fourteen policemen, from which the following is an extract:

Group of Irish Volunteer officers photographed at the officers' training camp, Sheares Street, Cork, 1915.

In this motley assortment of uniforms are Black and Tans and Auxiliaries who operated in Cork city. Photograph was taken near Saint Patrick's Bridge, Cork.

Tomás MacCurtain, murdered lord mayor of Cork, and his successor, Terence MacSwiney, who died a martyr's death in Brixton Prison, are both included in this historic picture. BACK ROW (*left to right*): *David Cotter, Seán Murphy, Donal Barrett, Terence MacSwiney and Paddy Trahy.* FRONT ROW: *Tadg Barry, Tomás MacCurtain and P. Higgins.*

Tomás MacCurtain, murdered lord mayor of Cork, lying-in-state in the old City Hall.

The old City Hall, Cork, in which an important brigade council meeting was held on the night of the arrest of Lord Mayor MacSwiney.

The remains of Terence MacSwiney, Cork's heroic lord mayor and brigade commandant IRA, being removed from Southwark Cathedral, London, for interment at home. The coffin-bearers in front are his brothers, Peter and John MacSwiney.

Terence MacSwiney, lord mayor of Cork, lying-in-state in the old City Hall.

Bridges were blown up and roads trenched to impede the movements of Britain's armed forces.

General Sir Neville Macready, who commanded the British forces in Ireland during the months preceding the Truce.

A view of a well-known department store on Patrick's Street, which was destroyed in the burning of 1920.

Scenes of the devastion in Cork on the morning following the city's burning.

Cork City Hall after the fire.

Still smouldering ruins in Patrick Street, on the morning following the destruction of Cork city by the British. Many familiar landmarks were gone forever; many a remembered contour and skyline had given place to gaping cavities where whole buildings had collapsed; here and there a solitary wall, windowless and heat-blistered, leaned at some crazy angle from its foundations.

Thomas and Richard Kent and their home, Bawnard House. Richard was mortally wounded during the fight against British crown forces at the house.

Thomas (left) and William Kent on their way to Fermoy police barracks, under heavily armed escort of British military, following the heroic defence of their home. Thomas was court-martialled, sentenced to death and executed a week after the fight at Bawnard House.

Buildings burned in Mallow in October 1920 in reprisal for the attack on Mallow Barracks.

Three Volunteers, Michael McCarthy of Dunmanway, Jim O'Sullivan of Kilmeen, Clonakilty, and Pat Deasy of Kilmacsimon, Bandon, were killed in action at Shanacashel, Kilmichael. The cross overlooking the scene of the ambush records their sacrifice.

Mixed group of British army and navy known as the 'wireless section' photographed in Bandon in 1921. At that time the British were forced to maintain their communication by wireless, as their regular communications between garrisons were effectively destroyed. This is a picture from the captured album of Captain V. Sheldrick Brealy, district inspector of the Royal Irish Constabulary in the West Cork Riding who is shown in the centre of the front row.

Is there any need to introduce them? Recruited from demobilised officers with experience in the First World War, the Auxiliary division formed the spearhead of the British offensive against the IRA, from the latter part of 1920 to the Truce. Here is a typical group of the men who made up this infamous corps.

A photograph of the well-known painting 'The Men of the South' by Seán Keating. It is of the men of the Cork No. 2 brigade flying column which was commanded by Seán Moylan. Included are D. O'Sullivan, Knockalluggin, Meelin; John Jones, Glencollins, Ballydesmond; Roger Kiely, Cullen; Dan Browne, Charleville; James O'Riordan, Kiskeam; Denis O'Mullane, Ballybahallow, Freemount, and James Cashman, Knocknamucklagh, Kiskeam.

Witnesses at the military inquiry into the shootings at Mallow railway station on 1 February 1921.

On active service with the East Cork column, IRA, in 1920–21 were: Daniel Cashman, Michael Desmond (killed at Clonmult); Jack Aherne (died in 1923. His brother was murdered by British crown forces as a reprisal for a Midleton ambush); Thomas Buckley; James Glavin (killed at Clonmult).

Members of the East Cork flying column who survived the struggle against the British. BACK ROW *(left to right): Vice-Commandant Joseph Aherne, M. Murnane, Jack O'Connell (Clonmult O/C), T. Buckley;* FRONT ROW: *Captain P. Whelan, D. Cashman, J. Aherne, T. Riordan.*

The East Cork brigade men who fell in the fight at Clonmult. BACK ROW
*(left to right): Richard Hegarty (Garryvoe); Jeremiah Aherne (Midleton);
Christopher Sullivan (Midleton); Joseph Morrissey (Athlone); Michael
Hallahan (Midleton); Paddy O'Sullivan (Cobh).* SECOND ROW: *James
Glavin (Cobh); John Joe Joyce (Midleton); James Aherne (Cobh); Michael
Desmond (Midleton).* FRONT ROW: *Donal Dennehy (Midleton); Liam
Aherne (Midleton); David Desmond (Midleton); Maurice Moore (Cobh).*

Some of Seán Moylan's men. FRONT ROW: *Joe Morgan, Leo O'Callaghan,
Jack Cunningham, Seán Breen;* BACK ROW: *Jeremiah Daly, Father J.
Piggott, Tadg Burns, Michael O'Connell, Dan Burns.*

Unveiling of memorial to Commandant Diarmuid Hurley, commander of the East Cork flying column, who fell on 28 May 1921. The memorial cross was erected by his comrade, Tadg Morley, NT.

Round-up of civilians by Auxiliaries and Black and Tans.

Seán Riordan, photographed after the Truce.

Ned O'Brien and James Scanlan, both of Galbally, photographed when they belonged to the East Limerick brigade, IRA.

This typical group of Ireland's fighting men belonged to the East Cork brigade IRA. Left to right: Michael Desmond (with his brother, David, killed in action at Clonmult); Patrick Higgins (captured at Clonmult, sentenced to death and saved by the advent of the Truce); James Glavin (killed at Clonmult); Daniel Dennehy (killed at Clonmult); Vice-Commandant Joseph Aherne (his brother Liam, with first cousin Jeremiah Aherne were killed at Clonmult); Richard Hegarty (killed at Clonmult); Joseph Morrissey (killed at Clonmult); Michael Hallahan (killed at Clonmult); D. Stanton; Patrick White.

General Crozier.

General Tudor.

Major Percival.

Daniel Shinnick.

Mick Fitzgerald.

Patrick Burns.

*Cornelius J.
Meaney.*

*William
Heffernan.*

Diarmuid Hurley.

Richard Barry.

Michael Scanlan.

Paddy O'Sullivan.

Sinn Féin has had all the sport up to the present, and we are going to have sport now. The police are only strong enough to hold their barracks. As long as we remain on the defensive, Sinn Féin will have the whip hand. We must take the offensive and beat Sinn Féin at its own tactics. Martial Law is to come into force immediately, and a scheme of amalgamation will be complete on the twenty-first of June. I am promised as many troops from England as I require. Thousands are coming daily. I am getting 7,000 police from England.

Colonel Smyth then explained why it was necessary to quarter military in towns like Listowel. He is reported to have said:

Police and military will patrol the country at least five nights a week. They are not to confine themselves to the main roads, but to take across country, lie in ambush, and when civilians approach shout 'Hands Up!' Should the order not be immediately obeyed, shoot and shoot with effect. If persons approaching carry their hands in their pockets, or are suspicious-looking, shoot them down. You may make mistakes occasionally, and innocent persons may be shot, but that cannot be helped. No policeman will get into trouble for shooting any man. Hunger strikers will be allowed to die in jail. Some have died, and it is a damned bad job all of them were not allowed to die. That is nearly all I have to say to you. We want your assistance to wipe out Sinn Féin. Any man not prepared to do so had better leave the job at once.

Colonel Smyth then asked the first man in the file if he were prepared to serve. This constable referred the divisional commissioner to the men's leader or spokesman, who said: 'By your accent I take it you are an Englishman. You forget you are addressing Irishmen.' The spokesman then took off his cap, belt and bayonet, and laying them on the table said: 'These, too, are English. Take them as a present from me, and to hell with you, you murderer.'

Colonel Smyth immediately ordered the arrest of the spokesman, but owing to the threatening attitude of the other policemen he left the barracks, which remained in the hands of the mutineers. Five of the men concerned subsequently resigned. Because of the number involved, the fact that the men concerned were the first to give publicity in a signed statement to Colonel Smyth's speech, and the raising of the matter in the British House of Commons, the Listowel barrack incident became famous. But there were others, though not in the same dramatic setting.

On a Sunday evening in June 1920, Colonel Smyth, a tall man of impressive appearance, wearing full military uniform and staff cap, his breast ablaze with medal ribbons, arrived at the Milltown (County Kerry) barracks of the Royal Irish Constabulary, and summoned the sergeant and six men to the day-room. Having taken an automatic from his pocket and placed it on the table, he directed the men to sit down. He prefaced his remarks by stating that he was responsible to no man in Ireland; that he was directly responsible to the prime minister. The Royal Irish Constabulary, he said, had been on the defensive too long and were now going to take the offensive. Block houses would be erected and barracks fortified. The houses of leading Sinn Féiners would be taken over. The police were to go out and not hesitate to shoot and if mistakes were made, he would break no man for doing so. Rubber shoes would be provided for patrols so that they could move along the roads noiselessly. He outlined a scheme under which Royal Irish Constabulary men dressed in khaki would accompany military raiding parties to identify Sinn Féiners. British recruits for the Royal Irish Constabulary and military reinforcements would be brought over from England. He said that the scheme which he had outlined would be issued as an order in the course of a week or ten days.

The Royal Irish Constabulary men, three of whom were middle-aged, did not quickly realise what Colonel Smyth was about, and were inclined to look on his visit as one of the 'comings and goings' of highly placed officers. The barrack orderly, one of the younger men, said that when he joined the force he did not anticipate having to shoot anybody. Colonel Smyth said that times had changed and tactics had to be changed with them, and from that out things would be different. He made little of the arguments advanced by the young policeman, and suggested that cowardice was at the bottom of them. Dominion Home Rule, he said, was coming, and after a few years Royal Irish Constabulary men who continued to serve would be awarded big pensions. After a stay of about an hour in the barracks, Colonel Smyth departed.

In a few days the barrack orderly received notification to Rathmore. He refused to accept the transfer. On 29 June, County Inspector Poer O'Shee came to Milltown accompanied by two lorries of Royal Irish Constabulary men armed with rifles and bombs. He spoke to the young policeman in a fatherly way and asked him why he would not take his transfer. 'Well, if you want to know,' came the reply, 'I did not join the police to lead around Black and Tans and the scum of England which have been brought into the force.' The officer tried to soften his subordinate and drew a picture of his bright prospects in the force, at the same time pointing out that such an attitude as he (the policeman) was taking up would create disaffection among the other men. Seeing that the young man was adamant, the county inspector, after an interview lasting two hours, declared he would have to suspend him. 'Take that and that,' said the policeman, throwing his revolver, belt and jacket on the table in front of the county inspector. After spending a few days around Milltown the suspended constable went to Killarney, where he was well known, having previously served in Beaufort. There the district inspector reasoned with him and pointed out that he was going out into a hostile people who would treat him as a spy. 'I understand well what I am doing and I'll take what is coming,' was the spirited reply.

In the British House of Commons on Wednesday, 14 July 1920, Mr T.P. O'Connor asked for information regarding the incidents in the Listowel police barracks and the speech delivered there by Divisional Commissioner Smyth. Sir Hamar Greenwood, chief secretary for Ireland, replied:

> The recent events presumably refer to the resignation of five constables in Listowel, County Kerry. On 19 June last the Divisional Commissioner, Colonel Smyth, made a speech to the members of the force, eighteen in number, stationed at Listowel. I have seen the report in the press, which, on the face of it, appears to have been supplied by the five constables already mentioned. I have myself seen Colonel Smyth, who repudiates the accuracy of the statements contained in that report. He informed me that the instructions given by him to the police in Listowel and throughout the division were those mentioned in a debate in this House on 22 June last by the attorney general for Ireland, and he did not exceed these instructions. The reason for the resignation of the five constables was their refusal to take up duty in barracks in certain disturbed parts of Kerry. They had taken up this attitude before the visit of the divisional commissioner. I am satisfied that the newspaper report is a distortion and a wholly misleading account of what took place.

Subsequently, Mr T.P. O'Connor asked and was refused leave to move the adjournment of the House to discuss the incident and the remarks attributed to Divisional Commissioner Smyth as calculated to produce serious bloodshed in Ireland.

The scene shifts to Cork city, where in July 1920, the Volunteer organisation was already reaching a high state of efficiency and the development of its intelligence department was receiving special attention. The County Club, resort of the landed families and high military officers, had a staff as loyal as its frequenters who engaged its first-class club and residential amenities. All efforts of the IRA intelligence department to penetrate into the staff were frustrated until contact was made with a young waiter. Thereafter the names of

British officers, military and police, who stayed at or visited the club, were known to the IRA. Colonel Smyth was staying there during the first fortnight of July. This information was conveyed to the IRA. It was decided to shoot him on Friday evening, 16 July. That day he packed his bags and announced his intention of going away for the weekend, so that the arrangements for shooting him fell through. He returned unexpectedly the following evening, and the receipt of this information caused the IRA to mobilise hastily a squad of six armed men. They entered the County Club at 10 p.m., held up the waiter, who was expecting them, and passed down the passage to the lounge, where Colonel Smyth was seated with County Inspector Craig of the Royal Irish Constabulary. Advancing into the lounge the leader of the armed party confronted Smyth, saying: 'Were not your orders to shoot at sight? Well, you are in sight now, so prepare.' Fire was opened. Smyth jumped to his feet and ran towards the door. Despite two bullets in the head, one through the heart and two through the chest, he succeeded in gaining the passage, where he dropped dead. He had attempted to draw his automatic, but apparently his strength failed him. The county inspector received a slight bullet wound in the leg. The armed party quickly withdrew.

In the scenes which followed the shooting of Divisional Commissioner Smyth, Cork city experienced a foretaste of what it was eventually to suffer. When Smyth's body was being removed by the military, police fired on the crowd which gathered. Armed parties of military took possession of the streets and fusilladed indiscriminately. An ex-soldier, James Burke, was bayonetted on Sunday night at North Gate bridge by military, who also inflicted bullet wounds on about forty persons, including a Volunteer who was assisting a woman. He died subsequently. An inquest opened at Cork military barracks on Monday into the circumstances surrounding the death of Colonel Smyth, divisional commissioner for Munster, fell through as sufficient jurymen, though summoned, did not attend. The remains were removed on Tuesday morning. At the same time a proclamation was issued by Major General E.B. Strickland, ordering that curfew be observed in Cork city from 10 p.m. to 3 a.m.

THE AMBUSH AT TOUREEN

by CON CROWLEY

IN THE AUTUMN of 1920, two companies of the Essex Regiment stationed at Bandon were playing havoc in our area, that of the 1st battalion of the 3rd Cork brigade. Raiding parties of the British were out every day, picking up some of our best officers and men, who were sent to Cork jail. Among those so imprisoned was Commandant Mick O'Neill, the battalion O/C. Arrests were one thing, but murder was another; so, when an unarmed Volunteer, John Connolly, of Bandon company, was taken from a house in Kilbrittain and found dead weeks afterwards in the park near his native town, the time had come to teach the Essex a lesson.

While the British were pursuing their career of raiding and murdering, the Volunteer organisation was not idle. Training camps had been established during successive weeks at Clonbogue, Kilbrittain and Knockavilla, where, under the direction of Commandant Tom Barry, an intensive course in the use of firearms was preparing the IRA for coming events. The growing confidence of the men in their own ability to go into action, and their commandant's anxiety to lead them into it to put a halt to the daily raids, arrests and shootings, boded no good for the Essex. Scouts sent to Bandon to get a line on troop movements, reported after a few days' observation that three, sometimes four, lorries left the barracks there every morning between eight and nine o'clock for Cork, travelling by the main road and returning between four and five o'clock in the evening. These lorries, it was observed, generally moved rapidly about forty or fifty yards from each other. Having considered this information, the brigade decided to lay an ambush for the lorries, and with the object of selecting the most suitable position, some of the officers traversed the route taken by the British and decided that Toureen presented the necessary advantages for a surprise attack which was to be delivered from a farmhouse, then owned by a Mr Roberts, and later by Mr Hyde, of Knockauley. Preparations were set on foot right away. Thirty Volunteers from the 1st battalion area were mobilised at Knockavilla, about two miles from Toureen, on the evening of 25 October. Under the cover of night a land mine was brought to within a short distance of the scene of operations, escorted by armed men with scouts thrown out along the road for further protection. Meantime the column was resting in billets. At 3 a.m. on 26 October, there was a general stand-to. The brigade O/C told the men their objective and outlined the plan that was to be followed. He invited any man who did not wish to participate to step out, but the ranks remained unbroken. All were anxious to strike a blow at the British who were murdering and imprisoning their comrades.

In the darkness of a late autumn morning, the column moved off towards Killeady, crossed the old road between Bandon and Cork and came on to the railway line which runs into the main road about a hundred yards from Toureen. Charlie Hurley and I, with a few men, then went ahead to take possession of the farmhouse. The occupants were frightened and disturbed at our intrusion, but eventually we succeeded in calming them and getting them all into a back room on the ground floor where they were quite safe. The house is situated about twenty yards from the main road, beside which runs a long range of out-offices. We ascertained from Mr Roberts the number of men he had employed and the time they arrived to work. When the main body came up, a section was detailed to lay the mine in the centre of the road about fifty yards from the out-offices on the Cork side. Positions were then taken up to deal with four lorries. One section was posted at the out-house gate, another about forty yards on the Bandon side of the mine, and a third on the Cork side. The plan was to allow the first lorry to proceed as far as the mine, of which Charlie Hurley had charge; the second lorry was to be fired on by half of the men in the out-offices, the remainder of whom were to engage the third lorry, while the section on the Bandon side of the mine was to attack the fourth or rear lorry. A few men were detailed to keep a way of retreat open to the south.

All were in position about 6.30 a.m., and time dragged slowly until 8 a.m., when Mr Roberts' three workmen arrived and were placed under guard with the occupants of the house. The diversion which their arrival caused had hardly ended when a scout signalled that two lorries were coming from Bandon. There was a feeling of tension as the leading lorry swept past the position of our first section, followed by the second lorry, forty yards behind. At this point all of us could follow the approach of the lorries by sound, and some by sight. As the leader careered along towards the mine, the men of the column braced themselves for the explosion that would pitch a lorry and its human freight into the air and gripped their rifles for the action that was to follow. No explosion occurred. The mine had failed to explode, and through the ambush position drove what all had counted a doomed lorry. The men in the forward section fired at it as it moved away from them and wounded some of the soldiers seated at the back. It put on speed and was soon out of view and harm's way around a bend of the road, nor did it stop until it reached Cork city. Its occupants had left their comrades to fight alone. The section of ten, which was to attack the second lorry, was waiting behind a timber gate. When the first lorry had passed, the gate was thrown open, revealing five men kneeling and five standing, who poured a deadly volley at seven yards' range into the second lorry. The driver was riddled, and when his lorry came to a stop at the opposite fence thirty yards distant, the men of the IRA section came out on the road and opened fire on it. Some Volunteers and the British were then engaged on the open road with no cover for either party. The British returned the fire under the direction of Captain Dixon, who blazed away with his revolver from the centre of the lorry. Another volley from the IRA quickly crashed into it, killing Captain Dixon and three soldiers, and wounding several others. This hail of lead was too much for the Essex, now officerless, so they flung their rifles on the road, chanting, 'We surrender, we surrender.'

The IRA section ceased fire and took the surrender of fourteen rifles, one revolver and about 2,000 rounds of ammunition, all valuable equipment for the rapidly growing column that was to win undying fame in numerous fights until the Truce. The lorry was set on fire, and as it sent flames into the morning air, the column fell into line and marched away across country to Shippool, from where we rowed across the Bandon river to Kilmacsimon Quay. There we had a short rest before proceeding to Ballinadee and on to Clonbogue for a much-needed meal and rest while the local Volunteers stood guard.

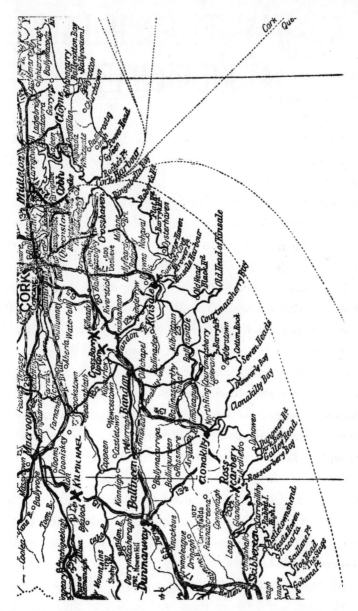

Map of the 3rd Cork brigade area over which the famous West Cork column, under Commandant Tom Barry, operated with great success against British crown forces in the years 1920 and 1921. Places mentioned in the stories of the fights at Crossbarry, Kilmichael and Rosscarbery are clearly indicated.

AUXILIARIES ANNIHILATED AT KILMICHAEL

by STEPHEN O'NEILL

OF THE MANY hard blows struck at the English by the West Cork column of the IRA under Tom Barry in the 1920–21 period, the ambush at Kilmichael was, in many respects, the most decisive. Up to the autumn of 1920, the system of war waged was in the nature of spasmodic attacks on police and soldiers by small numbers of men in the different areas. The success of these small coups compelled the enemy to move in greater numbers, and about this period never less than two lorry-loads travelled from one enemy post to another. The brigade council was obliged to take measures to meet this new situation, and a brigade column was formed. Each of six battalions supplied six fully-equipped and armed Volunteers. The idea was that the battalions should persist in their operations on a small scale, while the brigade column would tackle, in conjunction with the local battalion, any big operation.

About September 1920, a company of Auxiliaries was drafted to Macroom and took up their headquarters at the castle. This body had been specially recruited from ex-British officers and had had considerable fighting experience in the Great War. From their advent they had been tireless in their shootings and burnings, and repeatedly raided the district about ten miles south of Macroom, which was in the West Cork brigade area. On the first three Sundays of November, two lorries of 'Auxies' travelled the main Macroom-Dunmanway road as far as Coppeen, and this regularity in their movements was carefully noted. The West Cork flying column was mobilised on 21 November, and after less than a week's training the O/C decided to attack those Auxiliaries (a force which up to this time had not been attacked in Ireland) on Sunday 28 November.

The finding of a suitable position was not an easy matter, as the road runs through flat, boggy country; but he eventually chose a spot at Shanacashel, about a mile north of Gleann in the parish of Kilmichael. Shortly after midnight on Saturday the column moved on the long journey to its appointed position. A considerable number of the column had never before participated in a military operation. The arrival of the late John Lordan, vice-commandant of the Bandon battalion at dawn on Sunday morning at the ambush position was most welcome. Even at this early period, he was renowned for his great qualities as a fighter. He had heard on the previous evening of the O/C's intention, and hurrying to the scene was typical of him. The position was occupied about 9 a.m. The morning was frosty and foggy. As the day progressed, our condition, lying on the wet ground for many hours after the long march and sleepless night, was not an enviable one. We waited on. About four o'clock the scouts signalled the approach of the lorries. There were a few tense minutes. The first lorry appeared, and then the second, one hundred and fifty yards behind.

They moved unsuspectingly into the ambuscade. The silence was broken by the O/C's whistle, which was the signal to open fire. Simultaneously a bomb struck the first lorry which put more than its mechanism out of action and rifle fire was opened on the lorries from both sides of the road. The first lorry being in the ideal position from our point of view, many of the occupants were either killed or wounded in the first few minutes. The remainder took what cover was available and fought courageously, even though wounded, but within five minutes they were all accounted for.

As can be readily understood, the second lorry, though coming within the ambush, was not in such a suitable position when fire opened. The Auxiliaries were able to take cover afforded by rocks on the roadside, and replied to our fire. Their expert marksmanship and long training made itself felt, and for some time we failed to dislodge them. The O/C, with three of the section responsible for the destruction of the first lorry, came to our assistance, with the result that the attack was intensified. On being called on to surrender, they signified their intention of doing so, but when we ceased at the O/C's command, fire was again opened by the Auxiliaries, with fatal results to two of our comrades who exposed themselves believing the surrender was genuine. We renewed the attack vigorously and never desisted until the enemy was annihilated.

The arms and ammunition so precious to us, were carefully collected. The lorries were burned; seventeen Auxiliaries lay dead on the road. As we retired the rain, which had been threatening all day, fell in torrents. After many hours of weary marching we crossed the Bandon river at Manch and billeted at Granure. An unoccupied labourer's cottage, containing a plentiful supply of straw, enabled us to secure a well-earned rest.

Victories, such as ours on that day, cannot be achieved without sacrifice. On 28 November 1920, three young Irishmen, as noble and unselfish as any who ever fought, lost their lives at Kilmichael in this dour encounter. Michael MacCarthy of Dunmanway, and Jim O'Sullivan of Kilmeen, Clonakilty, were killed outright. Pat Deasy, Kilmacsimon, Bandon, a heroic youth of under sixteen years, was so seriously wounded that he died a few hours later. They lie buried in the graveyard at Castletown-Kenneigh. The cause for which they died is still unattained. And when our thoughts go back to the three gallant men who died for Ireland at Kilmichael, there is one other who was with us on that day, who has died since and whose memory will always be ever dear to us: 'Flyer' Nyhan of Clonakilty. 'Flyer' was one of the best loved and most gallant Volunteers of the West Cork brigade. He, too, has passed on; his life shortened by his wounds and his years of service to his country. May he and all the others who died for Ireland, rest in peace.

THE BOYS OF KILMICHAEL

Whilst we honour in song and in story
The names of Pearse and MacBride,
Whose names are illumined in glory
With martyrs who long since have died.

Chorus:

Forget not the boys of Kilmichael,
Those brave lads so gallant and true,
Who fought 'neath the green flag of Érin
And conquered the Red, White and Blue.

On the twenty-eighth day of November,
The Tans left the town of Macroom;
They were armed in two Crossley tenders
Which led them right into their doom;
They were on the road to Kilmichael
And never expected to stall,
They there met the boys of the column
Who made a clear sweep of them all

Chorus

The sun in the west it was sinking,
'Twas the eve of a cold winter's day;
The Tans we were wearily waiting
Sailed into the spot where we lay;
And over the hills went the echo,
The sound of the rifle and gun,

And the flames from their lorries gave tidings
    That the boys of the column had won.

Chorus

    The lorries were ours before twilight,
      And high over Dunmanway town
    Our banners in triumph were waving
    To show that the Tans were gone down;
    We gathered our rifles and bayonets,
      And soon left the glen so obscure,
    And never drew rein 'till we halted
    At the far-away camp of Glenure.

Chorus

THE FIGHT AT BURGATIA HOUSE, ROSSCARBERY

by JACK CORKERY

IN FEBRUARY 1921, most of the small barracks occupied by the Royal Irish Constabulary throughout West Cork had been evacuated owing to the attacks on them by the West Cork brigade of the IRA. In very few towns, except those garrisoned by English military or Auxiliaries, did the British attempt to retain a police barracks. The only one I can call to mind was the barracks in Rosscarbery. This seaside village is situated about eight miles from Clonakilty, twelve miles from Dunmanway and thirteen from Skibbereen. Clonakilty and Skibbereen were then British military posts, whilst about a hundred Auxiliaries occupied the workhouse at Dunmanway,

There was only one barracks occupied within this fairly large area, approximately two hundred and forty square miles – Rosscarbery – and if this were gone, it was obvious that a fairly large area would be available as bases, or retiring country, for the West Cork brigade active service men. The barracks was occupied by a strong force of the Royal Irish Constabulary and Black and Tans, and as several barracks had been attacked in West Cork, the police were very wary. Another difficulty was that the surrounding district at that time held a number of families, generally non-Catholics, who were hostile to republicanism and friendly with the British. So our leader – Tom Barry – moved off a flying column of about thirty-five riflemen one night, and we guessed before long that we were moving for Rosscarbery. The plan was that the column would move about fourteen miles through the night, occupy a large house near Rosscarbery, rest all the following day, come fresh for the attack the following night, and be fit to protect ourselves after smashing the barracks, in the event of our meeting reinforcements of British military and Auxiliaries.

We arrived about 3.30 a.m. at the house of one Thomas Kingston, JP, a large farmer and good British supporter. Kingston was openly hostile to the IRA, and was very much in touch with the British. Actually at that time, when motors were scarce, he used to volunteer to drive the police mails to Clonakilty, to prevent the possibility of their capture by the IRA, who had many times raided the mails on that route. His house was situated about one mile from Rosscarbery, on the Clonakilty road, and about two hundred yards up an avenue from the road. The house was surrounded and Kingston was called. On being informed that it was the IRA who were seeking admittance, he replied that under no circumstances would he admit us. Needless to say, we were soon in the house, had sentries posted, and we sat down to a good meal, which was badly wanted after our tiring march. We rested around on the floors until morning, and then when Kingston's workmen came along they were all arrested and not allowed to leave the house. Kingston himself was of course under close arrest all the time. About 11 a.m. a pretty problem presented itself in the arrival of a British official whose detention for any length of time would arouse suspicion as to our presence in the neighbourhood. He was released with instructions to continue his usual duties after he had given a solemn undertaking not to divulge to a living soul that the

IRA were in occupation of Burgatia House. The day wore on, and double sentries were mounted. About 1.30 p.m. a local Volunteer, Sonny Maloney, arrived and reported that the official who had been permitted to go two hours previously had gone straight to the Royal Irish Constabulary barracks at Rosscarbery and had remained there. Maloney further reported that British military were arriving from Skibbereen and Clonakilty. The column stood-to and Maloney was sent off on another intelligence mission, but we had scarcely been placed in positions when the enemy were reported coming.

Now, the reader should know that geographically we were situated in a very difficult position if the intelligence report of troops from Clonakilty and Skibbereen was correct. Here we were, one mile from Rosscarbery; at our back the sea was only a few hundred yards; on our front we could see the Black and Tans. To our left was Rosscarbery – probably held by troops as well as police – and, surely our only remaining way out on the east would be held by troops coming from Clonakilty. To make matters more difficult, the fields around Kingston's house were very large, and it was at least four hours before darkness would set in. The order was given that no shot was to be fired until the O/C blew his whistle, no matter whether the enemy was closing in or not. In a few minutes a volley was fired at us from the road, but we did not reply.

Up the avenue, a short distance came some Tans. Another volley was fired at the house – still we did not fire – no whistle sounded. We remained crouched in our positions. The British then started to advance up the field on our left, firing as they came, but they did no damage to us. By this time they appeared puzzled as there was no reply to their fire, and must have wondered if somebody dreamed about an IRA column at Kingston's. Meanwhile the O/C had sent out scouts to ascertain if the British had closed the remaining line of retreat, and he remarked to me that even if they had us completely surrounded, we would hold them 'till nightfall, and then break through them. He warned me to see that the house, to which we would eventually retreat (but only when forced to), did not catch fire. The scouts returned from the east and reported that the way out was clear.

The British continued to advance slowly and were still peppering the house behind us, when all of a sudden the whistle went and we opened rapid fire at the enemy. They broke and ran. Out we went onto the avenue and fired after them. After a few minutes rapid fire, to hasten their retreat, the order was given for one section to double away to the east and hold the road until the remainder passed out. And so, whilst the enemy was running, we moved off without delay across that road to the east, which, if held by the British officer in command before he attacked our front, would have made impossible our retreat until nightfall. On we marched until we had put about three miles between us and the scene of the fight. We halted. The main portion of the column was sent on to billets north-east, whilst the O/C took a section back to the town of Rosscarbery, which was entered after nightfall. The idea of a section returning was for two reasons, namely, to be on hand if the British were attempting any reprisals, and, secondly, because of the fact that it would have a good morale effect on the IRA, and the people generally, to give the English another rattle up a few hours after they thought they had us surrounded. All was quiet in the town, and, after waiting some time, we were ordered to open fire on the enemy posts. We kept it up for a bit, and then moved off to join the remainder in billets.

Those who remember reading the newspapers of the time will recollect the British headlines on the following day: 'Michael Collins Shot off a White Horse at Burgatia.' The horse was a bay mare belonging to Kingston which was being taken for IRA work. Billy Sullivan, who was told to bring her along, was on her back. She stumbled and came down, but was not hit. Collins was not in the area at all. *An t-Óglach* – the IRA organ – for some weeks following waxed very sarcastic at the expense of the British claims for compensation arising out of the fight. One sergeant was at that period awarded £1,000 compensation for the loss of his moustache, which was shot away, whilst other equally fabulous amounts were granted to those killed and wounded at this fight at Burgatia, Rosscarbery. And so ended our first attempt to get close enough to attack Rosscarbery barracks, but its destruction was only postponed.

THE MEN OF BARRY'S COLUMN

I.

When British terror failed to win
Allegiance from our people then,
The Black and Tans they were brought in,
They thought they'd teach us manners;
Instead of teaching they were taught
A lesson which they dearly bought,
For when Kilmichael's day was fought,
Low was their bloody banner.

II.

They sought to wipe the column out,
From east to west, from north to south,
'Till at Crossbarry's bloody rout,
They woke from their day-dreaming.
Though ten to one they were that day,
Our boys were victors in the fray,
And over the hills we marched away
With bagpipes merrily screaming.

III.

The Essex brutes who tortured Hales,
They scoured the land to fill the jails,
Thought their ugly deeds would pale
The cheeks of Irish mothers.
Paid dearly for their deeds were they
When passing by Toureen one day,
We dearly made the Essex pay
And well avenged our brothers.

IV.

When Barry saw the Tans efface,
The spirit of his fighting race
Right through his soul did madly chase
His blood went boiling over.
He marched his men to Ross' town
And burned that famous fortress down,
And never again will Britain's crown
Her foothold there recover.

Chorus:

So piper play a martial air
For the gallant boys who conquered there.
No merry tune to banish care,
Or mournful or solemn.
The grander tune of all is played
By the fighting squad of the 3rd brigade,
Whose glorious deeds will never fade.
The men of Barry's column

ROUT OF THE BRITISH AT CROSSBARRY

by TOM KELLEHER

EARLY IN MARCH 1921, the flying column of the West Cork brigade was at full strength. The column was composed of the following officers and men: Tom Barry, brigade column commander; Liam Deasy, brigade adjutant; Tadhg O'Sullivan, brigade quartermaster; Dr Con Lucey, column medical officer; Dr Eugene Callanan (then a medical student), assistant medical officer; Seán Hales, O/C No. 1 section – fourteen men (inclusive); John Lordan, O/C No. 2 section – fourteen men (inclusive); Mick Crowley, O/C No. 3 section – fourteen men (inclusive); Denis Lordan, O/C No. 4 section – fourteen men (inclusive); Tom Kelleher, O/C No. 5 section – fourteen men (inclusive); Peter Kearney, O/C No. 6 section – fourteen men (inclusive); Christy O'Connell, O/C No. 7 section – fourteen men (inclusive). Florence Begley, who played the pipes during the ambush at Crossbarry, completed the personnel of the column, which altogether amounted to one hundred and four men. Commandant Charlie Hurley (killed at brigade headquarters on the morning of the Crossbarry ambush, about four miles from it) was at the time recuperating from wounds received at the Upton ambush on 15 February 1921.

About 4 a.m. on the morning of 17 March (Saint Patrick's Day), the column lay in ambush at Shippool, Innishannon, for a convoy of British, comprising three hundred military, who were being moved from Kinsale to Bandon. The military had barely left the barracks and were proceeding on their way, when they were informed that we were waiting for them. They returned immediately and got in touch with their command headquarters in Cork. Thus was put in motion the British move to round-up the West Cork brigade flying column, which failed at Crossbarry less than forty-eight hours afterwards.

At 5 p.m. the column commander was informed of the British return to barracks, and accordingly the column was moved off just as darkness fell, to the townland of Skough, near Innishannon. It rested on the following day and at 10 p.m. moved northwards to Crossbarry. This was a cautious movement, as the column commander felt that an enemy round-up was again at hand, and I, who was in charge of the advance guard, was instructed to see that part of the advance guard would travel inside the ditches on both sides of the road. Onward, step by step, marched the gallant men of the column, little dreaming that before another day was over they would have fought and won one of the greatest fights ever fought against British tyranny in this country.

At 1 a.m. on the morning of 19 March, the column arrived at Crossbarry and billeted in the surrounding district. John O'Leary's of Ballyhandle was made headquarters, and the column O/C and senior officers retired there. Section O/C Mick Crowley and I then went in search of local scouts and suddenly, when near Brinny Cross, we heard the distant buzz of lorries from the direction of Bandon. It was about 2 a.m. at this time; the night was clear and fine, and the noise of the lorries was distinctly audible to us. Bandon is about seven miles from Crossbarry, and to show the slow rate at which the lorries travelled, it took them about six hours to travel from Bandon. It was about 10 a.m. when they arrived at Crossbarry.

The British were on a round-up expedition. At Kilpatrick they arrested a man named White of Newcestown. White, who was in one of the lorries as a hostage when the ambush took place, jumped out of the lorry unscathed and joined the republican forces inside the fence. When we heard the noise of the approaching lorries we turned back to headquarters. On the way we aroused the men billeted at John MacCarthy's, Lissaniskey. We then reported to Tom Barry and the staff officers. Barry issued an order to have every man stand to arms. In a very short time the whole column was mobilised in a field adjoining the Bandon–Crossbarry main road. The sound of the lorries could be distinctly heard in the clear air, seemingly, sometimes near at hand and then again dying away in the distance. This variation was apparently due to the continuous moving and stopping of the lorries on the way from Bandon.

The column commander ordered all ranks to fall in and delivered a short spirited talk, in which he pointed out that it was the duty of every man to give his best that day and to obey the orders of his superior officers. As they stood there in the fresh morning air, their rifles firmly grasped in their hands, the men of the 3rd Cork brigade felt a thrill of satisfaction at the prospect of another fight with the ancient enemy. Madly the blood coursed through their veins, as the words of their commanding officer rang out clear and vibrant. Proud they were, that on their shoulders rested the avenging of the wrongs committed by a merciless foe on a proud but helpless people. Some of them had fought at Kilmichael, others at Toureen, Bandon and Burgatia, and the memories of those fights were fresh with them. Yes, they were anxious to deal with the British forces again that day.

The column then moved towards Crossbarry and preparations

for the ambush began. Barricades were built, mines were laid down and positions were allocated to the different sections. No. 1 section was placed to the right enfilading the main road; No. 2 section at the left of No. 1 section, in Harold's house and farmyard; No. 3 section to the left of Begley's house; No. 4 section was placed at the extreme end of the ambush position near Crossbarry bridge; No. 5 section was placed at the rear of the whole ambush position near Driscoll's Castle; No. 6 section was placed to the right of No. 4 section, and some of this section on the other side of the road; No. 7 section was placed at the extreme right flank of the ambush position. Three men, detached from different sections, were sent back straight behind to give an ample warning of any enemy approach from our direct rear. Thus it will be seen that the disposition of the IRA had about seventy men facing the immediate front (Bandon–Cork road), and that the remaining thirty-five men were deployed for enfilading and protection at both flanks at our rear. It was not possible for the British to surprise the column.

On this morning then, 19 March, all the British forces at the disposal of the command in Cork, north, south and west, were mobilised with orders to converge on Crossbarry. No fewer than twenty-four lorries of military left Bandon; six hundred military came from Cork and Ballincollig, and three hundred from Kinsale. Men from Clonakilty and Auxiliaries from Macroom were also called out on the round-up. The Macroom Auxiliaries travelled by mistake to Kilbarry, seven or eight miles north-west of Crossbarry, and so did not come into action until later in the day. This mistake was undoubtedly a great advantage to the column.

During the preparations for the fight shots were heard in the distance at the rear of the ambush position. This was the first intimation of the enemy's approach from another direction. I recognised the shots as coming from the direction of brigade headquarters. A few hours before, Tom Barry had instructed two local scouts, Bill Hartnett and Bill Desmond, to go to brigade headquarters and bring Charlie Hurley and Seán Buckley to the column. As they neared headquarters they were accosted by British soldiers and arrested. When the British military surrounded headquarters (Humphrey Murphy's house at Ballymurphy) on that fateful morning of 19 March, Charlie Hurley was lying wounded upstairs. He had been wounded about one month before, at the Upton train ambush on the 15 February, and had not fully recovered from the wound. During the Upton fight Charlie had been fighting side-by-side with me. Early in the fight I noticed that a bullet had pierced Charlie's face between the cheekbone and the nose on the right side and had come out under the lobe of the left ear. When the fight was over and the Volunteers were retiring, Charlie suddenly remarked: 'Tom, I'm wounded.' It was only then he noticed his wound. This little incident, when he had fought for a full half hour without feeling the slightest pain from his wound, characterises the wholehearted vigour with which he threw himself into the fight for Ireland's freedom.

The loud knocking at the door was the first intimation Charlie had that Murphy's house was being raided. He hurriedly dressed, snatched a pair of Webley revolvers and rushed down the stairs. Before he got to the bottom the hall door was burst in and military rushed into the house. Charlie fired at them from the stairs, wounding three of them seriously. The remainder immediately retreated to the yard for cover. Charlie then rushed to the back door firing with both guns as he went. Just as he reached the back yard a bullet through the head ended the life of one of Ireland's most gallant and fearless soldiers. He died as he wished – an Irish soldier fearlessly facing the enemies of his country to the last.

He had trod the thorny way,
For Ireland and for you,
Pray for his country and pray
That all his dreams come true.

Preparations were now complete for the fight at Crossbarry. Suddenly the enemy arrival was signalled, and the hum of lorry engines sounded close at hand. The column leader had stressed to me the responsibility which my section would have in the fight. The section (No. 5) which was at the left rear of the main body was ordered to ward off attack and so protect the main body. In case I was to retire on the main body, the column commanding officer arranged for signals by means of a Peter the Painter (a gun which has a report which is easily distinguished from that of any other gun). By means of these signals the main body kept in touch with No. 5 section throughout the fight. All sections were then in position. The lorries were very near. It was now only a matter of minutes until the British and IRA would be in deadly conflict. One, two and three volleys and the pipes began to play 'The Men of the West'. The great fight of Crossbarry had begun.

Six sections of the flying column were in action. The cracking of the rifle fire, the bursting of bombs, rent the quiet morning air. It was then 7.30 a.m. Above all other sounds could be heard the crack of the Peter the Painter, held in the hand of the column leader; this sound encouraged the men and gave them renewed energy. Quickly the rifles were loaded and unloaded. The first convoy of the British were getting the worst of it. Their nine lorries were out of action. The remainder of the convoy 'about turned' and fled. Dr Con Lucey used his rifle that day with as much enthusiasm as he had wielded the camán in the hurling field. A bomb rebounded off a tree and fell at the feet of Dr Eugene (Nudge) Callanan; lucky for him it failed to explode. The sections were now ordered out on the road and opened fire on the fleeing soldiers, who were escaping down the fields towards the railway. Florrie Begley marched up and down Harold's yard playing the bagpipes. Back at the rear of the right was No. 5 section, disappointed, because the men had heard the din of the fierce battle and the tune of the pipes playing the old war songs and they had not yet fired a shot. The crack of the rifle fire was incessant. After a time it died down. Single shots then sounded. The fight was nearly over on the main road, and still it seemed that No. 5 section would not be needed that day. Tom Barry had issued an order to collect all guns and ammunition. Amongst the captures was a Lewis gun. Then the lorries were burned, and were being blazed when rifle fire broke out at the rear of No. 5 section. At last this section had got its wish.

After the shooting at Ballymurphy, the British forces from Cork and Ballincollig, six hundred strong, had divided into two columns with the definite object of surrounding the column. One division, under Major Percival (as General Percival he surrendered Singapore to the Japanese in the war just ended) of the Essex Regiment, took up position on the east and south of the IRA. One line of the British extended east to the road to Crossbarry bridge from Brien's bridge, a point directly one mile north of the ambush position. The other line, reinforced by a contingent from Kinsale, extended from Crossbarry bridge along the main Cork–Bandon railway line. This line was almost parallel to the position of the right flank of the IRA. Westward of this again the three convoys of the enemy who had fled earlier in the day had taken up position so that the southern front of the enemy was about two miles in extent in all. By attacking the enemy the column had succeeded in breaking up the British encircling movement. One of their attacking groups had been nearly wiped out on the Crossbarry–Bandon road.

Now came the other British attacking columns on the right and left flanks. They were met by Christy O'Connell's section (No. 7) on the main body of the column's right flank; by No. 4 section under Denis Lordan on the left front flank; and by my section (No. 5) on the left rear flank. No. 7 section was grandly placed to let them have it, lying on a position overlooking the crossroads. They blazed at them and drove them back eventually. No. 4 section, under Denis Lordan, was also heavily engaged by a column of about one hundred and fifty British. On several occasions the British were driven back before they gave up the attempt of breaking through this section. Here a fine Volunteer – Peter Monohan – was killed, holding the position, whilst Dan Corcoran of Newcestown was badly wounded through the hip. I may mention one of the outstanding feats of bravery by the Volunteers. When Corcoran was wounded the English were only about twenty yards away, but Dick Spencer of Castletownbere jumped out and brought him to safety on his back.

My section, No. 5, met the enemy on the left rear. About two hundred strong, the British advanced through O'Driscoll's farm at Ballyhandle in extended sections. They advanced towards our position and were met by rapid fire, which they returned. The firing continued for some time. Some British fell, but we did not escape either, as Volunteer Jeremiah O'Leary of Corrin, Leap, and Volunteer Con Daly of Carrig, Ballinascarthy, were killed, and two more were wounded. O'Leary and Daly died gloriously in the act of firing their rifles. The enemy was by this time in the 'Castle Field', a large field full of heights and hollows and in the centre of which stood an old castle ruin which was occupied by Den Mehigan of Bandon and Con Lehane of Timoleague. These two did great work firing continuously at the British as they advanced. The enemy poured lead into the castle, but the remainder of the section kept up rapid fire and prevented a further advance on this position.

Meanwhile, the column commander, Tom Barry, reinforced our section by sending on to us two officers, 'Nudge' Callanan and 'Spud' Murphy, and ten Volunteers. Spud had his arm in a sling, having been wounded in a previous encounter. With the arrival of these reinforcements my section advanced, and the enemy retired from a withering fire. We followed up and our two men who had been firing from the castle walked out and joined us. Leaving 'Spud' in charge of the remaining Volunteers, I set out with a few Volunteers to attempt a flanking movement on the British, and discovered a counter-flanking attempt on their part. They did not observe us and we waited until their leaders were within fifteen or twenty yards and then opened fire. The leading officer was killed and a number of his men. Immediately the remainder turned and ran, providing an easy target.

Just as our section had routed the flanking party, Commandant Barry at the head of the remainder of the column arrived. The enemy had been routed on three sides; the party of British engaged by our section were attempting to reform about three hundred yards away. We were ordered 'Fall in'; the whole column was deployed along a ditch facing the enemy, who were attempting to reform. The order was rapped out: 'Get ready. Target – enemy concentrations on your immediate front. Range – three hundred – three rounds, Fire!' Three times in quick succession a hundred rifles barked. Helter-skelter the English broke in all directions except those knocked out. One section of the IRA column continued to fire at individual soldiers until no more were in sight. The battle of Crossbarry was over.

The column fell in again. The order to march was given to each section commander. Advance, flank and rear guards were put out in extended order. The order 'March' was given, and over the hills moved the victorious West Cork brigade flying column, bringing their wounded and captured munitions with them. On through

161

Crosspound, through Raheen into Crowhill, where our flankers encountered a body of Auxiliaries and killed four of them. We had no casualties. On for Rearour, where our advance guard was also fired on by a British military reinforcement party. None of our party was hit, but two goats on the bridge at the time were shot dead. The column was then swung away and crossed further down, but the enemy did not attempt to follow up. On to Killbonane, where we had our first meal since the previous day, when we arrived at four in the evening. Our wounded were got to safety by this time.

A strange mixture was this band of Volunteers, for they were jubilant at their success, but sorrowful for their dead comrades. Sadly they mourned those great sons of Ireland who had died in battle that day – Charlie Hurley, Jeremiah O'Leary, Con Daly and Peter Monohan. Brave, patriotic men they were, the flower of our manhood, tested well on many occasions against the ancient enemy, in arms and in jails. May their souls rest in peace and their objects be soon achieved!

CHARLIE HURLEY'S WORK AND DEATH FOR IRELAND

by TOM BARRY

ON 19 MARCH 1921, an Irish patriot was shot to death by British soldiers at Ballinphellic, Upton, County Cork. His name was Charlie Hurley of Baurleigh, Kilbrittain, and he died alone, pressing the trigger of his half-empty gun, attempting to fight his way through forty English soldiers. His name is not mentioned in any of the many books written about the Anglo-Irish war; no words of his are handed down to us, no ballads (except one West Cork one) recall his name and his deeds; and shame on us, even his lonely grave in Clogagh graveyard remains as yet, unmarked by a tombstone. Yet, this Volunteer commandant of the Irish Republican Army was not less great than any of our great, for in patriotism, in courage, in effort for his people's freedom, and in his ultimate sacrifice, he stands for all time with Clarke, Connolly, Pearse, MacCurtain, MacSwiney and all the others who strove and died for Ireland. Fifty-eight West Cork men died of enemy bullets in the fight for the Republic, and it is no easy task to select one of their number as the subject for a tribute which may well apply to all of them. They were all great Irishmen, but I have no doubt that, could they select one of their number as a model of all that was best in the Volunteer movement, Charlie Hurley would be their unanimous selection. Owing to lack of space this article can only be a brief sketch of a man whose work and sacrifices for Ireland would, if chronicled, fill many pages.

Charlie was born in Baurleigh, Kilbrittain, on 19 March 1892. At an early age he went to work in a store in Bandon, and whilst there he studied and sat for an examination as a boy clerk. He passed and was appointed to Haulbowline. There he served from 1911 to 1915, when he was promoted to Liverpool. This promotion he refused, as its acceptance entailed conscription in the British army, and Charlie was even then a Volunteer of the Irish army. Since his boyhood in Bandon he had also been an active member of Sinn Féin, the Gaelic Athletic Association and the Gaelic League, thus being grounded to the faith of Irish separatism for which he was to work so hard and eventually to die. He returned to West Cork and started to organise the Volunteers, and in early 1918 he was arrested, charged and found guilty of possession of arms and of the plans of the British fortification in Bere Island. Sentenced to five years' penal servitude, he served part of it in Cork and Maryborough jails, but was released with other hunger strikers under the 'Cat and Mouse Act' towards the end of 1918. Back again in West Cork where he was appointed brigade commandant early in 1920 on the arrest and torture of Tom Hales. This post he held until his death nearly twelve months later.

Charlie was the idol of the brigade. He was loved for his patriotism, his courage, his sincerity, his generosity, good humour and his unassuming ways. He was a natural leader with an un-common power of inspiring men in dark and difficult days. There was a stubbornness in him on the issue of Ireland's freedom which was not based on any material factor, but on a mysticism of which one only got a glimpse on rare occasions. That mysticism of the

Celt made Charlie's love of country a religion – a faith – which only allowed him to visualise two ends, either his country's freedom, or his own death in attempting to achieve that freedom. Usually gay and of good spirits, sometimes he would brood if matters were not going too well. Then one would get a glimpse of the real man. His jaw would set, his eyes shine and his whole face light up as he would drive home the doctrine of 'Hit Back and Hit Harder'. He had the highest and most noble combination of courage – moral courage and courage in defeat and courage in attack. He was generous to a fault, wholly unambitious and in his unassuming way continually urged that he should be allowed to relinquish the command of the brigade and be left free for whole-time fighting with the brigade column. He had a premonition of his death, for several times he told me that he would die alone fighting against the English when none of us was near. And he died in just that way.

Charlie was wounded in the nose during an attack on British military at Upton railway station on 15 February 1921, by a group of eight IRA men. He recovered and sprained his ankle which was not completely cured on 18 March, when, with Seán Buckley (a brigade staff officer) he returned from O'Mahony's, Belrose, at midnight, to his headquarters at Forde's, Ballinphellic, four miles away. Seán Buckley went on to O'Connell's, about a mile across country from Forde's, where Charlie slept that night.

Meanwhile, the brigade flying column had come on to Ballyhandle, near Crossbarry, where they were to fight on the following morning. The column was roused at two o'clock on the morning of 19 March, as the brigade column commander received reports of British troops advancing on them from all directions – Cork city, Ballincollig, Macroom, Bandon and Kinsale. The Volunteers assembled at the pre-arranged assembly point at Crossbarry, and immediately two scouts were sent to bring Charlie and Seán Buckley straight on to the column, as they were of course in the line of the British advance. The scouts were captured by the British and the message was never delivered. And so, about half an hour before the dawn, Charlie was awakened not by his comrades, but by the noise of British soldiers battering in the front door of the house with their rifle butts. As ever thoughtful of others, he told the people of the house to remain upstairs in safety, and down the stairs he walked, clad in his shirt and trousers only, with his guns in his hands, to meet his death like the great Irishman he was.

The English were in the kitchen when Charlie walked into view, firing as he rushed them. They fired and broke, leaving one dead and two wounded, so Charlie made for the back door. Out into the back he rushed to be met immediately by a volley from a dozen rifles, and he fell dead into the farmyard with several bullets in him, chiefly through the head. About four miles away at Crossbarry, where we were about to be engaged, we heard the volleys, and I remember remarking that Charlie was gone. Somehow one knew that his fate was to die in such a way, and that it had come at last.

Late that evening, the British nosed their way back to Crossbarry with reinforcements to collect their dead. There, too, were three of our dead: Jeremiah O'Leary, Leap; Con Daly, Ballinascarthy, and Peter Monohan of Bandon. Charlie's remains were collected also, and those four Volunteers were brought into Bandon military barracks. Later Charlie's body was thrown into the workhouse morgue where he lay until the following day (Sunday) when he was taken out by subterfuge to the church at his burial place at Clogagh.

Owing to the war, it was not possible to have the fighting men of West Cork at a public funeral. We had to choose between giving him a public funeral or one where only armed Volunteers would be present. We chose the latter, as we knew he would wish it to be so. So we marched and marched all Saturday and Sunday night, although already weary and tired after the long fight at Crossbarry on Saturday morning, until 2 a.m. on Monday, when we arrived at Clogagh village. Armed sentries were thrown out, the priest was called, and a hundred riflemen filed into the church to pray that their comrade would have eternal peace. After a short time the column again formed up outside the church and slow-marched to the graveyard with Charlie's body in their midst. I have seen many pathetic scenes in a not uneventful life, but the memory of that night's burial remains foremost. Perhaps it may be that because Charlie was my great comrade and that I loved him greatly, that the scene was seared into my memory. It is still fresh and clear – the dirge of the war pipes played by Flor Begley, the slow march of the brigade flying column, the small group of only six other mourners, the rain-soaked sky and earth, and the wintry moon that shone, vanished and shone again as we followed him to his grave. The grief-stricken faces of the riflemen as I gave the order for their last salute to a gallant patriot leader – 'Present Arms' – and the three volleys and the 'Last Post' ringing clearly in the night air, are still vivid. The final tribute in an oration by the column leader was given, and we turned from his grave and marched away to the west to cross the main Bandon–Clonakilty road before the dawn broke.

Some day – soon it is hoped – when the Irish people again make paramount the virtues of patriotism, courage, truth and sacrifice, then will the memory of Brigadier Charlie Hurley, patriot and leader, be suitably enshrined and handed on to future generations as an example of all that was best in the Volunteer movement of our times. This tribute cannot be closed in any more fitting manner than by a verse of a ballad written by his friend and comrade, Seán Buckley:

In the lonely graveyard of Clogagh, he sleeps his last long sleep,
But in our homes throughout West Cork, his memory we will keep,
And teach our youth his love of truth, his scorn of wrong and fear;
And teach them, too, to love our land, as did our brigadier.

IN MEMORIAM

To Brigadier Charlie Hurley, of Baurleigh, Kilbrittain, who was killed in action near Crossbarry on the morning of 19 March 1921.

A few blades of grass, and the leaf of a daisy,
With a small shamrock spray from the grave where you lie,
Your battle for Érin now gallantly ended,
Inspiring your comrades to conquer or die;

These, these, shall I cherish through sunshine and shadow,
Like the spring blooms around you, dear Charley, so true,
And whenever of Érin and Freedom I'm thinking
With a prayer I'll remember these tokens and you.

In memory I'll see you on hill-side and valley,
Through good and ill-fortune still leading along;
When, many despairing, you carried on cheering,
Through the grim gap of danger all fearless and strong.

Your name and your grave will be honoured forever,
And we'll keep on the memories of days that have been,
'Till the bright dawn you died for, our dauntless young Fenian,
Shines forth round the banner of Dark Rosaleen.

DESTRUCTION OF ROSSCARBERY POLICE BARRACKS

by TIM O'DONOGHUE

MANY BETTER AND braver men of the Cork 3rd brigade of the IRA could write the account of the capture of the Royal Irish Constabulary stronghold of Rosscarbery in April 1921. Before setting down the details of that fight it would be well for readers to have some idea of situation existing at that time in the West Cork area.

The brigade area extended from Kinsale on the eastern side to the coastline at Berehaven, and from a line running across via Crookstown on the north to the sea in the south. The Cork 3rd brigade of the IRA operated in this area. It consisted of seven battalions and its active service flying column on parade numbered approximately one hundred riflemen. The full column was not taken into service on each operation. In the column were men from all grades – farmers, students, tradesmen, labourers; West Cork men all, loyal and staunch comrades, equipped with the arms and ammunition fought for and captured in attacks on British crown forces, and all armed with that deadly hatred of England and imperialist oppression. The column leader or O/C was Tom

Barry. Under his leadership the column had attacked, disarmed and defeated the British forces and Auxiliaries at Kilmichael, Toureen, Crossbarry and other places.

The enemy numbered thousands and held important posts right over the whole area. The civilian population was of the type found in almost every other area in Ireland at the time; the Irish backing the column and the fighting men to the last man; the mixed breeds and the imperialists openly hostile. Those of the civilian population who were good could not have been much better. They were of the best this country or any other country ever produced; old and young of them gave their all to the army of the republic. Night and day saw them standing-to behind the men of the column. Enough credit can never be given to the old folk who sat up at night to give their beds and accommodation to 'the lads', who scouted and acted as sentries often all night as the column rested. The true history of their unselfish and marvellous support could never be told in a short article. Ireland has reason to remember them and leaders who today say they move towards the national goal as fast as the people want them, libel those of our race who proved in 1920–1921 and later that they will always move as fast as honest leadership will take them.

On 19 March 1921 (one year to the day after the brutal murder of Brigade Commandant Thomas MacCurtain, lord mayor of Cork), the West Cork brigade flying column had attacked and inflicted a crushing defeat on the British column rounding up at Crossbarry. It had then moved west, and in the following month, April, had billeted in the 2nd battalion area near Ballinascarthy; the intention being to attack a convoy of enemy troops which usually travelled to Clonakilty Junction on Wednesday morning. The attack was called off as the military did not travel, and the column moved further into my area, the 2nd battalion. I was then vice O/C. Immediately the column arrived I was responsible for their billeting and other arrangements. I took them to the Kilmeen company area, fifteen miles north of Rosscarbery. The following morning the column O/C, Tom Barry, sent for me and gave me orders as to the preparation of the material required for his next operation – a mine, crude bombs – all to be manufactured for the following Monday evening. He told me the 1st battalion quartermaster, Dan Holland, would detail from where the explosives would be got and then he moved off in a zig-zag direction towards his next objective, Rosscarbery Royal Irish Constabulary barracks.

The material for the mine and bombs was scattered over a large area. It had to be, so that it would always be at hand for the column. This time, however, it had to be collected from Crosspound and Berehaven. Men had to travel for it with care so as to avoid capture and it was well into Monday night when all were back and we were in full swing preparing the mine and bombs. We worked at the house of John O'Mahony, Ballinvard, and anyone listening to the banter and joking as we worked would never have realised that we were going into action in such a short time. We finished our job by Tuesday. The column O/C was by this time growing impatient. He had to move each night and was getting closer to Rosscarbery than he liked. On his orders to proceed to Benduff, we got there through snow at 7 p.m. Wednesday night. (Benduff is about three miles from Rosscarbery.) On arrival I reported to the O/C, and was questioned as to the condition of the mine, and other matters, and was told at the same time that Jim Hurley (later secretary University College, Cork) and myself were to be in the storming party. Barry then addressed the column, telling them their objective was the capture of Rosscarbery barracks. He said at the same time that the garrison in occupation was expecting the attack. He named the storming party of ten men, each to be armed with two guns; a torch party of ten more to light torches and throw them in, this party to be in charge of Seán Hales. He, himself, took charge of the storming party and it formed the advance guard; the explosives were to bring up the rear. In this formation the column O/C led off to Ross. About a mile from the town the order 'All boots off' was given. We moved slowly up and then No. 1 section handed over the mine. Barry crept up to the gate to slip the latch, but it was too dark and the torches had to be lit; then Mick Crowley (Kilbrittain) and myself were ordered to jump with him over the wall if the gate were not open. The front wall was about twenty feet back from a line of houses and barbed wire was everywhere. The fuses were lit and we moved up quickly as they began to splutter like fireworks. Barry snapped the latch and to our joy it gave with him. We placed the mine against the door and then ran back thirty yards and lay flat with our palms to our ears. The mine went off with a deafening roar and sent up a cloud of blinding dust. By the time the dust had cleared the garrison opened fire. To rush in blindly we could not, as we could not see whether there was a breach or not, and inside the building it was dark. Now I have already stated the barracks was standing back, clear of all houses, a huge stone building, no building touching or overlooking it. It was well stocked with machine-guns and bombs, and it was the boast of the garrison that it was the only barracks that could not be taken. Indeed, that night it looked a hopeless task to take it, and I think any other man but Barry would have thrown in the sponge.

Instead he ordered Neilus Connolly (Skibbereen) to take three men across the street to the house opposite and open rapid fire with rifles, and ordered another party to procure petrol and paraffin oil. From the corner of the house on the left as one would go from the barracks, he opened fire to cover the party who rushed across the street. Shortly after they had taken up position the petrol and paraffin arrived, and he unscrewed the caps of four or five tins and pitched them towards the building. When the garrison got the smell of the petrol they immediately guessed what was to happen and they concentrated all their fire on the corner where Barry stood.

The bombs were the most dangerous. I often wondered how he sensed their coming. He could not see them, and I do not know how he could have heard them coming with the continuous rifle fire, four rifles in the house across the street and at least twenty cracking from the barracks and only fifty feet apart; but as each bomb came he always shouted just in time, 'Bomb, get down', and each of them came to either three or four feet from him. There was a stout telegraph pole close by and I stood behind it to shelter from several of the bombs. Barry's back was to me and he did not see me. Had he seen me I would have heard something I would not forget. It worked fine until one bomb rolled out further than the others and exploded at the same side as I was. That taught me a lesson, and I got down as quickly and as flatly as the others from then on. When he had the petrol tins pitched into the building he got a bag, folded it, stuck a bayonet through it and dipped it in paraffin, lit it and pitched it in by the point of the bayonet. This set the whole building alight. Then we saw the effect of the explosion. The door and windows had been blown in and all the steel shutters were off, but otherwise the building was intact, and it was necessary for the blaze to be kept up. There was plenty of light, of course, and while this was an advantage to Barry to see the bombers, he was plainly in view every time he went round the corner to throw in a bucket of paraffin. Each time this action brought a hail of bullets. At one time I remarked to Jim Hurley that we would be soon minus a column leader. Jim said, 'Not at all; he has a charmed life.' The column O/C certainly had a busy time for hours, dodging bombs, throwing in bombs, paraffin, without rest.

The ceilings were of plaster and were not catching fire, so Barry shouted for four charges. The fuse was lit. Jim Hurley pitched one and failed to get it in the window. I tried the next and fell short. Barry then said, 'Keep me covered; open up on the bombers who are at the far side of the windows.' Jim opened up on them and Barry rushed in and heaved the charge through the window. He did the same with the remaining one and they brought down the ceilings. The floors caught fire and then it was only a matter of time until the whole building was on fire. It was heartbreaking to hear the ammunition we badly needed exploding in the flames. It was daylight then and we left the town.

Openly singing the songs of our country, we marched through the town, on for the west. We halted to put our boots on, then off to the north and then we wheeled back east, passing north of Rosscarbery and on to Rossmore. We reached there about 8 a.m. Meanwhile British columns moved into the town where they were told we had gone west. Ponderously with artillery they swept west while we prepared to move to temporary safety across the Bandon river. Other fights were carried out by the IRA in Rosscarbery and its vicinity, but it is not my task to detail those. It is sufficient to say that for two months before the Truce no English policeman or soldier was in occupation of this historic old town.

UPTON AMBUSH

The ambush at Upton Junction, County Cork, took place on 19 February 1921, when members of the West Cork IRA attacked a train conveying British soldiers. Three members of the brigade, Jim Whelan, Patrick O'Sullivan and Batt Foley, were killed in action.

Many homes are filled with sorrow and with sadness,
Many hearts are filled with anguish and with pain,
For old Ireland now she hangs her head in mourning,
For the men who fell at Upton for Sinn Féin.

Chorus:
Let the moon shine tonight along the valley,
Where those men who fought for freedom now are laid;
May they rest in peace those men who died for Ireland,
And who fell at Upton ambush for Sinn Féin.

Some were thinking of their mothers, wives and sweethearts,
More were thinking of their dear old Irish homes;
Do they think of how they drilled along the valley,
Or when they marched out from Cork city to their doom.

Chorus

The morning cry rang out: 'Fix Bayonets',
And the gallant lads, they fixed them for the fray,
Gallantly they fought and died for Ireland,
Around the lonely woods at Upton far away.

Chorus

THE HEROIC DEAD OF WEST CORK

THE STORIES OF the fights at Kilmichael, Crossbarry and Rosscarbery in *Rebel Cork's Fighting Story* were written respectively by section leaders Stephen O'Neill, Thomas Kelleher and Timothy O'Donoghue of the 3rd West Cork brigade column IRA. This, the most famous brigade active service unit of the Anglo-Irish War, won undying fame under the leadership of Commandant Tom Barry, for its many victories over British military, Auxiliaries, Black and Tans and Royal Irish Constabulary in 1920–21. These contributors took outstanding parts in the actions they describe. Their contributions have been read by Commandant Barry, who directed the column's operations with masterly skill, and to whose daring and resource high tribute has been deservedly paid by the men he led into action. The sacrifices made by the manhood of West Cork for Irish freedom are eloquently recalled by the following brigade casualty list (giving rank and name, address and date and place of death respectively):

Volunteer John Hurley, Clonakilty; Easter 1916, General Post Office Dublin.
Lieutenant Tim Fitzgerald, Gaggin, Bandon; 29 August 1920, Brinny.
Lieutenant John Connolly, Shannon Street, Bandon; 1 October 1920, Bandon.
Vice-Commandant Michael McCarthy, East Green, Dunmanway; 28 November 1920, Kilmichael.

Lieutenant Patrick Deasy, Kilmacsimon Quay, Bandon; 28 November 1920, Kilmichael.

Lieutenant James Sullivan, Knockawaddra, Rossmore; 28 November 1920, Kilmichael.

Volunteer Michael Tobin, Ballineen; November 1920, Grattan Street, Cork.

Captain John Galvin, Main Street, Bandon; 3 December 1920, Bandon.

Lieutenant Jim Donohue, Shannon Street, Bandon; 3 December 1920, Bandon.

Section Commander Joe Begley, Castle Road, Bandon; 3 December 1920, Bandon.

Lieutenant Michael McClean, Lowertown, Schull; 8 December 1920, Gaggin, Bandon.

Volunteer Timothy Crowley, Behigullane, Dunmanway; 14 December 1920, Dunmanway.

Captain Jeremiah O'Mahony, Paddock, Enniskeane; December 1920, Paddock, Enniskeane.

Volunteer Patrick Donovan, Culnigh, Timoleague; 17 January 1921, Timoleague.

Volunteer Denis Hegarty, Clashfluck, Timoleague; 21 January 1921, Courtmacsherry.

Volunteer Daniel O'Reilly, Granassig, Kilbrittain; 24 January 1921, Bandon.

Lieutenant Patrick Crowley, Kilbrittain; 4 February 1921, Maryboro, Timoleague.

Section Commander Patrick O'Driscoll, Mohana, Skibbereen; 7 February 1921, Mohana, Skibbereen.

Volunteer Patrick Coffey and Volunteer James Coffey, Breaghna, Enniskeane; 14 February 1921, Kilrush, Enniskeane.

Lieutenant John Whelan, late of Liverpool; 15 February 1921, Upton.

Lieutenant Patrick Sullivan, Raheen, Upton; 15 February 1921, Upton.

Section Commander Batt Foley, Ballymurphy, Upton; 15 February 1921, Upton.

Volunteer Cornelius McCarthy, Kilanetig, Ballinadee; 16 February 1921, Crois na Leanbh, Kilbrittain.

Volunteer John McGrath, Rathclarin, Kilbrittain; 16 February 1921, Crois na Leanbh.

Volunteer Timothy Connolly, Fearnagark, Kilbrittain; 16 February 1921, Crois na Leanbh.

Volunteer Jeremiah O'Neill, Knockpogue, Kilbrittain; 16 February 1921, Crois na Leanbh.

Brigadier Charles Hurley, Baurleigh, Kilbrittain; 19 March 1921, Ballinphellic.

Volunteer Peter Monohan, Bandon; 19 March 1921, Crossbarry.

Volunteer Jeremiah O'Leary, Corrin, Leap; 19 March 1921, Crossbarry.

Volunteer Con Daly, Carrig, Ballinascarthy; 19 March 1921, Crossbarry.

Volunteer Timothy Whooley, Carrycrowley, Ballineen; 22 March 1921, Shannonvale.

Captain Frank Hurley, Laragh, Bandon; 9 May 1921, Bandon.

Volunteer Geoffrey Canty, Scrahan, Newcestown; 9 May 1921, Morragh.

Volunteer Daniel Crowley, Behigullane, Dunmanway; 7 June 1921, Behigullane.

Lieutenant Con Murphy, Clashfluck, Timoleague; 11 May 1921, Cloundreen, Kilbrittain.

Volunteer Matthew Donovan, Quarries Cross, Bandon; 10 June 1921, Quarries Cross.

Volunteer John Murphy, Cloghane, Bandon; 22 June 1921, Cloghane.

Commandant Michael O'Neill, Maraboro, Kilbrittain; 29 April 1922, Ballygroman.

Section Commander Patrick McCarthy, Monahin, Kilcoe, Ballydehob; August 1922, Skibbereen.

Commandant Gibbs Ross, Glandart, Bantry; 30 August 1922, Bantry.

Captain Patrick Cooney, Bridge Street, Skibbereen; 30 August 1922, Bantry.

Lieutenant Donal McCarthy, Carrigbawn, Drinagh; 30 August 1922, Bantry.

Lieutenant Michael Crowley, Reenogreena, Glandore; 30 August 1922, Bantry.

Volunteer Patrick Pearse, Kinsale; 4 October 1922, Upton.

Volunteer Daniel Sullivan, Kinsale; 4 October 1922, Upton.

Volunteer Michael Hayes, Shannon Street, Bandon; 4 October 1922, Upton.

Volunteer Daniel Donovan, Clogagh; 4 October 1922, Timoleague.

Section Commander Tadhg O'Leary, South Square, Macroom; 4 November 1922, Ballineen.

Volunteer John Howell, Clonakilty (late of Doneraile); 4 November 1922, Enniskeane.

Volunteer Patrick Duggan, Kilbrogan, Bandon; 17 November 1922, Glengarriff.

Assistant Quartermaster General Richard Barrett, Hollyhill, Ballineen; murdered 8 December 1922, Mountjoy.

Volunteer George Dease, Castlehaven; 8 December 1922, Kealkil.

Volunteer J. Dwyer, Castletownbere; 8 December 1922, Kealkil.

Captain Timothy Kennefick, Fairhill, Cork; 11 December 1922, Coachford.

Captain Laurence Cunningham, Clonakilty; 15 February 1923, Lyre.

Volunteer John O'Connor, Innishannon; 7 March 1923, Ballyseedy, Tralee.

Lieutenant Denis Kelly, Scart Road, Bantry; 17 April 1923, Kealkil.

NORTH CORK FROM 1915 TO THE TRUCE

by VOLUNTEER

IN SEPTEMBER 1915, a Millstreet Aeridheacht, which marked the beginning of a page of Irish history, was held in the football field, mid-way between the town and the railway station. P.H. Pearse was billed to speak there. The local Royal Irish Constabulary had instructions to keep a sharp look-out for this Irish felon. They did not, however, have the satisfaction of hearing him speak, nor of taking mental notes of such portions of his speech as they would have considered likely to cause disaffection amongst His Majesty's subjects. Whilst the members of the 'Force' were dutifully carrying out their instructions, Pearse passed through them unnoticed, down the main street of the town and on to the football field. He addressed a crowd of several thousand people gathered together to enjoy a real Gaelic day and also to listen to the gospel of Irish patriotism by its greatest exponent of the time. When the Royal Irish Constabulary found that Pearse had evaded them and, worse still, had addressed the people without a policeman being present to take a note of the sedition he was bound to preach, their chagrin can better be imagined than described.

Pearse's address at the Aeridheacht gave the multitude much food for thought. It reawakened in the hearts of many the dormant chords of Irish patriotism inherited from an unyielding and freedom-loving ancestry. Many took a secret resolution that day to strive and, if necessary, to die, that Ireland might be free. Amongst the organisers of the Aeridheacht were men who remembered the stirring events of 1867; men who were themselves members of the Republican Brotherhood; others were young boys who had learned the history of their native land. Amongst the older men were the late Jim Buckley, Church Street, and the late Jeremiah O'Riordan, 'The Corner House', stalwart veterans still carrying on the traditions of the Fenians. When the Land War was fought, they did more than their part to end the degrading system of landlordism which prevailed from the Plantation to the 1880s.

Amongst the younger element associated with the formation of the Aeridheacht were the late Cornelius J. Meaney, Coolinaree, and the late Jeremiah Crowley, Drishanebeg, subsequently commandant and adjutant respectively of the Millstreet battalion until the Truce. Following a conference with Pearse, these men, as well as others still living in the district, set to work to organise the Volunteers. In a short time the Millstreet, Keale, Rathduane and Mushera companies were in being. There was an average of fifteen men for each company or corps. The companies were attached to the 4th Cork brigade. Training, arming and equipping were started in earnest. The patriot-martyr, Terence MacSwiney, lord mayor of Cork, was a frequent caller to the district on organisation work. At the Manchester martyrs' celebration in Cork in November 1916, and again at the Saint Patrick's Day celebration, 1916, the Millstreet district was represented by a contingent of Irish Volunteers.

On Easter Sunday 1916, the various units paraded with full equipment and marched through the town as far as Kilmeedy. The officers and men were unaware that anything unusual was afoot, nor did they know of the capture of Roger Casement, or of the arms ship, *The Aud*. On Easter Sunday evening, when the parade had been dismissed, the officers got a hint from the Kerry side that the hour for action was at hand. They waited, but no word came from their Cork headquarters. At midnight on Easter Sunday, acting on information from Kerry, the Mushera company, whose headquarters was four miles east of the town, mobilised and marched to the outskirts of Millstreet. There was a deluge of rain at the time. The town company was not called out, but the officers were ready to mobilise it at a moment's notice. Rathduane company, with its headquarters midway between Rathmore and Millstreet, and Keale company – three miles on the Kanturk side – were not ordered out, but arrangements were made for mobilisation if they were needed. About two o'clock on Easter Monday morning, a dispatch messenger, who had been sent to Rathmore, arrived back in Millstreet and reported that there was nothing doing. The Mushera company returned home, every man drenched to the skin, and thoroughly disappointed by the course of events.

On Easter Monday evening, a report reached Millstreet that the Irish Volunteers were in action against the British in Dublin. A member of the Millstreet company, Jimmy Hickey, cycled to the Volunteer Hall, Sheares Street, Cork, to enquire for orders. In the meantime, mobilisation of the companies proceeded through a wet and stormy night. Mushera company occupied the Priest Cross, three-quarters of a mile north-east of the town. Early on Tuesday morning, Keale company was in readiness near the railway arch at Drishanebeg; whilst Rathduane company marched and took up positions at Kilcahane, about half a mile south of the town. The town company, acting on instructions, did not mobilise; the men were ordered to stay near their homes and if possible to observe any movements made by the enemy. They were also instructed to be prepared to mobilise at a moment's notice.

Also early on Tuesday morning, Jimmy Hickey returned from his forty miles' bicycle dash to Cork, with the information that brigade headquarters had no orders to give. The Volunteers, however, were instructed to arrange to receive any which might be issued during Tuesday. They waited until nightfall, but no orders arrived. As the Royal Irish Constabulary in Millstreet barracks having heard, doubtless through some of their friends, that armed men were concentrated in the vicinity, the Volunteers were sent home with orders to mobilise for action when called upon. The remaining days of Easter Week passed slowly and painfully by, and still no orders came for the waiting men. Ultimately, on the following Sunday, came news that the Rising was smashed and that Pearse, the man who had spoken to the people of Millstreet on the previous September, was a prisoner in the hands of the enemy.

On Thursday 2 May, a party of military swooped upon the town and, guided by the local Royal Irish Constabulary, they arrested three men from the town; two were members of the Volunteer organisation: Jim Buckley, Church Street, and Jerry Twomey, Main Street. The British also arrested a third man who lived some miles outside the town, but who was not in the Volunteers, although an active sympathiser. Again, in the early hours of Friday 5 May, there were further raids by British military and Royal Irish Constabulary. Jeremiah O'Riordan, 'The Corner House', and his son Michael, were arrested and taken to Cork. The homes of other prominent Volunteers were also raided, but the men sought were not found. There were further raids on 10 May. This time Con Murphy, Ballydaly, and his brother Tim, both active Volunteers, together with Con Callaghan, Mill Road, Millstreet, were placed under arrest. The homes of the other men sought were again raided unsuccessfully. All of those arrested, including the non-Volunteer, were deported to Frongoch, where they were kept until December 1916. Not a rifle, cartridge or bandolier was given up by the Millstreet men, though bribes and threats were used against them during the weeks following the Rising.

By Christmas 1916, the Millstreet deportees, together with the few who luckily escaped arrest, had returned to their homes. Steps were taken to re-organise, train and equip the young men of the district, to carry on the fight. The determination that Ireland should take its proper place amongst the nations was stronger than ever.

The Volunteer movement in Millstreet found many recruits from 1917 to 1920. In the latter year, practically every young man of military age in the battalion area had joined up. There were almost eight hundred men on the roll in July 1921. In Millstreet parish alone, there were seven companies averaging over ninety men to the company. Not alone was there a large number on the battalion roll, but the discipline maintained was excellent, whilst the standard of military proficiency was very high. The battalion commandant, the late C.J. Meaney, and the battalion adjutant, the late Jerry Crowley, were responsible for this satisfactory state of affairs. Both were exceptionally efficient officers who, by their tact, prudence, self-sacrifice and untiring work of organisation, built up as fine a fighting machine as was possible, considering time and circumstances. Their courage and coolness in the face of danger, inspired the other officers and men of the battalion. Above all, their honest patriotism made them beloved by those who considered it an honour to serve with them. Even the enemy had a secret admiration for these two men, who knew neither fear nor injustice.

In 1917, Mrs Jack O'Sheehan and her troupe of singers and dancers visited Millstreet. Her husband was at that time serving a sentence of imprisonment for singing patriotic songs. The performance in Millstreet, a national one, was a huge success and crowds of admirers would escort her home each night after the show. One night, as the crowd passed the Royal Irish Constabulary barracks in processional order, some parties, not in the procession, threw stones at the barrack gate, and thus put the machinery of the law in motion. C.J. Meaney, commandant, Patrick J. Healy, battalion vice-commandant, John O'Connell and Denis A. Hickey of Main Street, all of whom had been in the procession, were arrested. They were charged under the Unlawful Assembly Act and were sentenced to a term of imprisonment. A fifth man who was also arrested, was discharged, having given evidence that he was not in the street at the time of the incident. The prisoners went on hunger strike and were released under the 'Cat and Mouse Act'. Indignation because of this action by the authorities spread through the district and from that time onwards the Royal Irish Constabulary were despised and hated by all, whilst the men who suffered were admired and respected.

During 1917, 1918 and 1919, the work of organisation, the training and equipping of the Volunteers went on steadily. In 1920, the British intensified their 'campaign of frightfulness' against the Irish Volunteers, as well as against the Irish race in general. Millstreet district was specially marked for attack. In the summer of 1920, Jeremiah O'Riordan's 'The Corner House', was fired into from a 'tender' of mixed Royal Irish Constabulary, Black and Tans, and military. Mr O'Riordan, then an old man, had a miraculous escape from flying bullets. This was the first night of terror in Millstreet by the newly arrived Tans. There was indiscriminate firing by the police and military all over the town, both before and after the incident at O'Riordan's. From that time onwards, outrages of this kind became general by the crown forces, who made unsuccessful attempts to murder Volunteers.

The battalion adjutant, Jeremiah Crowley, had a narrow escape when his father's house at Drishanebeg was raided by masked and armed men in the autumn of 1920. Having fired one shot at his brother Tom, who retreated upstairs, unharmed, the raiders, deeming discretion the better part of valour, departed hastily. They were wise in this, as a few minutes' delay would have meant disaster for them.

Another person marked out for special ill-treatment at this time was the late Fr Joe Breen, CC, who was curate in Tralee in 1916. A man of high patriotism, he was a member of the Irish Volunteers, and his sound advice and able assistance were much appreciated by all who worked with him in the movement. After the Easter Week Rising, he was transferred to Millstreet, as chaplain to Drishane convent. In Millstreet he found full scope for his Volunteer sympathies, and his counsel and valuable aid were availed of by the officers of the battalion. Following an attempt on his life by the British in the autumn of 1920, he went 'on the run' and did not return until the Truce. Whilst on the run, he maintained close contact with the officers of the battalion and the men of the column. He was in a large measure responsible for the successful way in which the fight was carried on in the district.

By November 1920, matters were indeed bad with the unhappy townspeople. None but the bravest dared to venture about after nightfall. There were searches, holds-up and highway robberies committed by the Royal Irish Constabulary and Tans, not to mention the danger from the flying bullets of those drunken hirelings of the British government. On 22 November, a party of Volunteers took up positions in the town, with the view to checking the onslaughts on peaceful townspeople. A fight ensued in which two of the Tans were wounded. The Volunteers lost one of their best men when Paddy McCarthy was killed at Upper Mill Lane. A chance shot fired by a passing Tan hit him on the head and the bullet, apparently a dum-dum, ended his life immediately. Fr Breen, CC, attended to his spiritual wants, and the remains were placed in a motor car and removed from the town to the house of the late Eugene O'Sullivan, Gortavehy, a distance of five miles. Members of the column kept vigil over the body at the wake, which was held that night and next day. The column again took up positions in the town on Tuesday night, and remained until four o'clock on Wednesday morning. But the Tans had learned a lesson and decided that it was unwise to carry on further night attacks against the defenceless citizens. On Wednesday night the funeral procession of Paddy McCarthy moved off from O'Sullivan's house at eight o'clock. It was, indeed, a sad occasion for his comrades who bore the remains through the long boreen to the public road. The late General Liam Lynch had personal charge of the arrangements. When the procession reached the main road, the coffin was transferred to a waiting motor car, and accompanied by three other motor cars; the remains were taken to Lismire graveyard, where the interment took place with full rites of the Holy Church, Fr Breen, CC, officiating at the graveside. When the funeral had left for Lismire, the column again marched to the outskirts of Millstreet, but having been in position a few hours, the men were allowed return to their billets.

EXECUTION OF CON MURPHY

TOWARDS THE END of 1920 nine members of the Millstreet battalion whose names were on the 'murder list' of the Tans, formed a flying squad or small flying column. The late Jeremiah Crowley was in charge of this body of men and under his direction training in military operations was carried out. The squad was reinforced considerably later on and an effective column of close on forty men was formed. On the night of 3 January 1921, the squad, which then consisted of nine men all told, arrived in Rathmore. The late Con Murphy, having arranged billets, went home to his father's house in Ballydaly – a quarter of a mile from the nearest house where the squad was in billets. At about nine o'clock on the morning of 4 January, the scouts protecting the squad reported the presence of a considerable force of military and Royal Irish Constabulary raiding in Ballydaly. The little squad immediately got into a position of defence. Retreat was out of the question as the only way out was occupied by the enemy. There was another line of escape if circumstances were favourable, by crossing the River Blackwater. On this day it was flooded, so that the only alternative in case of attack was to fight to a finish. With this end in view positions were taken up in the old rath. There was not, however, any raid or attack at Rathduane. After a few hours scouts brought the information that the raiders had departed in the Millstreet direction, taking Con Murphy, his father, Denis Murphy, and his two brothers, Tim and Denis, with them as prisoners. Con was later tried by court martial and found guilty of having a revolver in his possession. He was executed at Cork military barracks, and was the first man in the campaign to suffer the death penalty for carrying arms.

SUCCESSFUL TRAIN AMBUSH

IN JANUARY 1921, it was noticed that small parties of armed military travelled occasionally by train between Mallow and Tralee. The Dooneen and Coolinarna companies made preparations to ambush one of these parties. The first plan was to get the Volunteers to take up positions adjacent to Millstreet station with the view to rush either the seven o'clock train from Mallow or the eight o'clock train from Tralee, if any of the parties of military were aboard. The danger to this plan soon revealed itself. It was next arranged to bring off an ambush on the nine o'clock train, at a 'cutting' in the line at Drishanebeg, about a mile to the east of the station. The plan was to get the engine boarded by two armed men and to compel the driver to stop at the ambush position, where elaborate preparations had been made.

It was, however, found after about a week that the chances of any party travelling on the 8 p.m. train were getting remote. It was also observed that they occasionally travelled on the 7 p.m. train from Mallow. Early in February the battalion column took on the task. Plans were laid. Dooneen, Coolecross and Rathcoole companies under Commandant C.J. Meaney, co-operated with the column which was in the charge of Adjutant J. Crowley. On the night of 2 February, the column which at that time had only eight rifles (the remainder having shotguns filled with cartridges of homemade slugs) took up their position at 6.30 p.m. at the appointed place. In the meantime other important details were receiving attention elsewhere. At Rathcoole and Millstreet stations two Volunteers awaited their respective trains – ready to board the engine should either train carry armed military. At Banteer station, four miles on the Mallow side of Rathcoole, a Volunteer awaited the arrival of the Tralee-bound train. His duty was to inspect the trains thoroughly for armed military, then board as an ordinary passenger and report to his comrade at Rathcoole. At this time the train from Mallow to Tralee used to stop fairly long at Banteer. It would not stop at Rathcoole unless it carried a passenger for that place, or unless signalled to do so by the stationmaster; hence the necessity of sending a man to Banteer to await the Tralee-bound train. Both trains passed the ambush position on time, night after night, but there was no party of military on board.

On the night of 10 February, the Volunteer at the Rathcoole end reported six soldiers on board, with uniforms, but without arms or ammunition, whilst the officer commanding the Dooneen company, who had charge of the Millstreet end, reported the arrival of the train there later with six armed Tommies aboard. It was evident that the rifles and equipment had been hidden beneath the seat of the carriage whilst the train was passing through Rathcoole and Banteer stations. As the days were now lengthening, the battalion commander and the O/C of the column decided that unless something turned up the next night, the column would be withdrawn and some other method adopted to capture the troops who were known to be getting through by train.

On the night of 11 February the column took positions as usual at 6.30 p.m. (It was then nearly dark.) They were in position about twenty-five minutes when the seven o'clock train was heard approaching from Rathcoole. There was tension amongst the members of the battalion. Would the waiting prove fruitless as on the other nights of the week, or would there be a fight? These were the thoughts uppermost in every man's mind. The engine sounded a long and shrill whistle while nearly a mile off. This was the pre-arranged signal, in case a party of the enemy was aboard the train. It caused intense excitement amongst the Volunteers. Shotguns and rifles were loaded and held at the ready. A bicycle lamp which had lain covered by a sack on the side of the rails, was uncovered and placed in position between the rails, its bright light shining in the direction of the oncoming train. The train slowed up and stopped as it approached the ambush position, the rear of the engine just over the bicycle lamp. As it had travelled a few yards further than was anticipated, the column moved up into fresh positions. The commandant then called out loudly to the military to surrender to the Irish Republic. For answer a rifle shot rang out in the still night air. The column was ordered to open fire on the carriages containing the military. For about fifteen minutes the calmness of the night was broken by the crack of rifle, revolver and shotgun fire, above the din of which could be heard the groans of the wounded Tommies. The slopes of the cutting were lit up by oil torches prepared in advance by the column and thrown down outside the carriage in which the military were travelling when the fight began. The positions of the soldiers were clearly shown up by the torches, whilst the attackers were covered by the darkness. The fight was one-sided from the outset and the British duly surrendered. Fourteen soldiers came out, one other was dead and practically all were wounded. The column collected the rifles and seven hundred rounds of ammunition. Just at the surrender, a man in the uniform of a British soldier left the train a few carriages back from where the armed men were situated. He advanced up the slope, with his arms above his head, towards the column and asked for 'a rifle to fight for Ireland'. It was then noticed that he was an unarmed Munster Fusilier who spoke with a strong Kerry accent. Needless to state, his request was not granted. It transpired, however, that when he reached his native Kerry he discarded the foreign uniform, joined the Volunteers, fought bravely for Ireland and is today hale and hearty, living somewhere round Tralee. When the military had been disarmed they were put back on the train, which moved off for Millstreet station. Some civilians on the train shouted 'Up the Republic' to the column, who answered with a parting cheer. The column did not suffer any casualty.

TUREENGARRIFFE AMBUSH

TUREENGARRIFFE AMBUSH, WHICH took place on 28 January, resulted in serious losses to the enemy. Major-General Holmes was shot dead and six staff officers were wounded. Tureengarriffe is a wild, rocky district midway between Kingwilliamstown and Scartaglin, County Kerry. It was known that officers of the British army had gone west and the IRA waited at this place for two days to intercept them on their return. A trench had been cut across the road and the driver of the first car seemed to sense trouble ahead and tried to jump his powerful car over it, but failed. A challenge from the IRA instantly rang out; the military party got into action and put up a desperate resistance. It was only when General Holmes was shot dead and practically all the other officers wounded that they surrendered. Seán Moylan, who was in charge of the ambushing party of North Cork and East Kerry men, had the wounded attended to by the First Aid corps and conveyed in a passing motor car to Castleisland. One of the cars was badly damaged and was destroyed; but the other was driven off by the IRA in the Kingwilliamstown direction. On the following days enraged parties of Black and Tans swept into the village, but the inhabitants had wisely fled into the hills. Three houses were bombed and burned. One belonged to Mr Timothy Vaughan – whose son, Captain Dan Vaughan, afterwards became TD for North Cork. He was at this time a prominent man in the IRA. The others belonged to Mr T. O'Sullivan, post office and general drapery, and the residence of the late Willie McAuliffe.

Men from Rathmore took part in the Tureengarriffe ambush. On the Sunday following the engagement, lorries with crown forces swooped down on Knocknagree. They opened fire with machine-guns on some youths who were playing football in a field. A boy named Kelliher was killed and two others were wounded. This dastardly act was undoubtedly intended as a reprisal for Tureen-garriffe.

CLONBANIN AMBUSH

ABOUT 4.30 P.M. on 4 March 1921, the North Cork column, which had its headquarters at Lackadota, two miles south of Millstreet, mobilised and got ready to move against the Tans stationed in the town. A messenger arrived from Seán Moylan, who was commandant of the Newmarket battalion area. Arising from the message, plans were altered and cars were procured to take the men of the column as far as Drishanebeg. There they fell into marching formation and proceeded across the Blackwater by Keale bridge. Taking to the fields, they went via Derinagree to Clonbanin. When the column was passing through Derinagree, an old man and his wife emerged from a cabin. Their faces reflected the joy they felt in their honest Irish hearts at seeing the fighting soldiers of Ireland. As the rearguard passed, the woman could not restrain herself longer. She shouted: 'I suppose ye have the mischief done last night?'

'Yes,' they assured her. 'You will hear of it bye and bye.'

This was within half a mile of the ambush position.

As the column arrived, other men already in position gave word that the military were approaching from the east in lorries. The column could now see, from the shelter of a fence, three lorries with military pass along the road beneath them, only a field distant. They passed on towards Kerry without a shot being fired.

Some days previous IRA intelligence had reported that a top rank military officer had left Buttevant barracks and proceeded to inspect the troops in Kerry. As the Williamstown–Castleisland road had previously proved fatal to an RIC officer of high rank when he and his escort were ambushed at Tureengarriffe by Seán Moylan's column, it was surmised that the apparently safer Mallow–Killarney road would be used by this officer on his return journey. Two days previously the Newmarket and East Kerry columns had lain in ambush at the 'Bower', between Rathmore and Barraduff. Owing to the possibility of information having reached the British, the officers in charge decided to abandon that position. They then took up a new one on the same road in County Cork. Clonbanin was selected as the most suitable place. It is about six miles from Kanturk, where a party of military were stationed, and about the same distance from Millstreet, which had a very strong garrison of Black and Tans as well as members of the Royal Irish Constabulary. Mines were laid during the night, and as the British convoy was passing through next morning the batteries connected to these were switched on, but failed to explode. Consequently, the Tommies passed through unmolested and utterly oblivious of their narrow escape from disaster. As soon as the military had passed on towards Killarney, scouts were posted on the hillsides for miles on the Kerry side, whilst the columns from Newmarket, Millstreet, Charleville and East Kerry were provided with breakfast, after which they again took up positions. Newmarket and Charleville held the northern side of the road. The East Kerry column, commanded by the late Humphrey Murphy, and a section of the Millstreet unit took positions south of the road. A section of the Millstreet men occupied the haggard of Mark O'Shaughnessy, where they placed a Hotchkiss gun, manned by the late Bill Moylan and the late Denis Galvin. The Kerry column was on its flank. The remainder of the Millstreet men occupied a position away from the ambush, covering the roads from Kanturk in order to prevent reinforcements from that direction.

About 3 p.m. the signallers announced five military lorries coming from the Killarney direction. A few minutes afterwards the leading lorry drove into the ambush. As it was passing Shaughnessy's the Hotchkiss gun opened fire on it. A little further on the same lorry was engaged by the columns on the northern side of the road, and having exchanged six or eight shots, was brought to a stand-still. About two minutes' silence followed, until the remainder of the convoy, which consisted of another lorry about a hundred yards ahead of a touring car, which was followed at a distance of about fifteen yards by a Rolls Royce armoured car, arrived. Another lorry, about a hundred yards behind, brought up the rear. All vehicles drove right into the ambush position.

The silence was broken by two rifle shots fired in quick succession and the touring car immediately swerved across the road, apparently out of control. The armoured car collided with the rear of the tourer and the driver, attempting to push on, got the armoured car bogged in the soft dyke on the side of the road. In the meantime the Hotchkiss engaged the second lorry with deadly effect, and heavy rifle fire was concentrated on all vehicles from both sides of the road. To the shout of 'Surrender' from the IRA a voice from the touring car was heard to reply: 'To hell with surrender! Give them the lead!' Immediately a tall man in officer's uniform was seen to leap from the car. He made a dive for cover on the north side of the road but never reached there, as a bullet from an ambusher's rifle blew out his brains. So fell Brigadier-General Cummins, the first British general to take prisoners as hostages on his lorries. That day at Clonbanin his party carried a hostage who escaped during the fighting. Apparently the occupants of the armoured car suffered initial shock and surprise, as almost five minutes elapsed from the moment that the tourer was fired on before the car's Vickers gun went into action, and even then the firing was wild for some time.

On the battle raged, man for man, the trained and specially picked soldiers of England against the raw and badly armed Volunteers of the IRA columns. Above the crack of the rifle and the rattle of the Vickers and Lewis guns which were used by the military, could be plainly heard the moans of the dying and wounded soldiers. The IRA

Hotchkiss gun went out of action early in the fight and our rifles had to fight the Vickers in the armoured car as well as the Lewis gun and opposing rifles. The rifle fire from the roadway gradually grew weaker, until about an hour-and-a-half from the opening of the battle, not a military rifleman dared to fire a shot, though the Vickers gun in the armoured car swept the hedge tops with a leaden hail. It was clear that the military must have suffered heavily, and it was equally obvious that as the armoured car, although stationary, held a position which dominated the road through the full length of the ambush position (about a quarter of a mile long), its capture was out of the question. So the IRA gradually retired, unscathed, leaving thirteen of the enemy dead and fifteen wounded.

Tureengarriffe, Clonbanin, and the train ambush – the latter the only successful one of its kind in the Anglo-Irish War – struck a severe blow at the British military prestige in Munster and caused consternation in the minds of its highly-ranked officers. They realised that not alone did the King's Writ no longer function, but that His Majesty's direct military communications between Cork and Kerry were completely severed. Worse still, all attempts to restore them were hopeless.

Other tactics were resorted to, and 'rounds-up' were amongst the new methods by which the British hoped to gain lost ground and, if possible, to defeat the IRA. Again British militarism was doomed to failure. The area over which the Millstreet battalion IRA operated was 'rounded-up' by large forces of military, numbering from one to six hundred men, no fewer than four times between April 1921 and the Truce, but the battalion did not suffer any casualty of consequence. In order to prevent the British from using armoured cars and lorries for transport, the IRA demolished bridges and trenched roads. Several attempts were made to keep the roads open, but when a bridge was temporarily repaired or a trench closed by the British during daytime, they were again re-opened at night by the Volunteers. The IRA in the Millstreet area had a very successful system of signalling by means of beacon lights at night and horn blasts by day. Also their intelligence department was so efficient that the enemy was confronted at every move with a counter move which outwitted him.

On 16 May 1921, a large force of Auxiliaries arrived by special train at Millstreet and took over the Union premises and subsequently Mount Leader House, where one hundred and twenty of them were stationed until the Truce. Some of their stores remained in the train overnight following their arrival, and when their transport arrived the following morning to cart them to headquarters, only the charred framework of the wagons was found; strewn around were the ashes of their stores. The local company (Dooneen) had attended to these during the night. Soon afterwards, Millstreet workhouse (which had been occupied by crown forces) was burned down by the Claragh section of the town company. The Dooneen company also took part in this operation, which was carried out on the night of 2 June, as a result of an order from GHQ, who had information that it was to be used as a base for British military.

On 5 June, the military and Black and Tans, with cavalry and aeroplanes, took part in what is known as the 'Clydagh Round-Up'. The Millstreet column escaped unnoticed although hemmed in by about seven hundred military proceeding to the 'round-up' near Cullen. On the following day, cavalry were sniped at near Lackadota by Volunteers of Kilcorney. The military afterwards combed the hills very carefully from dawn to dusk, but failed to get any wanted men, though a few had narrow escapes. Following the arrival of the Auxiliaries in Millstreet, curfew was proclaimed and the British tried to intensify the 'campaign of frightfulness' to which the IRA had put an end on the previous November. Again the military genius whose thoughts ran on these lines was doomed to disappointment. The IRA proved harder nuts to crack than was anticipated.

RATHCOOLE AMBUSH

WHILST THEY OCCUPIED Mount Leader House, the Auxiliaries procured their supplies from Kanturk and Banteer stations, about twelve and eight miles distant, respectively. Owing to a long spell of dry weather, the fallen bridges proved unable to prevent them travelling twice daily to these places, as the rivers were passable to the Crossley tenders. It was then determined by the IRA to attack them on the road. Early on the morning of 16 June 1921, the column of the Cork No. 2 brigade was mobilised in Laught Wood overlooking the Millstreet–Banteer road, about a mile to the west of Rathcoole. The following is the official IRA report as it appeared in *An t-Óglach* of what is known as the Rathcoole ambush:

Since the Auxiliaries took up quarters in Millstreet, they have travelled in lorries on this road a couple of times a day, as they were getting nearly all their supplies from Banteer. The strength of this convoy varied from two to five lorries and nearly always they had a car scouting in front. The manpower of the convoy varied from twenty to forty men. It was decided to attack this convoy and this meant perhaps, to attack a Ford car, two lorries and two armoured lorries manned by forty men. It was apparent that nothing could be done with a convoy of such strength without the use of high explosives. It was decided to get the road mined. Six mines were set along one-and-a-half miles of road. Each mine was covered off by a party of rifle and shotgun men; and there was a flanking party of riflemen a quarter of a mile to the east and west of the minefield, so that our men held a front of about two-and-a-quarter miles. Other men were engaged in barricading the roads leading to the place selected for the ambush. The orders issued to these men were that as soon as they heard the firing they were to throw up the barricades. The men carried out their work effectively, although the Auxiliaries travelled this road a couple of times a day. It was decided not to attack them until their return journey from Banteer at 6 p.m. This hour was selected because it would be much easier to get away such a large number of men during the night. All the men were mobilised in the wood overlooking the road. The movements of the enemy could be seen from this wood. The British passed to Banteer at 3.30 p.m. It was decided to attack them on the return journey. Four cars passed, comprising one armoured lorry and three Crossley tenders. All the men moved into position at 5 p.m. The sections and mines were numbered off from west to east, one, two, three, four, five, six. It was decided that Number One section should attack the first lorry; Number Two the second lorry; Number Five section to attack the third lorry; Number Six to attack the fourth and last. The lorries arrived back at 6.30 p.m. on their return journey, so the attack commenced at this hour; the first lorry had got as far as Number Two position when the last got into Number Six and was blown up. None of the other lorries had got into the positions in which they were to be attacked. When they heard the firing on the last lorry they tried to get back to its assistance. The first lorry got back to Number Three position and was blown up. The second and third lorries stopped in their positions and opened heavy rifle, machine-gun and grenade attack on our position. The men attacking the last lorry were ordered to charge and disarm the occupants, when machine-gun fire was opened on them from the third lorry. The enemy, having got their machine-guns in position, were now directing heavy fire on our men, who continued returning it for three-quarters of an hour, hoping to capture the lorries. Five Auxiliaries jumped from the third lorry and advanced along the road, hoping to flank our men. They were blown up by the mine and are believed to have been killed. Our men on the fifth and sixth positions retreated with difficulty. All our men escaped without a scratch.

This engagement, in which Paddy O'Brien, Liscarroll, had charge, exploded the theory that this convoy was 'unambushable', and helped to demoralise the enemy further. The whole four lorries were put out of action. There was excitement and consternation amongst the crown forces that night, not only in Millstreet, but in Macroom, Kanturk and Buttevant. Just after nightfall on the following day, the Auxiliaries' headquarters at Mount Leader was fired on. This added further to the confusion of the Auxiliaries who already had three of their officers killed and fourteen wounded at Rathcoole.

On 24 June, a huge 'round-up' took place at Kilcorney and in the adjoining townlands of Tooreenbawn and Aubane in Mill-street parish. It was estimated that 1,000 troops took part in this operation, but the battalion quietly slipped through the hands of its enemies. Early on the morning of the 'round-up', Michael Dineen, a Volunteer of the Kilcorney company, was taken from his brother's house at Ivale, Kilcorney, by members of the Auxiliary force. Rifle and machine-gun fire was heard shortly afterwards, and when the Auxiliaries moved towards the hills, Dineen's mangled remains were discovered on Mr Kelleher's land at Tooreenbawn, a distance of three hundred yards from his home. Apparently he was tortured before being murdered, as his arms and legs were broken as if by blows from rifle butts. His funeral two days later to Millstreet was attended by thousands, including his comrades of the column.

On the evening of 1 July the Auxiliaries opened fire on two Volunteers who had finished cutting hay at Murphy's farm, Rath-coole. Bernard Moynihan, a member of the Kilcorney company, was killed. As the enemy could not get the better of the column, they burned the wood at Rathcoole. The Volunteers were not in the least disturbed by these antics, and plans were laid to give them a bigger shock than they had received at Rathcoole. Doubtless, if the Truce had not intervened, a smashing blow – worse than the Kilmichael ambush – would have been given to the Mount Leader gang.

About a week before the Truce, the military decided on another comb-out of the area lying between Headford and Cahirbarnagh and the main road from Millstreet via Rathmore to Killarney. Though horses were employed on this occasion, it turned out a greater fiasco than the former big round-up. In fact the colonel in charge was so nervous that he expected to be attacked by the

IRA instead of attacking them. He sent out strong flanking parties when he came to the 'Bower' to test the position there, before he attempted to move his main body. The success of the IRA in Rathmore, and this applies to every district in North Cork and East Kerry, was due mainly to their marvellous intelligence branch. Every move of the enemy was known beforehand. And whilst the crown forces rightly distrusted each other, the utmost confidence existed amongst the Volunteers, who looked on themselves as brothers in a sacred cause.

On the night of 7 July, Jeremiah Long, column commander, and a few others, sniped the 'Auxies' at Mount Leader. Later, an order came to proceed to West Limerick. The column was organised at once and fourteen of the Millstreet men proceeded by car to King-williamstown, where they were joined by other sections, and all proceeded to Rockchapel. The position selected for the coming ambush was at Barnagh, between Abbeyfeale and Newcastlewest. Having waited two days, without contacting the enemy, the plans of the combined columns were interrupted by the advent of the Truce at twelve o'clock on 11 July 1921.

IN THE BARONY OF DUHALLOW

THE BARONY OF Duhallow has produced so many sons eminent in the Volunteer movement, that it would require a complete volume to do credit to their exploits, which can only be dealt with briefly in this short article. To mention but a few of the men who made history, the names of Jack O'Connell, Paddy Clancy, Liam Lynch, Charlie Reilly, Paddy McCarthy, Dan O'Brien, Liam Moylan, Seán O'Riordan, Ned Winters and a host of others come charging over the ramparts of memory as they themselves charged against the enemy over a quarter century ago. Their unsurpassed courage and glorious self-sacrifice does much to keep alive our racial pride. For many years previous to the Great War and until after the Rising of 1916, the patriotic ardour of the people of Duhallow was dormant. The district had suffered severely during the political wrangles of the O'Brienite and Redmondite parties, and these squabbles disgusted the people who ceased to take interest in public affairs.

The Rising of 1916 had a tremendous effect throughout North Cork, and soon afterwards Sinn Féin clubs began to be formed here and there throughout Duhallow. Not, indeed, that the people understood or bothered much about the teachings of the new movement. Rather they saw that its leaders and adherents were so sincere that they counted even their lives of little value when the advancement of the national interest was at issue. Such sincerity rapidly won converts, and when the grave menace of conscription developed, the people, particularly the men of military age, threw themselves heart and soul into the Volunteer movement. In the beginning, however, they were only an untrained rabble, as proved by the famous march from Kiskeam to Newmarket in which about two hundred young men took part. They were practically unarmed, and Seán Moylan, who met them at Coolagh bridge, advised them to return home as it would be madness to attack the well-armed military and Royal Irish Constabulary. Acting on this advice the boys returned home, and commenced training and acquiring arms. Many of them played a brave and valiant part in the struggle for national freedom during the critical years which followed.

Soon the development of the national movement was greatly helped by the holding of Aeridheachta in various centres. The British authorities proscribed these gatherings. One to be held at Cullen was proscribed and military and aeroplanes were used to prevent it taking place. It was held later at Glashakinleen bridge about eight miles to the north of Cullen, when the address was given by the late Fr Breen, Millstreet. It is interesting to recall that this patriotic priest was the only person in Kerry, except the late Austin Stack, who knew of the proposed landing of Casement at Banna Strand on that fateful Good Friday morning, 1916. The British employed aeroplanes on the occasion of the Aeridheacht at Glashakinleen bridge to frighten the people. Their plans miscarried; the people were not stampeded and the reverend speaker was delighted at their *sang froid* in the face of the enemy. About this time also, Countess Markievicz and Paudin O'Keeffe addressed an Aeridheacht at Kiskeam which, to confuse the authorities, was billed for Newmarket. The Countess was arrested in Cork afterwards and spent many weary months behind the walls of an English prison.

BALLYDROHANE AMBUSH

BALLYDROHANE AMBUSH WAS the first important engagement in which the Volunteers of the Duhallow district took part. Bally-drohane bridge lies midway between Kanturk and Newmarket. It was then the usual practice for the military at Kanturk to take rations to their comrades at Newmarket. The ambush was laid at an acute bend on the road, onto which an old farm cart was pushed at the psycho-logical moment as a block. When the lorry containing the military came to the farm cart it stopped; immediately the cry of 'Hands Up' rang out from the IRA positions. The military jumped off the lorry and put up a stiff resistance, but eventually surrendered to the IRA who captured nine rifles and much military material. Owing to the proximity of the army at Kanturk and Newmarket to the ambush position, the Volunteers having secured their booty beat a hasty retreat towards Drominarglin. Seán Moylan and the late General

Liam Lynch were in charge of this ambush. Fearing a reprisal they placed a guard of IRA over Allen Bridge Co-operative Creamery on the following night. Seán Moylan was also in charge of the Clonbanin ambush, already described, when the attackers comprised some two hundred North Cork men of the 4th Cork brigade, with some East Kerry detachments under Humphrey Murphy. In the evening after the Clonbanin engagement Captain O'Brien, whilst in charge of the Liscarroll section, came face to face with a British military detachment and after an exchange of shots forced it to retreat.

SHOOTING OF CHARLIE REILLY

THE SHOOTING OF Charlie Reilly, Newmarket, caused the greatest sorrow throughout North Cork, where his family was so well known. On an evening of March 1921, 'Cha' Reilly, Seán Moylan and John D. O'Sullivan, had been taking measurements at Coolagh bridge which was closely guarded by military. The little party had gone some distance along the Line Road, when Seán remembered that he had left a spirit level on the bridge. He jumped out of the pony-trap in which they were travelling, ran back and got it. Rejoining the party in the trap, all were surprised by a party of military who ordered them to put up their hands. All jumped out immediately and got over the fence on the left-hand side of the road. The military opened deadly fire on them with a machine-gun and as 'Cha' Reilly was crossing the bog adjacent to the bridge, he fell, badly wounded. He crawled along to a nearby cottage, where he remained during the night. Next day he was removed to his home in Newmarket, where he died a few days later. Seán Moylan and John O'Sullivan providentially escaped.

THE CAPTURE OF SEÁN MOYLAN

On Sunday evening, 16 May 1921, a large detachment of the Gloucesters arrived in Boherboy, seemingly on their usual business of searching and rounding up. Having remained until nightfall, they then moved off, as though returning to Kanturk. This, however, they did not do. Instead they divided into small parties, one of which put up in a disused farmhouse belonging to Mr O'Connell. Another went along the Kilnahulla road and took possession of the farmhouse of Mr Dwane. When night had advanced they renewed their search of the locality. The IRA scouts sensed that something was wrong; they gave the alarm to Seán Moylan and James O'Riordan who were taking a much-needed rest in the district. Both men succeeded in partly dressing and getting out of the house where they were billeted. They were, however, met a short distance away by the military who shouted 'Hands Up'. O'Riordan replied with a volley from his rifle and the soldiers took cover. This gave both men a chance to get away and although the place from which he fired was raked with machine-gun fire, O'Riordan succeeded in escaping and reached Tureenduve. Moylan, having escaped until dawn, was then captured and was, with several others, taken into Boherboy. Here he was bound with chains, thrown into a lorry, conveyed first to Buttevant and from there to Cork. He was tried by court martial and sentenced to death. At the court martial, high British officers in the Cork command spoke highly of Moylan's chivalrous conduct towards wounded Tommies in various engagements, especially at Tureengarriffe. His sentence was later commuted to penal servitude for life.

NIGHT OF MURDER AND ARSON IN FERMOY

by P.J. POWER

WHEN THE AUXILIARIES had blood in their eyes they spared neither age, sex nor condition. They were ex-British officers but they were not gentlemen. War-crazed drunkards many of them were and in their cups they were capable of the most fiendish cruelty and diabolical deeds. Alcohol turned them into savages and few incidents of their unwelcome stay in Ireland demonstrate this throw-back to the beast more than the murder of ex-Captain Prendergast, a gentleman of Fermoy, who himself had held the British King's commission with honour and whose body bore wounds received on the French and Italian fronts during the First World War.

Prendergast, a native of Wexford, was a scholar, a linguist and a most amiable man who in his earlier years had been a Christian Brother. He advocated the cause of the Allies during the war and proved his mettle by joining up and seeing service in France where he was wounded. Invalided home he offered his services again and this time with the rank of captain he fought on the Italian front and was so severely wounded that he was unfit for further campaigning. He settled down in Fermoy, married, became the proprietor of the Blackwater Hotel and professor of languages at Saint Colman's

College. Learned also in geology he was a delightful companion, willing to share his knowledge and experiences with those not so gifted. A charming conversationalist, he loved to spend his leisure hours quietly chatting with friends and this trait he indulged some times in the Royal Hotel where officers of the British military garrison foregathered. As one who had held a commission just as they did he was freely admitted to their company and conversation, exchanging stories of foreign service and military gossip, the usual small talk of such assemblies of serving and ex-soldiers. On the night of 1 December 1920, ex-Captain Prendergast might be found sitting comfortably in the Royal Hotel at peace with the world, altogether inapprehensive of the horrible fate that was shortly to overtake him.

A day or two previously, the Auxiliaries had got the biggest jolt in their Irish career at Kilmichael where a section of them were wiped out by an ambushing party of the IRA. The defeat rankled, so that when some of these ex-officers of his Britannic Majesty's army arrived in Fermoy in the evening on their way to the funeral of their fallen comrades, they were in an ugly mood. A broken-down lorry delayed them, so they promptly commandeered one from a local merchant instructing him to have it in readiness for them at 8 a.m. next day. Meantime they proceeded to load themselves with drink, visiting many public houses where, as was their wont, they ordered freely without the slightest intention of payment. In their peregrinations through the town they jostled, insulted and molested civilians and made their presence generally felt in the most objectionable ways that occurred to their befuddled brains.

It was night-time when they reached the Royal Hotel, crazy with drink. More drink and still more drink was consumed until round about eleven o'clock they were raging beasts. They argued and bragged of their own and their nation's valour in and out of the trenches in all the campaigns of the Great War. How Prendergast became mixed up with them is not clear. One version has it that he was standing at his own door at 10.45 p.m. when he was recognised by some Auxiliaries with whom he had served abroad, and that he accompanied them to the bar of the Royal Hotel. If they were friends or acquaintances of campaigning days they did not stand by him in his hour of direst need. The trouble apparently started in the hotel lavatory where scuffling was heard and the door of which was smashed. Four Auxiliaries and Captain Prendergast returned to the bar when everything seemed amicable. Things were not, however, to remain long so.

An officer of the Royal Engineers, serving in town, came down the stairs and on approaching the bar pointed a finger towards Prendergast and said, 'Beware of that man, he's a traitor'. Immediately one of the Auxiliaries, commonly known as 'Jock', seized Prendergast by the coat lapels and demanded of him if he was a 'Shinner'. Prendergast refused to answer the question saying he was an Irishman. Next they ordered him to fall on his knees and swear he was not a 'Shinner'. He refused to comply. One of them shouted: 'Pull him out'. Three of them then roughly caught him by the arms, he resisting as best he could. They dragged him to the steps of the main door leading onto Pearse Square. 'Jock' was seen to raise his hand and hit Prendergast on the back of the head with great force with his revolver which appeared to cause instant death, as the unfortunate man collapsed immediately. They then seized him by the collar of his coat, at the back, and dragged him on his back, head hindmost, across Pearse Square towards the River Blackwater at O'Neill Crowley Quay, where they hoisted the body onto the wall and roughly pushed it into the river which was then greatly swollen owing to heavy rain. The marks left on the roadway by the dragging of the body remained for some time afterwards.

When they had disposed of the remains the four 'Auxies' proceeded to the Grand Hotel at Ashe Quay, and further imbibed, as if the brutal murder they had just perpetrated was with them an everyday occurrence.

Alarmed because of her husband's absence, Mrs Prendergast accompanied by her assistant, visited the Royal Hotel and was told he was not there. She then proceeded to the Grand Hotel and one of the Auxiliaries, overhearing her enquiry, answered: 'Try the Blackwater', which she understood to mean the Blackwater Hotel. It was not until some days had elapsed that the rumour became current that the body had been thrown into the river, and eventually after one month, the remains of Captain Prendergast were found three miles away caught in some bushes below Clondulane.

The Auxiliaries were not, however, through with their dreadful deeds that night and were next heard of again at the Royal Hotel at midnight, where they tried to hold a dance. They were informed that some of the neighbours objected to any noise at such a late hour and immediately demanded the name of the objector and were, it is stated, told it was Mr Dooley, who kept the draper's shop around the corner on MacCurtain Street. Utilising long poles to which paraffin-soaked rags were attached, and flashlamps, they scanned the names over the adjacent shop fronts until they located Mr Dooley's premises. They then smashed in the door of the shop and ordered Mr Dooley out, just allowing him time to put on his trousers. His premises as well as those adjoining – Mr John O'Keeffe's, bootmaker, and Miss Flavin, tobacconist and newsagent – were given to the flames. When the fires were under way they marched Mr Dooley, whose wife had escaped through a window, to the spot on the quay from which a short time before they had hurled the body of Captain Prendergast. Mr Dooley was similarly treated. He was not a good swimmer, and while struggling in the river three shots were fired at him, but luckily all missed their mark. He struggled to the corner of the Mill Island, adjoining the weir, and, managing to grasp some ivy, he succeeded in reaching land, and made his way by the Lower Inches, which were flooded, to the Fermoy Hospital, guided by the lights of the institution. He was in a sorry plight following his terrible ordeal. Consternation was caused in the town by his disappearance, and when daylight dawned bodies of civilians and Royal Irish Constabulary began to search the debris of the burned-out houses expecting to find his remains. It was not until some time later that word was conveyed to those engaged in this work that he was safe. They were not, however, made aware of his whereabouts.

Indescribable scenes were witnessed during the efforts to ex-tinguish the fires started by the Auxiliaries. These spread alarmingly, and it was thought that the flames would reach the Royal Hotel and the hardware shop of Mr Walsh adjoining, where oil was stored. Several of the Auxiliaries drew their revolvers and when the local fire brigade, with volunteer workers, attempted to lay the hose through the Royal Hotel they were ordered to desist. Just to be contrary, other Auxiliaries ordered people to use the hose. No officer seemed to be in charge of the Auxiliaries, the cause of all the terrible destruction of life and property that fatal night. One of them even cut the hose in his desire to see the conflagration develop.

After some time about thirty soldiers arrived in the square in charge of an officer, and the Auxiliaries disappeared for the time being. The military remained in charge until daybreak. About eight o'clock the following morning the Auxiliaries secured Mr McGowens' lorry and left the town about nine o'clock. On their way through MacCurtain Street, one of them, apparently not satisfied with the damage they had caused, attempted to take another life. He was seen to draw the bolt of his rifle and aim at a civilian standing by his door. Luckily the vehicle swerved around a corner before he had time to put his murderous intention into effect. On leaving Fermoy the Auxiliaries were highly intoxicated and were later heard of that evening in the vicinity of Macroom, where they shot dead the Venerable Canon Magner and a young boy.

Staff Officer Murray of Kilworth camp conducted an inquiry into the Fermoy incidents as a result of which 'Jock' was arrested. Several people gave evidence at the inquiry, which had not, however, concluded when the Truce came which was fortunate for the Auxiliary known as 'Jock', as Staff Officer Murray was determined to bring the actual murderers to justice. The 'Boots' at the Royal Hotel disappeared immediately after the murder of Prendergast and was much sought after by the officer in charge of investigations, but he could not be traced. As a matter of fact, on two occasions he was located, and when the Royal Irish Constabulary got instructions to apprehend him he mysteriously vanished. He was believed to have been threatened with death if he attempted to give his evidence which Staff Officer Murray was confident would be the means of convicting 'Jock'.

At the time of his murder, a base rumour was circulated that the late Captain Prendergast was a spy for the British. This falsehood was, however, definitely countered later. Captain Prendergast, it should be said, was well disposed to Sinn Féin.

NIGHT OF TERROR AT MALLOW RAILWAY STATION

by DAN GRIFFIN

HERE IS THE first authentic account of the terrible ordeal which Mallow railwaymen had to undergo on the night of 1 February 1921. Following an ambush in which the wife of County Inspector King was killed, Black and Tans shot three railway men dead and wounded several others. Many workers escaped to Buttevant on a pilot engine.

On the fatal night, the county inspector and his wife visited the railway station at about 9.40 p.m., and shortly afterwards went to the Royal Hotel, which is close by. As they were returning down Railway Hill fire was opened on them, and Mrs King fell mortally wounded. The county inspector emptied his revolver in the direction of the attackers. Leaving the dead body of his wife on the hill, he hurried into the town. At the time of the tragedy, upwards of a hundred railway men were at the station. Night workers had to reach the station before 10 p.m., curfew hour, while men coming off duty had to wait in the station until curfew ended at 3 a.m. A company of military rushed into the station premises and arrested all the men they could find. The prisoners were taken to the barracks and brutally treated. Twenty minutes later, sixteen

Black and Tans, under a head constable, entered the station as the Thurles 11 p.m. goods' train arrived driven by George Allison. Ignorant of what had occurred, the driver and his fireman, P. Cotter, were on the point of descending to the platform when the Tans opened fire on them. Cotter had a miraculous escape, as a bullet passed under his arm, and sank half-an-inch into an iron rivet. Allison jumped down on the permanent way at the opposite side of the engine and disappeared. Cotter was arrested, but later managed to elude his captors. The Tans broke into the saloon-bar, and liberally helped themselves to drink. Crazy from drink, they searched all the buildings and shot at every man they saw carrying a lamp. Things became so hot eventually that work was suspended, every man seeking shelter from the rain of bullets. Richard Dunne, yard foreman, had a miraculous escape. Halted by a Tan, he dashed from the platform under the wagons of the Thurles goods' train. The Tan opened fire and perforated the wagon in four places over the fugitive's head. Dunne escaped to the fields above the station.

The loco men were at this time in their own waiting-room attached to the loco department. The men present were: Patrick Maher, driver; Paddy Howe, driver; Matt Cronin, cleaner; Michael Mahony, steam-riser; Daniel Mullane, fireman; J. Barrett; H. Martin, driver, and several others. They were making tea and preparing for work, when the Tans entered and gave the order 'Hands Up!' Thirteen men, including Chris Connell, night foreman, were marched to the station. Some of the men held tea cans over their heads as they were not allowed time to lay them down. Tans staggered out of the bar to look at the prisoners. Chris Connell told one of the most rational-looking of the raiders that he was responsible for all the engines and rolling stock, and that it would cost the railway company a lot of money if he was not allowed to do his duty. On this plea he was liberated. As he had not much respect for a Tan's word, he decamped quickly.

The remaining railway men were ordered out of the station. When they had reached the top of the hill they were told to run for their lives. The Tans opened fire on the retreating men. Few escaped the rain of bullets. Three men died of their wounds. They were: Cleaner Bennett, aged seventeen years, who was a great loss to his people and who was liked by everybody. He was killed outright before he had reached the bottom of the hill. Patrick Devitt, father of eight children, who was a redundant signalman and acted as a porter. He died a week later in the Mercy Hospital, Cork. Daniel Mullane, aged twenty-three, fireman, had safely reached the bottom of the hill and turned the corner when, on seeing his mate, Harry Martin, a driver, lying on the ground, he turned back and tried to lift his comrade. As he did so he received three bullets through the hips, but managed to go as far as the old Scotch church. He went through a window of the head constable's house and fell on the hall floor. The head constable's wife sent to the Tan barracks across the road for help. The wounded man was removed to Dr Vaughan's surgery, where he died at 6.35 p.m. on the following day. Harry Martin recovered from his wounds, but died four years later. Peter Morrissey, a carriage examiner, now residing in Dublin, was badly wounded. Matt Cronin, who received a bullet under the heart, survived his dangerous wound. Michael Mahony and Paddy Maher were both badly wounded in the back. Mahony, a native of Newmarket, crawled on his back up the hill and down O'Meara's Avenue. He was found lying on the back road, and was removed on a stretcher to his lodgings. Henry Greensmith, aged sixty-five years, was hurled from his signal cabin to the ground and died four years later from the effects of his injuries. A number of men escaped on a pilot engine, driven by P. O'Brien. The Tans followed the engine as far as P. Maher's house.

The railway service was completely disorganised until the following afternoon. The remains of Fireman Mullane and Cleaner Bennett lay in state in Saint Mary's church. The funerals were the largest even seen in Mallow.

Some weeks afterwards a military inquiry was held into the tragic incidents. The late Mr Tim Healy, KC, represented the relatives, who received large compensatory awards.

THE EAST CORK BRIGADE IN ACTION

by P. O'C.

SATURDAY, 5 JUNE 1920, was, in Midleton, County Cork, one of those glorious midsummer days when man, buoyed up by nature's blessed sunshine, finds so much happiness in life. Gleeful and carefree the workers toiled in the fields, whilst the townsfolk enjoyed the influx of shoppers so characteristic of Saturday in that rather prosperous period in Ireland.

The arrival in the town of a big detachment of Cameron Highlanders on that day gave rise to dark forebodings amongst the local IRA. Hitherto they had been on the offensive and the efforts of the Royal Irish Constabulary to cope with their initiative and to annul their activities had been a complete failure. The arrival of the Camerons was even more significant, because the Midleton company of the IRA had planned an attack on Ballycotton police barracks the following Sunday morning. Ballycotton is that beautiful health resort by the sea nine miles south of Midleton. In happy mood, however, with thoughts on the morrow, did the IRA relax on that eventful Saturday afternoon. The possibility of encountering a military force had not yet been conceived by these young soldiers of Ireland. Perhaps the opportunity would soon present itself.

Shortly after six o'clock that same evening a party of the newly arrived Cameron Highlanders left Midleton on their bicycles fully armed and with a Royal Irish Constabulary man, Constable O'Connor, as guide. Singular enough is the fact that the party numbered the proverbial thirteen – twelve soldiers and one Royal Irish Constabulary man, who was armed with a revolver, the others all bearing rifles fully loaded. They took a by-road leading by a circuitous route towards Carrigtwohill. Their thick Scotch accent was very noticeable as they gave way to idle banter once they had reached the open country.

Word of their movements was brought to Diarmuid Hurley, then captain of the Midleton company, IRA. He informed one of his trusted men at once and both readily saw the possibility of a coup. Having armed and left their lodgings about eight o'clock that night, they summoned the few Volunteers they casually met in the streets of Midleton to follow them along the Cork road. A scout, who had followed the military patrol, just then arrived with word that it was returning by the main road towards Midleton. Hurley and another having preconceived 'a score of bowls' as a ruse, now lined up for competition. The entire group numbering but nine in all were fully aware of the strategy to be adopted. As they approached a bend in the road, which brings into view 'The Mile Bush', a well-known corner, they observed the military coming, cycling in scattered formation and still about four hundred yards away. The Volunteers were also a little scattered, as they had to give the idea that some were watching the bowls while the contestants, having discarded their coats, kept on throwing.

As the military drew nearer, the IRA stepped onto the footpath, obviously to give a clear road to the patrol. As the leading cyclists came abreast with Hurley and his colleague, who were originally the men furthest from the approaching patrol, they (Hurley and his associate) fired two shots towards the fence at their backs from their folded arms and rushed the cyclists simultaneously with the shooting. The rest of the Volunteers acted similarly, making the rush instantaneous. The patrol presented a sorry spectacle as the British lay helpless on the road, scattered about a distance of sixty yards. The bicycles and rifles were immediately seized and heaped together by the attackers, and the soldiers were relieved of their ammunition.

One soldier, who had become detached from the main party, at this juncture approached within three hundred yards of the 'hold up'. Possibly having heard the shots and perceiving that something was amiss, he opened fire. His comrades were at once ordered to put up their hands. This had the desired effect and the soldier ceasing fire, took to the fields and, throwing his rifle into a hedge, made 'cross country' for his barracks, the first to bring the news of the occurrence. A passing motor was requisitioned to convey the captured war material to a place of concealment, and the military were allowed to proceed to their destination after half an hour.

The military, angered because they were so easily outwitted, left their barracks about 11 p.m. that night and fired indiscriminately volley after volley up and down the main street of Midleton. The Royal Irish Constabulary, believing the firing was an attack on their barracks, returned the fire, which lasted for a couple of hours, the only victims being a few stray donkeys. Pedestrians, however, were interrogated by the military, arrested and chained to posts in the military quarters during the night.

The following morning the Midleton company of the IRA proceeded to Ballycotton to capture the Royal Irish Constabulary barracks. To their dismay, however, they found military posted on duty beside the Royal Irish Constabulary barracks. The Volunteers passed through unchallenged, but they had to abandon for the time being the contemplated capture of the police barracks.

CAPTURE OF CARRIGTWOHILL POLICE BARRACKS

THE 1ST CORK brigade of the Irish Republican Army had arranged for simultaneous attacks on various Royal Irish Constabulary barracks throughout their area on Saturday night, 3 January 1920. Selected men from the Cobh and Midleton units, under Commandant Leahy, had planned a combined attack on the police barracks at Carrigtwohill, a rather prosperous village, on the main Cork–Youghal road, ten miles east of Cork. The barracks was situated towards the city end of the village, and its ruins today remind the passer-by of stirring times in Ireland. This was the first engagement of any magnitude undertaken by the hitherto inexperienced East Cork men, and its success enthused and heartened them for subsequent military encounters.

An experienced soldier would say that the task undertaken that night by these young Volunteers had not a hope of success, in view of the impregnable nature of the barracks, which had steel shutters and sandbag protections inside. The equipment of the Volunteers was limited, the Midleton unit having to rely on twelve revolvers with suitable ammunition previously purchased in Belfast through the foresight of Commandant Hurley. Their confreres from Cobh were more fortunate, having in their possession a few rifles, now much needed for the hazardous attack ahead.

At nine o'clock on that eventful night the attackers assembled in the vicinity of Carrigtwohill. Having got their instructions and the groups having been assigned their respective posts, they eagerly awaited the signal for attack. Meanwhile others were effectively cutting off telephonic communication with the barracks and the neighbouring districts. The cutting of the wires precipitated matters because those engaged in that operation were intercepted by two patrolling Royal Irish Constabulary men who hastened to interrogate them. The elusive 'lads' kept a safe distance and maintained their silence as well. This aroused the suspicions of the Royal Irish Constabulary, who quickly retraced their steps to the barracks to give the alarm of impending danger. Sergeant Scott of the Royal Irish Constabulary proceeded to telephone for reinforcements but found that he had been forestalled by the precautions of the IRA. This confirmed the seriousness of the situation, and the police at once threw their barracks into a state of defence, hastily closing their steel shutters and requisitioning all kinds of emergency aids.

The group of IRA at the rear of the barracks opened with a fusillade of shots, covered by a five-foot wall adjoining a hay barn partly filled with hay, on the top of which some of the Volunteers took positions. Through the apertures in the steel defences could be seen the flashes from the rapid fire of the besieged garrison. On the street side of the barracks there was little firing, because of the danger to the occupants in the houses opposite. Nevertheless, the Volunteers remained at the front, even approaching and firing through the barrack door at intervals. After an hour the firing became less rapid. The IRA was then convinced that the possibility of getting surrender from the safely entrenched Royal Irish Constabulary men was remote. But the group at the rear never relaxed, and intermittent firing continued up to midnight. A charge of gelignite was then inserted in the western gable-end wall of the barracks, which adjoined a stable. When it was fired, the noise of the explosion reverberated throughout the district, adding to the terror which had gripped the villagers. A breach was thus effected, which afforded passage into one of the rooms on the ground floor of the barracks. A light was hastily procured, but it revealed an empty room. Commandant Hurley and Joseph Aherne advanced through the breach, followed by a few others. It was obvious now that the police had retreated to the upper storey of the building. Fire was opened again by the invaders, and this had the effect of disconcerting and dislodging the Royal Irish Constabulary, and in a few minutes an improvised white flag answered a demand for surrender by Commandant Hurley.

It is difficult to conceive now the jubilation of these youths as the Royal Irish Constabulary came down the stairs with their hands aloft. The Volunteers gathered in, and from the day-room collected their booty, consisting of bombs, rifles, revolvers, ammunition and police files. A motor car was procured and the captured stores were transferred to a safe distance. Nocturnal travellers, intercepted earlier in the night by the IRA patrols outside the firing zone, were now ordered to proceed to their destinations. The Volunteers, having collected their personal belongings – coats, revolvers, bicycles – departed from the scene, lustily cheering and singing the patriotic songs then in vogue, and leaving the Royal Irish Constabulary garrison nonplussed by the awful suddenness and, for them, the unpleasant ending of the affair. Villagers stood at their doors, or peered through the open windows of their houses, whispering and sometimes venturing a commentary on the proceedings. Early morning brought curious enquirers, and throughout the day groups were here and there in the vicinity discussing the happening that had overtaken their peaceful hamlet. Throughout Sunday pressmen and photographers poured into the village and Monday's papers gave conspicuous headings and diverse accounts of the siege and capture of Carrigtwohill Royal Irish Constabulary barracks.

CAPTURE OF CASTLEMARTYR POLICE BARRACKS

CASTLEMARTYR NESTLES SNUGLY amidst sylvan surroundings,

five miles east of Midleton on the Cork–Youghal road. It is an up-to-date little town, harbouring a prosperous and contented community. Lord Shannon's demesne, now the property of the Carmelite Fathers, adjoins the town, which on 9 February 1920, had its calm serenity disturbed by revolver fire during the capture of the Royal Irish Constabulary barracks. The barracks – a spacious and pretentious building – was situated in the main street of the town, having private residences on either side, and almost opposite the Catholic church. It housed at the time a garrison of eight men, including two sergeants, namely Sergeant O'Brien and Sergeant O'Sullivan. Monday 14 February was Fair day in Midleton, where Sergeant O'Brien and Constable Collins were detailed for special duty. Diarmuid Hurley, the O/C Midleton company, IRA, was made aware during the day of the presence of these two men in Midleton. He arranged for their capture on their return to Castlemartyr that evening. He had in mind the capture of the police barracks at Castlemartyr, and this lessening of the garrison would increase his chances of success, as well as reduce the risks to be incurred.

About five o'clock Sergeant O'Brien and Constable Collins were cycling leisurely homewards, and when about to pass Mr Leahy's outside farm at North Churchtown, their progress was suddenly impeded by a farm cart speedily pushed through a gateway. The policemen had to dismount rapidly to save themselves from a collision with the cart, which partly concealed two men who then rushed at O'Brien and Collins with drawn revolvers and shouting 'Hands up!' It had been anticipated that the Royal Irish Constabulary would have been armed, but luckily they were not, and they became an easy prey to their three captors. The policemen were brought into the farmyard, blindfolded and carefully handcuffed, while one of the three Volunteers was dispatched to inform Diarmuid Hurley of the position. On the Volunteer's return he was left in charge of the two policeman, and his two colleagues went on to Castlemartyr to make a survey and, if possible, to arrest any Royal Irish Constabulary patrol in the hope of further weakening the garrison. Approaching 7 p.m. Constable Hanrahan emerged from the barracks apparently on his way to tea, when he was suddenly pounced upon by the two Volunteers, overpowered and hurried away to a place of concealment outside the town. In a further recognisance by one of these Volunteers – the other holding Hanrahan in safe custody – it was ascertained that Constable Hassett was in his own home in the town and that still another constable was on leave. This accounted for five of the garrison, the remainder being in the barracks.

Communication with Midleton was now rather difficult for the two Volunteers who had to keep watch on the barracks and hold Constable Hanrahan. At 8 p.m. one of them went to cut off telephonic communication with Castlemartyr. It must be remembered that Killeagh Aerodrome, holding a military garrison, was quite adjacent. In the meantime the Midleton company, having finished their work for the day, set out about 7 p.m., headed by Diarmuid Hurley. On their way they picked up their two police prisoners at Churchtown and advanced without delay to Castlemartyr. Disappointed at not seeing their two comrades in the vicinity of the Royal Irish Constabulary barracks, Diarmuid Hurley was apprehensive of trouble, and straightaway approached the barrack door, on which he knocked. A voice demanded, 'Who is there?' and Hurley immediately replied Sergeant O'Brien and the other fellow. He could not at the moment of tension recall Constable Collins' name. Constable Lee, the challenger, sensing danger, slightly opened the door, which had a running chain on the inside, and thrusting his revolver through the opening, fired it empty. Hurley thrust his right arm, holding a revolver, through, but his revolver failed to go off and he lashed with fury at his opponent's head splitting his eye with a blow of his revolver and bursting the chain with his boot. In a moment Hurley and his men were in possession. Sergeant O'Sullivan, realising the futility of further resistance, surrendered, and while the Volunteers eagerly sought out all the military equipment, Hurley had a priest and doctor summoned to attend to the wounded man. The doctor from the next house and Fr Murphy from two hundred yards away, were on the scene in a few minutes, and the IRA quickly decamped for their homes, scarcely having had time to realise the result of the engagement they had just carried out. Emerging from the town they encountered one of their two colleagues who had disposed of the wires and who was then on his way to the barracks to await the arrival of his comrades. He returned in gleeful spirits to acquaint the guard of Constable Hanrahan. The constable was immediately released to join Sergeant O'Brien and Constable Collins of similar fate. The Midleton boys, having shared the hospitality of their beloved and trusted friend, Mr Seán Kelleher of North Churchtown, journeyed homewards jubilant.

CAPTURE OF CLOYNE POLICE BARRACKS

The ancient and historic town of Cloyne was the scene of a successful attack by the East Cork IRA battalion on the night of 8 May 1920. The barracks was a substantial three-storey building, occupying a central position in the main street of the town. Business premises adjoined the fortress on either side and corn stores were situated directly opposite. The IRA arranged a concert and play to be held in the local concert hall on the night previous to the proposed barrack attack and consequently were enabled to transfer the arms and ammunition necessary for the Volunteers to the vicinity of the barracks, by including them with the scenery for the play.

It was eleven o'clock when Commandant Leahy, the O/C of the 4th battalion, directed the opening of hostilities, Volunteers having occupied vantage points in the corn stores. A small party of senior officers, including Commandants Leahy, Hurley, Aherne and Manley approached the barrack entrance adopting the role of 'drunks', lest the suspicions of the garrison might be aroused. The IRA O/C then called on the Royal Irish Constabulary to surrender in the name of the Irish Republic. Meanwhile Aherne and others were removing the outside shutters from the windows of the barracks and Commandant Hurley had a revolver inserted in the loophole of the door. The Royal Irish Constabulary refusing to surrender, Hurley blazed away through the loophole and simultaneously a heavy interchange of fire took place between the Volunteers in the opposite building and the besieged garrison. The reflection from the Verey lights fired by the Royal Irish Constabulary and the continuous rapid fire made the night one to be remembered by those who witnessed the scene.

The attack having been two hours in progress, Volunteers succeeded in entering houses adjacent to the barracks, and having bored holes in the dividing walls of the top storeys they poured petrol into the doomed building. The fire which spread when the petrol was ignited drove the defenders to the basement where, after a few minutes, they signified their desire to surrender by throwing a pillow through one of the windows. The members of the garrison were disarmed and marched to the suburbs of the town, where they were subsequently released. The victorious IRA retired from the scene, giving air to their happy feelings as 'The Soldier's Song' was sung around the blazing fire. The barracks and the business premises adjoining were gutted by the fire, which spread rapidly.

British reinforcements from Cork, under Major Yates, were held up by felled trees at Cobh Junction, and consequently did not arrive in Cloyne until the IRA had safely departed.

CAMERON HIGHLANDERS ATTACKED AT WHITEROCK

HAD A TREE at Whiterock, on the Castlemartyr–Midleton road, fallen a split second sooner on Friday 26 August, 1920, a lorry full of Cameron Highlanders would have been forced to surrender or die. A small group of Volunteers of the 4th battalion, under Vice-Commandant Joseph Aherne, occupied an ambush position two miles east of Midleton. One section lay behind a five-foot wall, while the second, which was detailed to pull down a tree as the enemy approached, had the protection of a broad covered bank, three feet high, on the roadside, with a drop of five or six feet on the inside. The British military were expected to come from Midleton where detachments of the Camerons were stationed at the time to enforce martial law. Volunteer Seán Kelleher, hearing that the lorry was coming from Castlemartyr, straightaway jumped on his motor-cycle and dashed off to warn the leader of the IRA party.

It was around two o'clock on a fine August day when Volunteer Michael Kearney, who had been detailed to act as scout, signalled the approach of the enemy. As the lorry moved at a brisk pace down the incline into the ambush position, fire was opened by the IRA. The first volley killed the driver, Private Hall, but did not cause the lorry to crash or go out of control as the wheel was immediately taken over by the auxiliary driver, who stepped on the accelerator. Under heavy fire from the IRA position on the left-hand side of the road, the lorry continued on its course while frantic efforts were made by the young Volunteers on the opposite side to pull down the tree that would bring it to a halt or wreck it.

As the Irishmen fired and tugged the Britishers fired and hurtled along anxious to get clear of the falling tree and out of the danger zone. Down it came at last, but failed by the length of the lorry to come down quick enough. It actually struck the rear of the lorry but did not cause sufficient damage to force it to stop. Away drove the Camerons with one dead comrade and two, Lieutenant Beggs and Private Wintern, badly wounded. The Volunteers suffered no casualties. A few of them, Volunteer David Desmond (killed subsequently at Clonmult), Volunteers Daniel Walsh and Michael Murnane, had narrow escapes.

WAITING FOR GENERAL STRICKLAND

AN IRA PARTY, withdrawing from a position in which they had hoped to ambush General Strickland, British GOC, in Cork, had the tables nearly turned on themselves. On 20 September 1920, a small IRA section, under Vice-Commandant Joseph Aherne, lay all day in ambush at Carrigtwohill for General Strickland, the British general officer commanding the Cork district. Information had been received that he would pass that way. He did pass, but it was not at the time the ambush party had anticipated. However, as the day wore on and there was 'nothing doing', the order was given to withdraw. On their way to Midleton the IRA men accepted a lift in a passing calf crib and were jogging along merrily when several lorries laden with enemy troops came suddenly into view at the Mile Bush. Out jumped the armed Volunteers and over the wall they rushed for the open country. Out jumped the British also and opened a heavy fire on the retreating Volunteers. The bullets were dropping uncomfortably close when Aherne, followed by his men, dived into a brake of furze. It provided a welcome screen but not protection against capture or death. So short a distance separated the pursuers and the pursued that the latter could distinctly hear the British officer vowing vengeance in lurid language on the heads of all rebels. A diversion of enemy interest in the occupants of the brake of furze was urgently called for. Out through the undergrowth crawled Volunteer J. Aherne of Ballyrichard and Volunteer T. Spillane of Cloyne. Jumping to their feet they dashed away. After them went the Britishers pell mell, firing as they went. The decoy had worked, Aherne and Spillane ran the gauntlet successfully, and the men in the brake of furze were saved. All escaped after an exciting adventure. General Strickland and his armed guard were later ambushed at Kilacloyne bridge near Carrigtwohill. The car in which the British GOC was travelling came under heavy IRA fire, but the general was not hit. Volunteer Deasy was fatally wounded in that encounter.

COLUMN'S ESCAPE FROM TRAP
WITHOUT CASUALTY

AN IRA COLUMN's escape without casualty from a house surrounded by British troops in the town of Cloyne is a remarkable tribute to fine leadership and resource in a critical situation. On Saturday night 11 December 1920, the East Cork column IRA occupied a house in one of the principal side streets of the town of Cloyne. Their presence must have been noted by an enemy agent who took prompt steps to notify his paymasters, for at eleven o'clock on the following Sunday morning the column's sentries raised the alarm that the house was being surrounded by British troops.

Commandant Hurley, the column O/C, received the news with characteristic coolness and immediately gave orders that strict silence should be maintained inside the house, as he wanted to give the British the impression that it was unoccupied. Having taken up positions that commanded the front and rear of the house the British O/C detailed a section of his men to search it. Meanwhile Commandant Hurley and Volunteer John Aherne (Ballyrichard) awaited the intruders on the stairway landing. Receiving no answer to their loud knocking at the front door the British troops promptly smashed it in and proceeded cautiously to enter. Not a living thing seemed to be within so complete was the silence. The Britishers advanced with rifles at the ready to the foot of the stairs. Crash! The silence was shattered by a volley from the rifles of Commandant Hurley and Volunteer Aherne. Confused by their reception the soldiers dashed out through the door, one of them turning to throw a hand grenade into the hallway. Volunteer Aherne with great daring and coolness kicked it out after the retreating troops thereby averting the tragedy that would certainly follow if it exploded in the confined space of the hall.

The British, now sure that they had caught a tartar, proceeded to direct heavy fire on the house. The IRA replied with vigour. Commandant Hurley, searching for a means of escape for his column, noticed that immediately opposite the house was an open gateway flanked on one side by a house and on the other by an old store or out-house. Through this gateway, he decided, the column must pass to safety. Suddenly appearing at the front door of the house, a revolver in each hand, he discharged the contents of them right and left in rapid fire in the direction of the British. These daring 'Wild West' tactics so nonplussed and scattered the British that a section of the IRA dashed unscathed to the gateway. Hurley gave the British no time to settle to their task until all his men had got safely across. The late Volunteer Jack Aherne, kneeling in the open street, covered off the retreat of the column and while doing so inflicted many casualties on the enemy.

OFFICIAL REPRISALS IN MIDLETON

SOME OF THE first official reprisals, the destruction with explosives of the houses of prominent residents, followed an ambush of Royal Irish Constabulary and Black and Tans in Midleton on the 29 December 1920. Patrols of British military and police were on the streets of all Irish towns after nightfall. It was their practice to walk on the footpaths at each side of the street in extended formation so that it was almost impossible for attackers in fixed positions to cover them all. The only alternative was to get into the open street and fight them and take the risk that some of them would get away. On 29 December 1920, a mixed patrol of Royal Irish Constabulary and Black and Tans, ten in all, were patrolling Midleton. Five black-coated figures, fully armed, moved cautiously along each side of the street, ten or twelve paces apart. In between the lines of crown forces there suddenly appeared, as if from nowhere, a line of IRA and as suddenly they opened fire. Constable Mullins of the Royal Irish Constabulary fell mortally wounded. Five Black and Tans went down, seriously wounded; two of them, Constables Dray and Thorpe, succumbing shortly afterwards. Two of the patrol escaped to the barracks. The arms and equipment of the others, precious booty at this stage of the struggle, were collected by the IRA.

Two miles out from Midleton reinforcements of Royal Irish Constabulary and Tans from Cork ran into an ambush prepared at the Mile Bush. A sergeant and constable were wounded, and Volunteer J. McCarthy was hit in the hand in the exchange of fire. Next day the British exacted reprisals, the first of their kind since they were official. Hitherto it had been the custom of the crown forces to run amok after they were attacked and wreak indiscriminate vengeance. This time the houses of certain residents were selected and after the service of formal notices the occupants were given time to remove their personal belongings, other than furniture, and the buildings were demolished with explosives. Those who had their residences so treated in Midleton by order of Brigadier General Higginson were Messrs John O'Shea, Paul McCarthy, Edmond Carey, Urban District Councillor, all of Midleton; Messrs Aherne and Dorgan of Ballyrichard; Messrs Cotter and Donovan of Ballyadam.

THE HEROIC FIGHT AT CLONMULT

THE STRUGGLE WAS entering the last and critical stage, and the fighting-men on both sides were determined to have it out. Gone were the days when the Irishmen could choose their objective, attack it and, whether they succeeded or failed, melt again into their civilian background, leaving the enemy to paw the air or take a vengeful reprisal on the nearest household. Events had so shaped themselves during 1920 that as many of the Irish as there were rifles and shotguns for in the IRA armoury had to stand permanently to them and use them no matter how, when and where the opportunity occurred. In every area the men who were naturally brave and fearless were the first to possess themselves of the arms taken from captured barracks, from disarmed British soldiers and police, or bought from individual members of the crown forces prepared to 'flog' their own or their comrades' equipment for ready cash.

In this way there were equipped in every enterprising brigade and battalion area of the Irish Republican Army a number of compact, mobile, fighting units which, acting alone, could harass, with the aid of their local knowledge and intelligence service, any British raiding party, and which, when brought together for a major operation, could hold their own with superior enemy forces. Thus there grew up to meet the military situation of the period the active service unit, or flying column, which gained the esteem and affection of the people over whose territory it operated according as it proved its worth and resource against the British enemy.

To go on active service with his brigade, battalion or company unit was the ambition of every Irish youth, fired with the desire to do his part to free his country. Supporting and encouraging these young men were the plain people of Ireland, from whom they were drawn, and the thousands of other young men who, for lack of arms, had perforce to remain in their own homes and perform the routine, and often hazardous, duties of unarmed sentries, scouts, intelligence agents, road cutters, tree fellers, dispatch carriers, and the hundred and one services, great and small, that fell to a nationwide organisation which had the cream of its personnel locked in a life and death struggle with an imperial army, fresh from the battlefields of France, Flanders, Macedonia and Palestine.

This imperial war machine was not without its friends, too. Vastly superior in equipment, training and resources to the sturdy little bands that opposed them, the forces of the British crown, military, police and Auxiliaries, had the slightly concealed sympathy of the foreign stock and the covert assistance of a native accretion. The British had not been in Ireland for seven hundred and fifty years without having struck their roots deep into the soil of Ireland. In and around the garrison towns Britain found a fertile recruiting ground for her army, and for her loyal set. Through the countryside were dotted many white-washed farmhouses from which had gone forth strapping 'six-footers' to give England one of the most reliable and efficient police forces in the world – the Royal Irish Constabulary. By patronage, by contracts, by pensions, by all the gifts that government can dispense, Britain had bound to her with hoops of steel a goodly section of the Irish people. After the British harrow had passed over the face of Ireland most of them returned to their allegiance to the old land, but there was still a number prepared to stake their all on the invader and give him what secret support they could in his war against the Irish nation. How one of this element within Ireland but not of it held out a grimy hand for blood-money – thirty pieces of paper – and sold those who would make him free, makes a sordid epilogue to the story of deathless courage that is here related.

In order to fit themselves thoroughly for the task in hand, the IRA active service units, in the seclusion of quiet retreats, went through courses in physical and military training with the full knowledge that they needed both if they were to match themselves successfully against the war experienced British soldiers. The IRA had to fight and learn at the same time; had to perfect themselves to a degree of discipline and skill that takes years to acquire in regular armies. Their Volunteer spirit, their zeal and their objective helped them to become proficient at arms in a short time, and turned them into soldiers who could act with high intelligence and cool self control in any emergency or enterprise, either collectively or individually.

So could be found the active service unit of the 4th battalion of the 1st Cork brigade, under the orders of Commandant Diarmuid Hurley, taking possession early in the month of January 1921, of a disused farmhouse in a secluded position overlooking the village of Clonmult, seven miles north-east of Midleton. The house was of the type with which we are all familiar, a long, low building with a roof of thatch. A large cow-shed stood at right angles to the front of the upper, or northern, side of the house, while the south of it adjoined a small grove of about twenty trees. A low fence and a number of trees were at the immediate rear of the house. Directly opposite the house, and some fifteen yards from it, a tree-fringed boreen ran parallel to the enclosed farmhouse. It was an ideal location for the purpose for which it was selected, the headquarters and training ground of an active service unit, composed of twenty young men drawn from various IRA companies in East Cork. It included among its members Volunteers who had been in action at Carrigtwohill, Cloyne, Castlemartyr and Midleton. Strong, healthy, clean-living boys, they revelled in the martial exercises and lectures designed to make them better fighters in Ireland's cause. The days passed quickly for this group of congenial spirits fired with a common purpose. Around the fire in the January nights they sang patriotic songs, played practical jokes on each other and generally indulged in the carefree pranks of their years. They went through the routine life of the camp, doing their share of fatigues and chores with a smile. A month of this intensive training and these boys, toughened to the trade of arms, were ready to take on twice their number of the enemy in a fair fight.

Satisfied with their progress and anxious to gratify their desire to measure themselves with the enemy, their popular leader, Commandant Hurley, cast his eye around his area for suitable employment for his eager young soldiers. He decided to ambush a military train, a pretty ticklish operation, at Cobh Junction on Tuesday, 22 February 1921. With this end in view, Commandant Hurley left the headquarters of the active service unit at Clonmult, taking with him Vice-Commandant Joseph Aherne and Captain Patrick Whelan to make arrangements for the transfer of the column to Dooneen and also to consult on the spot about the disposal of their forces at the proposed train attack at Cobh Junction. Before leaving Clonmult, Commandant Hurley appointed Captain Jack O'Connell of Cobh company, as acting O/C of the column and instructed him to march to Dooneen at dusk on Sunday 20 February.

The disued farmhouse at Clonmult was a scene of bustle and laughter that Sunday afternoon as the boys, having had their dinner, started to pack their personal belongings, clean up their equipment and prepare to evacuate, with all their gear, the building that had sheltered them and been their common home for over a month. Each man was busy at his task and all must have been nearly complete and ship-shape when towards 4.15 p.m. Michael Desmond and John Joe Joyce, taking their own and their companions water bottles with them, went to the spring well, about twenty yards from the house. They were engaged in filling the bottles when suddenly they noticed that a company of the Hampshire Regiment was surrounding the house. Drawing their revolvers, Desmond and Joyce attempted to fight their way back to the house through the military cordon that was closing in on their comrades. Gallantly they opened fire and as gallantly took the consequences. Though fatally wounded they managed to crawl to the rear of the house and with their dying breath gasped out: 'The house is surrounded and no escape is possible.' Their message was factual and prophetic. With the clarity of mind that comes before death, they correctly appraised the situation. The house was surrounded and no escape was possible.

What was to be done? Fight it out and make the house their tomb? Attempt a sortie with the hope that some might get through and organise local aid to relieve the others? A hurried council of war decided on the latter alternative. The surplus ammunition and grenades were distributed. A heavy fire was opened on the attackers as the five men, including the acting O/C, lined up for the desperate venture. Out from the bullet-riddled cottage they dashed, their comrades redoubling their fire and cheering them on to the defiant strains of 'The Soldier's Song'. The national anthem and the flying lead were the requiem of three gallant men. Michael Hallahan was mortally wounded almost on the doorstep; Richard Hegarty fell as he sought cover at the fence in front of the house; James Aherne received his death wound when jumping a fence 200 yards from the house. Jeremiah O'Leary having vainly attempted to fight his way through the enemy ranks, was fortunate enough to rejoin his comrades within the house. The acting O/C, Captain Jack O'Connell, alone succeeded in running the hazard and getting outside the British wall of death. He had achieved what his dying comrades, Joyce and Desmond, had branded as impossible.

A quarter of the column was wiped out! It was a cruel, testing time for the survivors. The British thinking that the fate of the sortie would dishearten the garrison, called on them to surrender. Intensified fire and 'The Soldier's Song' was the answer of the Irishmen, who had 'sworn to be free'. Outside the British lines the acting O/C, despite the unnerving experience he had lived through, got busy in an effort to organise the relief of his sorely tried comrades. A reconnoitre of the vicinity disclosed the dispositions of the British forces, and also brought him into contact with two local Volunteers, who were later joined by a third with a bicycle. Action was necessary and it was quickly taken. Six miles away at Ballinoe the North-East Cork column was billeted. If they could be summoned in time the siege at Clonmult might yet be raised. Away sped the cyclist on the most urgent mission he was ever called on to undertake. Arms in the hands of even a few men prepared to take the British in the rear might create the diversion of their forces that would break the circle of steel that enclosed the ill-fated cottage and its gallant occupants. Time was never so precious. Where were the arms? Shotguns were dumped in a cemetery some miles away. Off sped the local Volunteers to procure them. Help was being organised, but would it come in time to ease a situation that was getting more desperate every minute?

Around the cottage the battle raged relentlessly. The gallant defenders kept the British at bay, undaunted and undismayed. A volley in the distance raised their hopes. With the optimism of their race, the Irishmen interpreted the rattle of rifle fire as a message of good cheer from comrades hastening to their rescue. They did not know that it was the rattle of British rifles trained on their column O/C, who was still reconnoitring and keeping close to the scene of operations. It was the British that were reinforced and not the Irish. Within an hour of the start of the fight the Black and Tans arrived. Fearsome was the position of the garrison now. Clean death would find them unafraid, but death at the hands of human vultures was something too awful to contemplate. The fight must go on. How long could the defenders hold out? – as long as they had the life and strength to pull a trigger in a loaded rifle. They reckoned not with an element that could thrust them alive into British hands despite their resolve. The thatched roof of the cottage was ablaze. Were heroic men ever in more desperate straits? Over their heads a blazing roof was making the cottage a fiery furnace. At any moment it might fall in and become their funeral pyre. Outside was a ring of rifles, manned by the scum of England, hungry as wolves for Irish blood.

> On top of roof and window,
> Those boys stood up to fight,
> 'Till the burning of the cottage
> And no escape in sight.

Through the doors and windows British lead poured in a relentless stream. No hope of breaking through in face of that hail of death.

Why not try to breach the gable? A narrow opening was made. Volunteers Glavin and O'Leary tried to force themselves through. They fell back with serious bullet wounds in the head. The wily Britishers had left no means of escape uncovered. The game was up. The fire from the roof had now spread so that the entire house was involved. There was nothing the men could do now but surrender. Before doing so the heroic garrison broke their rifles and threw them into the flames. They then marched forth from the blazing cottage.

Volunteers Liam Aherne, Jeremiah Aherne, David Desmond, Christopher Sullivan, Donal Dennehy, J. Morrissey and J. Glavin, the first seven to emerge, were brutally massacred by the Black and Tans. It was typical British chivalry towards defeated but gallant foes. The wounded Volunteer, J. O'Leary, having lapsed into unconsciousness prior to the surrender, was removed from the house by three comrades, an action which saved their lives, as it gave time to a British military officer to stop the Black and Tans in their ghoulish work before the other prisoners, wounded and unwounded, reached the place of surrender.

The North-East Cork column on hearing of the plight of their East Cork comrades, marched immediately to their aid, but unfortunately did not arrive in Clonmult in time owing to the distance they had to traverse on foot. And so the British were the victors at Clonmult, from which they withdrew with two wounded prisoners, Captain P. Higgins and Volunteer J. O'Leary, and six unwounded prisoners, Volunteers P. O'Sullivan, M. Moore, O'Leary, Walsh, Harty and Garde. Commandant Hurley and his two senior officers were actually surveying the ground at Cobh Junction and making plans for the proposed train ambush when the lorries passed by on the return journey to Cork. Little did they think that that large convoy of military lorries contained all but one of the column they had left so recently in such fine fettle at Clonmult. The prisoners were tried by field general court martial and sentenced to death. The sentences on Volunteers O'Leary, Walsh, Garde and Harty were later commuted. Volunteers P. O'Sullivan and Maurice Moore were executed at Cork military barracks on 5 May 1921. Captain P. Higgins who was shot through the mouth after the surrender, had not recovered from his wound, otherwise he would have shared the fate of his executed comrades. The advent of the Truce in July, saved his life. Against the background of the deathless courage displayed by the East Cork column IRA at Clonmult, there stands out in ugly light the savagery of the British Black and Tans and the treachery of an Irishman. He, a British ex-serviceman, had been trapping rabbits at Clonmult and, noting the presence of the column, turned informer. When captured by the North Cork column he confessed to his treachery, and before execution, admitted that for his betrayal of his countrymen in arms he received the Judas-like sum of thirty pounds from the British.

An t-Óglach, the official organ of the IRA, published the following account of the battle of Clonmult in its issue of April 1921:

The Clonmult Conflict

Honour to the brave in misfortune. – Napoleon

It is possible to learn from a reverse, especially from a reverse that is not dishonourable. Such an encounter was Clonmult, near Midleton, on the twentieth of February, where a party of our troops, surprised and surrounded by superior numbers, fought to a finish. Our men were surprised by an enemy force which came up accidentally. Our column was to have moved at dusk and the men were getting ready when the enemy came up at four-fifteen p.m. In the circumstances there could not fairly be said to have been any carelessness, but it shows that only the most extreme and uncompromising vigilance gives real security. It should be a regulation in flying columns for half the column to pack at a time, the other half mounting guard. This would be particularly useful on or near main enemy routes, and would enable them to attack the enemy instead of being placed on the defensive.

Our report goes on: Each man at once rushed to his post and the enemy immediately opened fire. Our men started to sing 'The Soldier's Song' and everyone was quite cool. The extra ammunition was divided and six hand grenades distributed, our men waiting for targets all the time and doing very little firing. The thatched roof soon caught fire and our men made two sorties, the first being driven back and the second resulting in the death or capture of the garrison. Only one officer succeeded in breaking through. Our casualties were twelve killed and four wounded prisoners. We found afterwards loop-holes cut in the walls of the house, some of the dead bandaged and everything pointed to a splendid struggle against desperate odds.

The enemy numbered fifty at first, and were reinforced later. Their casualties are estimated at twelve killed and wounded, including two officers. There was an honourable and dogged defence. We can hold this up as an example – there is no comment.

As regards technical things, there are a couple of points: (a) A closer-knit machinery may have enabled the officer who broke through to assemble a local party to attack the assailants in the rear – communications, organisation, initiative are the lessons to learn (b) Tighter command within the surrounded column might have enabled the sorties to be better timed or handled perhaps. But this one can only suppose. There is no proof one way or another.

EAST CORK ROADS MINED

IMPROVISED LAND MINES sprung under lorries conveying crown forces through East Cork made the enemy wary of using the roads around Midleton prior to the Truce. Shells discharged by the British at target practice from the forts on the Cork coast were considered as having served their purpose. Fishermen collected them and used them for ballast in their boats. The IRA found another and more deadly use for them. Filled with explosives and sealed they made ideal and destructive land mines. On 10 April 1921, British troops suffered many casualties when a mine exploded under one of their lorries at Ballydekin, Churchtown, three miles from Midleton on the main Youghal road. Commandant Hurley, the officer commanding the IRA, had another of his many narrow escapes from death when retreating from the scene of the explosion.

As a reprisal for the mine incident the British 'shot up' the town of Midleton and in the early hours of the following morning they bombed the home of Volunteer Daniel Cashman, refusing the five women occupants of the house permission to leave.

Carrigshane Cross on the Youghal road, about a mile-and-a-quarter from Midleton, was the scene of a similar operation on Sunday, 3 July 1921. Many British soldiers were reported seriously wounded. As a reprisal, the enraged crown forces descended on the seaside village of Ballycotton, eight miles from the scene of the explosion, and shot two men, R. Cusack and J. Whelan, Cusack dying from his wounds.

'SHOOT AT SIGHT'

THE MASSACRE OF their comrades at Clonmult rankled in the minds of the Volunteers so that when the order to 'shoot at sight' was given on 14 May 1921, it was well and truly obeyed. In Midleton one Royal Irish Constabulary sergeant, two Tans and two Royal Marines fell mortally wounded. The IRA marched through the Main Street of the town calling on the crown forces to 'come out and fight', a challenge which was not accepted. In their own good time the British had their inevitable reprisals. Michael Aherne, Ballyrichard, Midleton; Richard Barry, Knockgriffin, Midleton, and John Ryan, Woodstock, Carrigtwohill, were taken from their homes in the early hours of the following morning by Cameron Highlanders. Later the bullet-riddled bodies of the murdered men were discovered in the district. Four nights afterwards, on Wednesday 18 May, at 2 a.m., the explosion of a land mine daringly placed beside the courthouse, which was occupied by enemy forces and adjoined the Royal Irish Constabulary barracks, heralded a prolonged 'strafe' by the IRA with the object of putting the 'wind up' the garrison. The British replied in kind and heavy fire was exchanged. The IRA withdrew when it was considered that the enemy had been sufficiently rattled.

The Volunteers of Youghal and Cork city took an active and prominent part in IRA activities in East Cork. Despite the presence of large British forces, successful ambushes of crown troops were carried out in Youghal. The explosion of a mine under a company of the Hampshire Regiment resulted in seven killed and twenty wounded. Constable Prendeville was fatally wounded when a section of Royal Irish Constabulary men were disarmed on the streets of Youghal. On different occasions Cobh company, IRA, attacked and disarmed British troops in the suburbs of the town. A party of military was disarmed while travelling by train from Cobh to Cork. In all the major operations in East Cork the Cobh company was well represented.

A SOLDIER'S DEATH

THROUGHOUT THIS RECORD of activities in East Cork the name of Commandant Diarmuid Hurley, the officer commanding the column is frequently mentioned and always for some valorous deed, some daring and resourceful exhibition of leadership, that marked him out from his fellows and made him the ideal fighting IRA officer. On his way from Midleton to Carrigtwohill, alone and on foot, he was surprised by a foot patrol of Royal Irish Constabulary and Black and Tans who suddenly appeared around a bend of the road. 'The Gaffer', as he was affectionately called, immediately made a dash for the open country. He had put a quarter mile between himself and his assailants from whom he was rapidly drawing away when the fatal bullet struck him. So died on 28 May 1921, a well-beloved and fearless leader.

His heartbroken comrades removed the remains to the house of Mr Patrick Daly, Gurteen, and later interred them temporarily in Churchtown cemetery. After the Truce full military honours were paid to the remains of the late commandant when they were re-interred in the republican plot at Midleton cemetery, beside many of his gallant comrades who are also taking their last long sleep there.

LAST LETTER OF A PATRIOT

HERE IS A copy of the last letter to his mother of Volunteer Patrick O'Sullivan, who was captured at Clonmult and executed, together with his fellow townsman, Maurice Moore, in Cork jail on 5 May, 1921.

Military Barracks, Cork,
April 27th, 1921

My Dearest Mother,
I sincerely hope and trust that God and His Blessed Virgin Mother Mary will comfort and console you and enable yourself and poor father to bear this trial with patience and to suffer all for the holy Will of God; also my loving brothers, relations and friends.

I am in great spirits and pray for the hour to come when I will be released from this world of sorrow and suffering. We must all die some day, and I am simply going by an early train. Jesus and Mary were my friends and supports in all the trials of life, and now that death is coming they are truer and better friends than ever.

You can rest assured that I will be happy in Heaven, and although I have to leave you in mourning, you will be consoled to think that I am going to meet God in Heaven and also my brothers and sister. Why should I fear to die, when death will only unite me to God in Heaven. If I could choose my own death, I would not ask to die otherwise. In fact I am delighted to have had such a glorious opportunity of gaining eternal salvation as well as serving my country. My death will help with the others, and remember that those who die for Ireland never die.

Don't let my death cause you too much unnecessary worry or grief, and then when I get to Heaven I will constantly pray to God for the kind and loving parents He gave me, to help them to bear this little Cross. Tell my loving brothers and friends that I will also remember them. Good-bye now, my dearest and best of mothers, until we meet again in Heaven with God.

Your fond and loving son,

Paddy.

TERRIBLE ORDEAL OF AN EAST CORK FAMILY

by P.J. POWER

IN THE MARTIAL law area during the Anglo-Irish war, families would retire to rest at night in terror of what the night or the dawn would bring to themselves or their neighbours. None dared be abroad after curfew so that the British might move freely on their raiding missions and find the members of every household gathered under their own roof and thus render easy identification, interrogation, arrest, or worse. This system of nightly visitation was calculated to test the morale of the bravest. In towns no one knew outside which house an approaching lorry was going to stop with screeching brakes, followed by stamping feet and grounding of rifle butts as its occupants jumped to the ground demanding admission. Loud knocks and foreign oaths would terrorise the victims of the unwelcome intrusion. Once inside the raiders spared neither sex nor age in their invasion of privacy, and fortunate was the household from which they departed without leaving cause for regret at their coming. In remote country districts these raids were infrequent but were, if anything, more terrifying because of the isolation of the homesteads and the unfamiliarity of the people with the ways and accents of the British forces.

In the townland of Currabeha, six miles east of Fermoy, the Mulcahy family retired to bed in their farmstead on the night of 22 March 1921. The list of names pinned to the back of the door in obedience to the British curfew order showed that the household consisted of William Mulcahy, father; Hannah, mother; Arthur and Denis, sons; Mary and Alice, daughters. They were peacefully asleep for some hours when the stillness of a cold, moonlit night was broken by a furious knocking at the door of their house. Jumping out of bed and hastily donning his clothes, the head of the family asked who was outside and received the dreaded answer: 'Military. Open quick.'

He opened the door and in rushed four British officers with drawn revolvers. One of them scanned the list behind the door while another rushed to the boys' bedroom and ordered them to dress. Arthur and Denis Mulcahy did as they were told and the officer left their bedroom and was heard holding a conversation with others outside the house. He returned to order Denis back to bed, saying that it was Arthur whom they wanted. By this time officers and soldiers had penetrated into the young men's bedroom and Arthur was ordered to hurry his dressing. While he was lacing his boots one soldier gruffly said: 'Your boots are all right. Come on, you dog.' Putting on his cap and overcoat the youthful prisoner left in the custody of British officers. His father, with a premonition of danger, asked: 'Arthur, have you your Rosary Beads?' and received an affirmative reply.

Arthur was escorted towards the road by a large body of military, some of whom were detached on the way to raid another house in the neighbourhood. While this was in progress John Caplis, who had also been placed under arrest in his house, heard shots, but little knew that they were being fired into the body of his neighbour, Arthur Mulcahy. Within a short distance of his home, which he had left a few minutes before, Arthur Mulcahy was riddled with British bullets and while still alive was thrown onto the bottom of a lorry. As the lorry passed through Glengoura the people heard the moans of a wounded man. Not satisfied with the effects of their bullets the British resorted to their bayonets to end the cries of pain of an Irish boy prisoner. At the spot where he was shot, his cap was found at daybreak beside a large pool of blood. The bullet-riddled body of Arthur Mulcahy was brought around during the night on the same lorry which actually stopped again near his home while the brothers Caplis, now prisoners, were being supplied with refreshments by the Mulcahy family who little thought that in an adjacent lorry lay the butchered corpse of their own kith and kin. William Mulcahy naturally enquired from the soldiers the whereabouts of his son and was informed that some of the lorries had returned to Fermoy, and perhaps he was in one of them. During the conversation the soldier was noticed casting uneasy glances towards the floor of the lorry in which he was standing.

Early next morning William Mulcahy and his daughter, Mary, went to Fermoy and were told by a prominent merchant that a party of military returned some hours before with a corpse in one of their lorries. Father and daughter went to the old military barracks and there the sad news was broken to them by the chaplain, who conducted the father to an out-house where lay the body of his twenty-two-year-old son. It had bayonet and bullet wounds back and front, mute testimony to the blood lust of British soldiery. Mary Mulcahy, who, until this stage, understood that her brother was a prisoner, received a most dreadful shock when confronted with his mangled corpse. A request by the father that the body be handed over to him was refused unless he consented to attend a military inquiry the following day. He consented and gave evidence of identification, but after that the proceedings turned into the usual farce when several of the soldiers who were at Currabeha on the fatal night came forward and swore that he was shot while attempting to escape. In the experience of the people it had long since outworn itself as an excuse for murder, but it served the British military to make a casual entry in a record book and cover up another of their dastardly deeds with the cloak of legality. When the huge funeral cortège was leaving for Tallow cemetery the Black and Tans could not refrain from making themselves objectionable and one under-sized brute with fixed bayonet charged forward to drag the tri-colour from the coffin. The bodyguard interposed themselves between him and frustrated his design. It was nothing new to Arthur Mulcahy's parents to feel the heavy hand of British misrule, for both of them had seen their parents evicted and thrown on the roadside during the land agitation. Their own greatest sorrow – the murder of their firstborn son – renewed for them the sacrifice which it seems the Irish people must make in every generation for social and political freedom.

CAMPAIGNING IN THE MITCHELSTOWN AREA

by P.J. O'B.

IT IS DIFFICULT now to recapture the atmosphere of the troubled period of the Black and Tan war in Ireland. Each parish and district has some memories, glorious or sorrowful, but time is dulling their clarity and even to those who took part in the attack and ambush, the details are rapidly becoming less clear. The tension of the period is gone. To remember details is not sufficient unless one can recall the electric atmosphere that prevailed. People were living dangerously then, none knowing what the morning might bring and growing used to such living so that ultimately it seemed quite natural. This state of acceptance had not developed suddenly. The germ of unrest had been small at first, and had grown greater day by day. Had the terrific strain come suddenly upon the people it is doubtful whether they could have stood against it, but coming gradually, it was accepted. To isolated incidents, raids for arms and baton charges, were added the rattle of shots. Shootings and more shootings, attack and ambush following each other at shorter and still shorter intervals. The dread sound of military lorries passing in the night, news of men dragged from their homes and shot, farmhouses blown up, counter-reprisal with unionist houses in flames, curfew, and troops stealing silently through the streets in rubber-soled shoes, the dreaded knock of the search-party, news of attack and the fear of drink-maddened marauders seeking reprisal, and all the while the civilian population standing stolid by under the strain. Such was the crowded period of the Black and Tan regime. To trace the course of events which led up to this state of affairs, it is necessary to turn back the pages of history to the months preceding the outbreak of the First World War.

A group of Mitchelstown men decided on forming an Irish Volunteer company in the town in 1914. They formed themselves into an organising committee and made affiliation with headquarters in Dublin. They appealed for recruits and the men of the town responded in no uncertain manner. After a time, the committee requested general headquarters to send down a drill instructor to Mitchelstown. The late Sir Roger Casement, then leader of the Volunteer movement, interested himself in the affairs of the newly recruited company, and recommended headquarters to send a drill instructor to Mitchelstown. Headquarters advised the local committee that an experienced man, Stephen Ward, would arrive in Mitchelstown by the 9.30 p.m. train on Easter Saturday 1914. A parade of the company was called for that night to meet Ward and extend an official welcome to him.

The company turned out in full strength and marched to the station, but great was the disappointment when Ward did not arrive. When Ward arrived at Mallow Junction he had to change trains and, unfortunately he entered the wrong train. He realised his mistake at Banteer station and, getting off the train there, he decided on walking to Mitchelstown that night. He reached there at 8 a.m. on Easter Sunday morning, having walked approximately thirty miles. On Easter Sunday a parade of the company was held in the Brewery Yard and Ward attended.

His first work was to have the company appoint officers, and the late Jim O'Neill was elected captain. The Mitchelstown company of the Irish Volunteers was then definitely established and, some time later, its officers decided on extending activities to the outside areas. They were assisted by Ward, and in a short time the necessary number of companies to constitute a regiment was available in the area. Ward visited those outside companies and instructed them in military matters about once a fortnight. The Mitchelstown company officers appealed to headquarters to hold a review in the town. Sir Roger Casement advised headquarters to hold a review there and decided on conducting it himself. The responsibility of organising the event rested with the officers and men of the Mitchelstown company, and right well the work was carried out by them. Sir Roger Casement was unable to attend on Sunday 29 July, 1914, to review the men of the 'Galtee Regiment', and sent down Colonel Maurice Moore (ex-senator) and Major Crosbie to deputise for him. Four thousand men paraded before Colonel Moore in the historic square of Mitchelstown on that day. He later read a message from Sir Roger Casement to the men of the 'Galtee Regiment', in the course of which special reference was made to the organising work done by the officers and men of the Mitchelstown company. Amongst the men who formed the committee, which initiated the Irish Volunteer company in Mitchelstown, were Seamus Hannigan, Jim O'Neill, Jackie Connors, Patrick Coughlan, CE, W.J. Ryan, David Walsh, Timothy Dwane, William English, Edmond Condon, Jim Condon, Mick O'Sullivan, Thomas Delarue, Christy Ryan, Jerry O'Mahony, painter, and John Burke.

In September 1914, the Mitchelstown company officers decided to procure rifles and small arms. An appeal was made to the members of the company, who could afford to purchase their own rifles, to hand in the necessary amount, and a public subscription to help the purchase of arms was opened in the town among the general public. Enough money was subscribed to purchase fifty rifles, and Captain Jim O'Neill was commissioned to go to England and negotiate the deal for the arms. Jim went across to Birmingham and succeeded in getting in touch with an arms factory there. He put the bogus case before the officials of the factory that he had a company of men who had volunteered for service in France and who were prepared to purchase their own rifles and one hundred rounds of .303 ammunition per man and go out to France under the command of their own officers. The armament firm and munitions people were only too delighted to supply the rifles and ammunition and, one evening in September, Captain O'Neill arrived by train in Mitchelstown with fifty Mark 1 Lee Enfield rifles and 5,000 rounds of .303 ammunition. The guns distributed among the company were not used in France during the years of the Great War, but were used against the British forces in Ireland in the Black and Tan war.

The Mitchelstown company was not seriously affected by the Redmondite split. On Whit Sunday, 1915, the company attended a monster parade of Irish Volunteers in Limerick city. This parade was held under most adverse circumstances, as the loyalist element in Limerick left nothing undone to prevent it. They did not succeed. Volunteer contingents from Counties Cork, Clare, Kerry, Tipperary and Limerick paraded in the Treaty city that day. Captain Monteith, GHQ, was in charge of the parade, and Éamon de Valera was in command of the Dublin contingent. The strength of the Mitchelstown company was sixty men, fifty of whom carried rifles.

The opening months of 1916 were uneventful as far as Mitchelstown was concerned. In February, Ernest Blythe re-organised the company. Jim O'Neill was again elected captain, Thomas ('Kirk') Walsh, first lieutenant, and Dan O'Keeffe, second lieutenant. On

Saint Patrick's Day, Mitchelstown company attended a Volunteer Parade in Cork city, which was confined to the Volunteer units within the county. Tomás MacCurtain was in charge of the parade.

On Good Friday 1916, the officers of the Mitchelstown company were ordered to have their men on parade at Finn's Grove, at 8 a.m. on Easter Sunday morning. They issued instructions to the men to this effect. There was an air of tension prevalent among the Volunteers during the week, and all realised that it would be no ordinary parade. The purpose of mobilising the 'Galtee battalion' was to destroy telegraphic and telephonic communications within the area, and to effect contact with the West Limerick battalion (Newcastlewest). Both battalions were to hold the railway line between Cork and Dublin, to allow the rifles to be landed in Kerry easy transit to Dublin.

On their way to the parade on Easter Sunday morning, two Volunteers, Paddy Roche and Seán Keane, were approached in Lower Cork Street by a motorist, who had just arrived in Mitchelstown. He put the following question to them – 'What Volunteers do you chaps belong to, "Irish" or "National"?' Roche answered 'Irish'. The motorist requested them then to convey him to their company captain. After consulting between themselves, they escorted him to Finn's Grove and handed him over to the local captain, Jim O'Neill. He produced his credentials, and, having satisfied Jim O'Neill with regard to his *bona fides*, handed him Eoin MacNeill's counter-order 'cancelling all Volunteer parades for that day, and until further notice'. Having done this the motorist then left for Cork.

The company officers decided, in the face of this order, to march their company to Duntryleague, Galbally, the battalion point of mobilisation. They arrived at Duntryleague about 1 p.m., having heard Mass in Anglesboro on the way. Liam Manahan, the commandant of the 'Galtee battalion', was already there and informed the Mitchelstown company officers that a conference of the battalion staff and company captains would be held immediately to decide their course of action. This conference decided to abandon their original intentions and hold battalion manoeuvres. I remember well the mock attack on Galbally village that day. I was one of the attacking force, and saw a Volunteer named Billy O'Dwyer leave the lower part of his boot in the bars of a gate when jumping off it. I think it was never decided who won this battle. I was taken prisoner by Ned O'Brien of Galbally and a party of his Volunteers.

In the evening Michael Colivet, of Limerick city, arrived in Galbally. Michael was in charge of the Limerick City Irish Volunteers. Another conference took place, and as a result of its findings every company was ordered to return to its own area, there to await further orders. Amongst the officers who took part in those conferences were: Liam Manahan, battalion O/C; Tadg Crowley, TD, battalion staff; Thomas Murphy, Ballylanders; Ned O'Brien, battalion staff; Bill Quirke, Galbally; David Walsh, battalion staff; Mick O'Sullivan, battalion staff; Jim O'Neill, Mitchelstown; Bill Howard, Anglesboro.

On Easter Monday night, news reached Mitchelstown that the rebellion had broken out in Dublin, and for the remainder of the night groups of Volunteers could be seen at various parts of the town discussing the possibilities. On Tuesday, Patrick Coughlan, CE, then in charge of operations in the Mitchelstown area, sent two Volunteers named Patrick Sullivan and Bob Noonan to Limerick. They were to try to get in touch with Colivet or some other of the leaders there. On Wednesday, Patrick Coughlan, CE, made arrangements with Fr Davy O'Connell (later Canon O'Connell) to hear the Volunteers' Confessions in Fr Davy's own house on that night. The Volunteers assembled at Seamus Hannigan's, next door to the priest's house, and went in through the back to Fr O'Connell. The last of the men making their Confession had not left Hannigan's when Patrick Sullivan arrived with a dispatch from Commandant Liam Manahan. Patrick Coughlan, CE, on reading the dispatch, ordered Patrick Sullivan, Thomas Delarue and Johnnie Condon, Ballinamona, to mobilise the company and have the men parade with rifles and ammunition as soon as possible at Bill Molan's Lios in Gurrane. The company was instructed to wait there for further orders. Patrick Coughlan set out with Mrs Seamus Hannigan in a pony and trap for Ballylanders to meet Commandant Manahan.

At three on Thursday morning of Easter Week the following were amongst the men of the Irish Volunteers company in Mitchelstown, each armed with a rifle and a hundred rounds of ammunition, who paraded in Molan's Lios in Gurrane: Jim O'Neill, Mick O'Sullivan, Patrick O'Sullivan, Tommy O'Sullivan, Paddy Clifford (Lower Cork Street), Patrick Walsh, Thomas Walsh, Dick Carroll, Bob Noonan, Davy Walsh, Dr Mick Walsh, Liam Casey, Paddy Roche, Bill Roche (King Street), David Dwane, Seán Keane, Mick Casey, Upper Cork Street; Thomas Roche (Ballybeg); Billy Coughlan, Mick Dunne (Kiltrislane); Johnny Condon (Ballinamona); William Hoare, Thomas Delarue and Bill Clancy (Upper Cork Street). They remained there until 7 a.m., and decided that as no word had arrived from battalion HQ, something had gone amiss. They returned to their homes. Raids and arrests by the British military followed, and amongst those arrested and interned in Frongoch were Seamus Hannigan, Liam Casey (King Street), Paddy Roche, Patrick O'Sullivan and Mick O'Sullivan.

In the re-organisation of the Volunteers in the winter of 1916–1917, Mitchelstown company was again to the fore. Pearse, Connolly, MacDermott and others had died that Ireland might live, and undoubtedly the resurgence which was taking place at this period proved that they had not died in vain. The revival in Mitchelstown was very noticeable. Men who, previous to Easter Week, were either hostile or apathetic to the Irish Volunteers, joined the organisation, and some of those men were amongst the best fighting material during the fight of 1920–21. In March 1918, a party of Volunteers from the Mitchelstown company travelled to Waterford to assist in fighting the by-election there. During their period in Waterford, they encountered the famous Ballybricken Pig Buyers. As a result of that encounter, two Volunteers, Christy Ryan and Mick Casey were seriously injured. Mick Casey died on board ship as he was entering New York harbour, as the result of the injuries he received that day in Waterford. Christy Ryan bears the mark of the fray to this day. Because of their activities in that by-election, the homes of the following Volunteers were raided by the Royal Irish Constabulary: Jim Dunne, Bill Roche (King Street), Bob Lewis, David Dwane, Seán Keane and Patsy Walsh. Bill Roche, David Dwane and Bob Lewis were arrested. Jim Dunne and Patsy Walsh were not at home at the time, and Seán Keane escaped from his house. When seven of the Royal Irish Constabulary were conveying Bill Roche from his house to the barracks, his brother Paddy made a daring, but futile, effort to effect his release.

During the period of the conscription threat, recruits flocked to the ranks of the Mitchelstown company. At one Volunteer parade, held in Clifford's in Gurrane, one hundred and sixty men numbered off. Another party of Mitchelstown Volunteers assisted in the general election in Waterford in December 1918. This concluded the activities of the company for that year.

Following the Soloheadbeg ambush in the spring of 1919, Seán Hogan, Dan Breen and Seán Treacy trekked across the Galtees, and arrived at Mick O'Sullivan's house in Mulberry two nights after the ambush. As Mick was wanted by the Royal Irish Constabulary at the time, he advised the three Tipperary men not to put up at his house and, on their accepting his advice, he brought them down to Christy Ryan's house in the New Square, Mitchelstown. Christy's business establishment is in one of the busiest parts of the town, and no one would ever suspect that men so badly wanted as Breen, Treacy and Hogan were beneath its roof. They remained at Christy's for the most of a week, until they had sufficiently recovered from the effects of their long tramp across the Galtees. Then Patsy Walsh conveyed them in his own horse and trap to Pat McGuire's house in Carrigturk, Ballylanders, where they remained a further period.

In May 1919, Ned O'Brien of Galbally, later a captain in the Volunteer regiment of Thomond, and Jimmy Scanlon of Galbally, were wounded in the rescue of Seán Hogan at Knocklong station. They were transferred to the Mitchelstown company area for refuge and treatment of their wounds. The Mitchelstown company was responsible for procuring billets and medical attention for the wounded men. They were housed at Will Bailey's of Ardglare, and whilst there Mrs Bailey attended to their wants and treated them as she would her own children. The Bailey's house was always open to the Volunteers from 1918 to 1921. Dr Jim Barry of Fermoy was procured to render medical aid to O'Brien and Scanlon. The Volunteers in charge of their safety and care were Mick O'Sullivan, Thomas Walsh, Patsy Walsh, Mick Corbett, Seán Keane and Seán O'Neill, Skeheen.

The year 1920 was introduced by a series of raids and arrests by the British authorities in Mitchelstown. W.J. Ryan, Seán Keane and Mick O'Sullivan were arrested and interned in Wormwood Scrubs prison, England. While there, they took part in a successful hunger strike for release. The military barracks in Mitchelstown was partially burned by the local company in May 1920. That operation was carried out under adverse circumstances, as at the time a large party of military from Kilworth camp, which is only three miles distant from Mitchelstown, regularly patrolled the town and district, accompanied by the local Royal Irish Constabulary. In spite of their vigilance, Dan O'Keeffe and his men succeeded in partially destroying the barracks. In May of that year also, a re-organisation of the company was effected. Dan O'Keeffe was appointed company captain, P.J. Luddy, first lieutenant, and Mossy Walsh, second lieutenant. Shortly afterwards P.J. Luddy was promoted to the rank of vice-O/C 4th battalion 2nd Cork brigade, and Mossy Walsh was transferred to brigade staff as secretary to General Liam Lynch. When Liam Lynch formed his active service unit, Jerry Clifford was transferred to the unit and assisted in the taking of Mallow barracks.

The IRA were waging against England, a desperate war in which capture in arms meant death. The IRA were winning their war, their ranks had grown, and the harder the fight the bigger they continued to grow. They continued to press the enemy and terror was the answer of the British; terror against the civilian population. The soldiers were beginning to shoot on every occasion that offered, and they shot to kill. Such a shooting took place at Coracunna crossroads about one mile from the town of Mitchelstown. The boys and girls of the country had gathered there for the customary crossroads dance one evening in July 1920. They were grouped at the cross, chatting, when they heard the sound of a lorry approaching from the direction of Cahir. They paid no attention, for at that period danger was not expected from a passing lorry. As the lorry swept past the crossroads, the occupants having sighted the group, opened fire and continued firing. The lorry pulled up a little distance beyond the cross and the soldiers, jumping out, lined the hedge, firing in the direction in which the people had run for shelter. After a short while the firing ceased and the soldiers drove away.

At the first shots the boys and girls rushed for cover and lay close against the ground until the firing ceased and the lorry had driven off, when they rose and reassembled. Two of them, however, did not rise. The aim of the soldiers had been only too accurate, and two men, McDonnell and McGrath, were dead on the road, their bodies close together. They had evidently been struck by the first volley, as their bodies were found on the road. They were taken to a nearby house. An inquest was subsequently held, at which the military attended. The soldiers swore that they were fired on and they only acted in self-defence. Such was impossible, as there was not an armed man amongst the crowd on that night, and the gathering was solely for amusement. Despite the fixed bayonets of the soldiers designed to overawe the jury, a verdict of murder against the military was returned. McGrath and McDonnell were buried with full military honours, and two simple crosses now mark the spot where they fell.

A state of war was rapidly being established, and Kildorrery village was the next scene of bloodshed in the area. The Royal Irish Constabulary in the barracks there were most active, and their vigilant patrolling of the countryside was a menace to the East Limerick column then in the locality and was a source of great annoyance to the inhabitants. Early in August 1920, it was planned to ambush the patrol on its way from Kildorrery to Rockmills, about three miles distant. A number of IRA men took up positions for the attack, but word of the intended ambush was conveyed to the patrol, which immediately returned to barracks and telegraphed Fermoy for military assistance. The attacking party, having learned of this development in good time, the ambush positions were evacuated.

On 4 August new positions were occupied by the East Limerick column, as close to Kildorrery barracks as two or three hundred yards. The column was reinforced by local men from the neighbourhood of Ballindangan and Glanworth, and the IRA had with them Miss O'Sullivan, a trained nurse, who had accompanied the column from County Limerick. She immediately proceeded to fix up an improvised hospital in the cottage of an old couple named Collins, both of whom were eighty-five years of age. When the IRA arrived Mrs Collins was preparing tea for her husband, who was then still in bed, until having learned what was about to take place old Collins jumped out, cheered for joy, and ordered his wife to seek protection in a neighbouring house, as this was then no place for women. He stoutly refused to leave himself, saying that he was glad of the opportunity to be present during an attack on the enemy. The IRA knew from previous engagements that the British would not hesitate to seek protection amongst the aged and infirm, so old Mr Collins was compelled to remain behind the barred doors of his own house whilst the fight was on.

During the hours of patient waiting for the enemy a farmer and his workers were engaged hay-making in the field inside which the IRA had taken up their positions. On the request of the column officer they continued about their work as though nothing unusual had taken place. Eventually, the Black and Tans appeared in the village street, trailing in the gutter behind them a tri-colour flag. They were in and out of their barracks a good deal before ultimately proceeding in the direction of Rockmills. In a few minutes the column leader's whistle heralded the moment for action and the British were called upon to surrender. Although surrounded, the police took up positions on both sides of the road and engaged the IRA. A brisk encounter followed but it was of short duration, and when the British surrendered six Black and Tans had been wounded, two of them fatally. Old Mr Collins who had cheered in his house whilst the fight was in progress was now allowed out to view the scene. The IRA nurse attended to the wounded for whose comfort everything possible was done. Two old Royal Irish Constabulary men, who were amongst the police party, were held as prisoners and placed temporarily in a labourer's cottage, having been warned not to attempt to leave for a specified time, as their knowledge of the country would be a great asset in the event of possible pursuit of the column by the British. Some months afterwards Black and Tans from Kildorrery murdered an unfortunate man named O'Donnell, in the cottage in which the police had been held prisoners.

The ambush at Kildorrery had been carried out within reach of large forces of the British, of whom thousands were stationed in nearby Kilworth camp, Mitchelstown, Buttevant, Fermoy and Ballyvonaire. The column armament having been increased by six rifles and two hundred and eighty rounds of ammunition, the men moved off in a direction between Shanballymore and Castletownroche. They had a difficult passage as rain fell in torrents and they were wet through when they reached Annesgrove, where they narrowly escaped a British detachment five times their strength. They spent that night in the neighbourhood of Ballyveelick and Shinakilla, and having evaded the enemy who scoured the countryside in large numbers on the following day, they marched across the hills, by-passing the British camp at Ballyvonaire, and ultimately arriving in Glenrue, County Limerick, where they were warmly received by Fr Bob Ambrose, PP, of Land League fame.

MITCHELSTOWN MEN IN BATTALION FLYING COLUMN

WHEN THE BRIGADE staff decided to form a battalion flying squad in October 1920, Jerry Clifford, James O'Mahony, BA, H.Dip, and

Paddy Joe Luddy, from the Mitchelstown company, were amongst those who volunteered for service in the column of the IRA.

By that time the Royal Irish Constabulary had been given the name of Black and Tans, owing to their ranks being reinforced by ex-soldiers so rapidly that there were not enough uniforms available for them, and they were dressed in khaki trousers with the black uniform coat of the Royal Irish Constabulary. There were soon a number of Black and Tans in Kildorrery, and they kept the civilian population in a state of constant terror, shooting, raiding and arresting. In the month of November 1920, a party from the barracks set out raiding. That night a young man named O'Donnell had gone to a cottage outside the village to sleep, as his own home was being constantly raided. The party visited the cottage, and finding O'Donnell there, shot him dead. Such shootings were becoming matter-of-fact and there was no danger that the murderers would be brought to justice. The stock excuse was that the unfortunate victim either attempted to escape or to attack, and the British authorities turned a blind eye towards such occurrences.

An inquest was held on O'Donnell, and a lorry and private car of military attended at Kildorrery from Fermoy. This party passed through Glanworth village on their way to Kildorrery, and word of the movement was conveyed to the IRA column. It was decided to ambush the party on its return journey. The column moved up around the village of Glanworth and decided to attack the lorry about a mile from the village at Labbacally, where there is a very steep hill. There was no opportunity to block the road and the column had barely time to get into position when the lights of the approaching lorry were seen. The attackers lined the ditch at one side of the road near the crest of the hill and waited. Up the hill came the lorry, its head-lamps lighting up the roadway. Bombs were thrown and bullets rained into the lorry, which swayed, slowed down, almost stopped, and then moved steadily on, its occupants blazing back at the ambushers. Up through the position forged the lorry, attackers and attacked firing steadily until the British drawing clear of the danger position, reached the summit of the hill, and swept on towards Fermoy, its occupants all the while blazing back at the IRA position.

The car, which had been following the lorry, stopped at the foot of the hill, and was abandoned by the British who set out across the fields for Fermoy. Two rifles were found on the road, evidently having fallen from the hands of the wounded or killed in the lorry. It was afterwards learned that the driver of the lorry was twice wounded but gallantly clung to the wheel and brought his charge safely through. Had he failed every one of the British would either have been killed or captured. The IRA withdrew from their position, but remained in the vicinity of Glanworth for some time, expecting the arrival of military from Fermoy. These did not come and the column ultimately withdrew.

The British were pouring troops into the country, and searches and raids were daily events. Only the strictest vigilance enabled the IRA columns to evade capture, yet they continued to maintain pressure on the British. An ambush was planned to take place at Glenacurrane, about three miles from Mitchelstown, in the month of December 1920. The original date fixed for the ambush was changed later and the Cork column which had moved up for the attack withdrew from the neighbourhood. A day after it had left, a party of military from Mitchelstown set out on foot and thoroughly searched the ambush position, which was at that time partly wooded.

On 17 December, the re-arranged date, the Cork and Limerick columns were lying in position at Glenacurrane shortly after dawn. The road to this spot runs through a glen or cutting in the hills, and the land rises sharply on either side. To the west the rise is sheer, but to the east there is a gentle slope and an excellent view of the road is obtained from the summit on this side. The IRA had selected this as their position. The day was cold and there was a considerable amount of frost. Outposts were widely flung and traffic towards Mitchelstown was diverted to a side road.

The object of attack was a large military convoy which frequently passed that way. Shortly after noon a fast Lancia lorry, accompanied by a touring car, approached from the direction of Tipperary, moving towards Fermoy. These were allowed to pass through unharmed, and the wait for the convoy continued. Evening was approaching with yet no sight of the convoy. Hope of a fight was fading when the Lancia lorry and car were seen returning from the direction of Mitchelstown. It was decided to attack and a tree was thrown across the road as the men got ready. The lorry and car dashed up to the tree and were immediately called on to surrender. For answer they opened fire, and an ensuing volley blazed down from the IRA position. The soldiers jumped from the lorry, seeking desperately for cover and firing towards the top of the rising ground. Bullets rained upon them from the summit; a machine-gun mounted by the IRA stuttered a burst of firing and the fight was over. The military raised their hands in token of surrender; the IRA ceased firing and silence settled upon the glen. Two soldiers were dead in the lorry and others wounded lay on the ground. The wounded immediately received attention, whilst the British rifles, ammunition and a case of bombs were taken by the IRA, who then retired, leaving the lorry in flames. Amongst mails taken from the lorry, were two medals which had been awarded a British officer and sergeant for 'Gallantry in Ireland'. These medals are still in the possession of men who took part in the attack.

After the fight there was hard marching for the IRA through

the bitter December night, and fear and anxiety for the civilians in Mitchelstown, which, however, escaped damage. The ambushed party were members of a regiment stationed in Tipperary, and it was on that town that reprisal was taken. When news of the ambush became known, the troops stationed there broke out of barracks, burned two houses and looted a number of shops. The only damage done in the Mitchelstown area was the burning of some hay, the property of a wanted IRA man. This was done by a patrol of the Royal Irish Constabulary.

The jails and internment camps were now being rapidly filled, as raids and arrests became more numerous. The British soon made their reprisals official, as part of a planned campaign of frightfulness. Houses of known republicans were visited by military, their occupants ordered out, mines laid and the houses blown up. Around Glanworth and Kildorrery, numbers of farmhouses were treated in this way. The IRA retaliated by burning the houses of known loyalists, and the British eased off their campaign.

In February the IRA column was again active. Some Lancers had been fired upon and the column took up position on a hill at Kilbrack, near Doneraile, to await a military search of the vicinity of the shooting. The column lined a ditch by the roadside and soon, in the dusk, a lorry came hastening to the scene. The intention of the IRA was to bomb the driver in the hope of ditching the lorry. The bomb was thrown when the lorry entered the ambush position, and at the same time fire was opened. The bomb struck the driver on the shoulder and fell back on the road, where it exploded harmlessly, and the lorry drove through the position under severe fire. It continued about two or three hundred yards past the ambush position and then came to a stop.

A machine-gun was immediately turned on the IRA position and its fire swept the ditch. The fire was hotly returned, but the position became untenable. Retreat while the machine-gun continued firing was out of the question, as its field of fire covered every possible line of escape. Further British reinforcements might at any moment arrive and hem in the small column. The leader decided that the gun must be silenced at all costs. Word was sent down the line and five men dropped out. Led by the column O/C, these five succeeded in making their way towards the flank of the position occupied by the machine-gun. There they gained a ditch near a labourer's cottage, from which point they had a view of the machine-gun, then maintaining rapid fire on the column's position. Word was given to cover the gun and the little party opened fire on the machine-gun, which was silenced. These new aggressive tactics compelled the military to change position. The moment the gun ceased firing the column retreated, as it was previously instructed.

The flanking party set out to retreat, having extricated the main body from its dangerous position. The machine-gun and rifles of the military were again in action, seeking the new position and the retreating five found themselves under heavy fire. Bullets cut the bushes and ploughed into the earth around them, but they came safely through. They eventually rejoined the column and a long march brought them to safety, though the district was immediately flooded with troops. Shortly after this engagement the column attacked Castletownroche and Kildorrery barracks, both of which attacks were unsuccessful owing to the defences of the barracks being considerably strengthened.

The British started the 'round-up' system at this stage and Mitchelstown district soon experienced these methods. During the night lorry after lorry would deposit troops at various points. These troops, drawn from different barracks and camps, would encircle a huge tract of country. Shortly after dawn the troops would close in, bringing with them every able-bodied man in the enclosed area. Clearing stations were established at various points and to those the troops would bring the men where they would be looked over by the Royal Irish Constabulary, and any wanted men picked out. Though a large area was included in the first round-up in the Mitchelstown district, only one wanted man was captured. Cavalry was used in the second round-up, which took place some time later over a different and larger stretch of country. In this round-up a South Tipperary column was nearly trapped, barely getting out of the net before it closed. Only a ditch separated the line of round-up from where the Tipperary column had thrown themselves into cover. It was soon noted that a column caught in such an encircling movement had no chance of escape. Many columns were disbanded and small parties sent to different areas.

On the evening of 23 April 1921, two Volunteers were cycling from Mitchelstown to Ballygiblin, about three miles distant. They had been mobilised to take part in the destruction of a bridge. Both men were armed with small revolvers of .38 calibre. At a turn on the road they ran into a British patrol, consisting of two armoured cars and an armoured lorry. This patrol had pulled up to pursue other members of the IRA who had been on the road and who had escaped across the fields on the approach of the military. The two Volunteers, Patrick Clifford and Michael O'Sullivan, cycled right into the patrol, under the guns of the armoured cars. They had no option but to submit to a search. The arms were found on them and they were immediately conveyed to Mitchelstown police barracks. A further search was carried out there, and a dispatch was found on Clifford notifying him to parade his section at Ballygiblin church that night.

Immediately that this dispatch was found the military sent armoured cars, lorries and cycling patrols to encircle Ballygiblin church. There was over eighty men, mostly unarmed, on parade at

Ballygiblin. The main body was drawn up near the church and a guard had been thrown out. The guard observed the lights of the lorries and immediately conveyed word to the Volunteers who took to the fields. They were not a moment too soon, as the lights of the lorries caught the last men to leave the road. Nobody was observed by the military, however, and the men managed to get across the fields and to elude the cycling patrols in the darkness.

Clifford and O'Sullivan were conveyed to Fermoy barracks and later to Cork, where they were tried by court martial. Both were sentenced to death, but a *habeas corpus* motion was immediately started in the High Court and the execution postponed. The fight for their lives finally went to the House of Lords. The result was not known until after the Truce, but the legal battle waged was responsible for saving their lives. Their graves had been dug, and after the Truce they had the pleasure of learning that they had been filled in again. Clifford and O'Sullivan were released at the general release of prisoners.

EAST LIMERICK COLUMN

A SHORT WHILE after the arrest of Clifford and O'Sullivan, the East Limerick column, which had come up to Knockanevin, received a severe blow. The townland of Knockanevin is in Cork county, but was part of the area covered by the operations of the East Limerick column. One Sunday evening a number of men of the column were gathered on the road which runs along the side of a steep slope. They were careless in their look-out, expecting no military movements. Two lorries containing military from Mitchelstown and travelling from the direction of Kilfinnane approached at rapid pace. The officer in charge of the military, taking in the situation at a glance, ordered fire to be opened. A heavy burst of shooting sent the IRA looking for cover, and taking advantage of this situation the lorries drove up as close as possible to the column, the troops maintaining rapid fire, jumping out and taking up whatever cover offered. The IRA ran up the hill seeking cover. A group of them turned to fight, but the military pressing home their advantage, poured volley after volley into them, advancing all the time. The IRA broke back up the hill leaving one man, Casey, a prisoner, and two others dead. The military quickly threw the dead into a lorry and set out for Mitchelstown. The remainder of the column rallied immediately and raced back to the attack, to find the military had gone.

Casey was taken to Cork in the same lorry as Clifford and O'Sullivan. He was immediately tried by court martial, and being caught in arms against the British, was sentenced to death. The execution was carried out immediately. A monument now marks the spot on Knockanevin where these men lost their lives. It is not far distant from the cross that stands where O'Neill Crowley was shot down by the British in 1867.

During the months of May and June isolated attacks took place and the British were constantly sniped. A party of military coming by train from Fermoy to Mitchelstown was attacked near Ballykinley bridge. Heavy fire was opened on the train and the military replied. The train pulled up some distance beyond the position taken up by the IRA and the military dashed out. As the number of troops was ten times larger than the attacking party, the IRA had to withdraw.

In the month of July the column reformed and moved around Mitchelstown seeking a chance to strike the British. Sniping posts were set up throughout the area, but the British were moving with greater caution and seldom left their barracks except in large bodies. Lorries travelled as seldom as possible and were invariably protected by armoured cars. The column operated under great difficulty round Mitchelstown, as the flat territory of the district offered no cover. Also, the town was occupied by a large body of military and a strong force of Black and Tans, in addition to which were large contingents of military stationed at Kilworth nearby. A military patrol consisting of about ten men regularly proceeded from Mitchelstown military barracks to the fountain, escorting a water wagon. The fountain is situated at the end of the town, some distance from both the military and Black and Tan barracks. It was resolved to attack this patrol as no other chance of an ambush offered, although the column had occupied various positions for about a fortnight.

Plans were laid for the attack. Before dawn on the morning fixed for the attack three men of the column were placed in a position commanding the military barracks, and three others took up a position in front of the Black and Tan barracks. It was the task of these two parties to delay the military and police long enough after the attack to enable the column to get clear of the flat country which is overlooked from Mulberry on the outskirts of the town. The remainder of the column consisting of nine or ten men armed with rifles and shotguns moved into Mitchelstown Creamery where they remained concealed in one of the stores. Four or five men armed with small revolvers had instructions to stay on the street and get as close as possible to any parties of military that remained up the street. From dawn the column in the creamery awaited the coming of the military. The usual milk supplies were handled and had been completed by the time the military came. When the military arrived the column split into two parties and opening both gates of the creamery they appeared on the streets calling on the military to surrender. The soldiers grasped their rifles and the IRA fired. Shots rang out from all sides. Soldiers who had been on the opposite side of the street took cover behind a low wall.

Bullets were flying from all sides. The men armed with the revolvers had been unable to get close enough to the soldiers and the soldiers under cover of the low wall poured volley after volley towards the IRA men. Three or four soldiers were lying on the ground before the military broke and fled towards their barracks. Two rifles were captured, and the column, with two wounded members, retired into the creamery. Getting over the wall at the back they started their retreat at the double, bringing their two wounded comrades with them.

At the first outbreak of shots the parties covering the barracks had opened fire, and kept up a constant fusillade to detain the military and police from being too quickly on the track of the retreating column. The military and police immediately returned the fire and the clatter of machine-guns rang out. Having held the British for a period considered long enough, both parties got quickly away. The military continued firing as they advanced out of their barracks. Armoured cars came speeding from Kilworth camp and raced into the country beyond Mitchelstown. Patrols set out on foot through the fields, but the IRA column had gone beyond their reach. Three civilians were severely wounded by military fire following the attack, one of them losing a leg.

The Truce came shortly afterwards and the country drew a breath of relief. The Treaty followed, and then the dark days of the Civil War. Then men of the column were off for the wars again and many of them did not return. When peace finally came, others were in want and were compelled to emigrate. Still, there is a bond of comradeship between those who fought together, no matter where they may be scattered now, and all will ever remember the men who died.

The following were amongst the men from the Mitchelstown company who served with the brigade active service unit and battalion flying column company during the Tan period: Mossy Walsh, Jimmy Walsh, Billy Gallaghue, Seamus O'Mahony, BA, H.Dip., Tim Fay, P.J. Luddy, Terry Clifford, Seán Keane, John O'Neill, Mick O'Sullivan, Paddy Clifford, W.J. Ryan.

CUMANN NA MBAN IN REBEL CORK

by P.L.

As THE ARMY of the republic continued to defeat the power of the British King's writ throughout the land there grew up, side by side with the military force functioning in the field, an organised body of patriotic Irishwomen without whose aid the success of the whole campaign might well have been doomed to failure. This organisation was known as Cumann na mBan and the help that its fearless members gave to the national cause under the most trying circumstances will long be remembered by all who participated in the fight. The activities of Cumann na mBan embraced the collection of intelligence data among enemy sympathisers, often inside the very ranks of the crown forces; the carrying of dispatches; the nursing in secret of wounded republican soldiers; the collection of funds to help the prosecution of the national effort; the provision of food, clothing, tobacco and other necessaries for the men on the run, and generally the organising of support and encouragement throughout the countryside and in the towns for all engaged in physical resistance against the crown.

Nowhere was Cumann na mBan more active or more effective than in the county and city of Cork where the young women were early behind the national forces and continued to render invaluable assistance as the fight grew in intensity. It would be impossible in anything but a large volume to cover the varied activities of these intrepid women even in one county. We must content ourselves here with a few brief references.

In the month of August 1920, a British aeroplane made a forced landing at Drominagh, near Clonbanin, and over it was placed an armed guard pending its repair or removal. The members of the Kanturk company, however, were quick to see that an attack on this plane and its guard would be a demoralising blow against the enemy, and plans were laid accordingly. The story of the success of the 'aeroplane ambush' as it came to be known has already been told elsewhere; also the murder of Connell and Clancy by the British machine-gun detachment, then stationed at Kanturk, as a reprisal for the aeroplane raid. Instrumental in conveying the intelligence reports of the enemy guard over the aeroplane was one of the most active members of Cumann na mBan in North Cork, Miss Nora Horgan of Drominagh, who, throughout the whole period of the struggle, rendered constant service of a similar nature. Others who were very active in that area during the period were Miss Katty Murphy of Kanturk and her sisters, Annie and Abina. Miss Alice Hayes, Miss Katty Moylan, Miss Nell Keating, Miss Annie Smith and Miss Molly O'Sullivan, all of Kanturk. These ladies, with the late Miss Ciss Courtney of Kanturk, were occupied throughout the fight as intelligence agents, dispatch carriers and in other forms of assistance.

Before and after the well-known Ballydrohane ambush their services were constantly at the disposal of the men of the fighting columns. In the Millstreet area Miss Eileen O'Leary of Cullen; Miss Biddy Bradley of Knockgurrane; Miss Madge O'Kelly of Ploverfield; Miss Elsie Andrae of Main Street, Millstreet; Miss

Bridget O'Riordan of the Corner House, Millstreet; Miss Nan Fitzgerald of Cloghoola; Miss Margaret Finegan of Lacknadotia; Miss Ellie Buckley of Aubane; Miss Nora O'Sullivan of Glenbeigh, Kilcorney; Miss Teresa O'Sullivan of Laharn; Miss Mary Fitzgerald of Gurraneduff; Miss Katty O'Sullivan of Rathduane, and Miss Ellie O'Leary of Milleen, were only a few of the many who were active.

In the Kiskeam and Newmarket areas, where many telling encounters with the enemy took place, Miss Nancy Murphy of Kiskeam, Miss Mamie Moylan of Newmarket and her sister, Greta, were constantly engaged in hazardous work. In Banteer and Nadd, women like Miss Bebe Mulchinock and Miss Ina Nagle rendered great assistance. Others who were constantly working and organising were Miss Nell Cronin of Ballyrushen, Kanturk; the Misses McAuliffe of Kilbrin; Miss Mem O'Brien and Miss Alice Canty of Liscarroll; Miss Molly Callaghan of Drominagh; Miss Nell Geary of Charleville; Miss Annie Callaghan of Drominagh and Miss Molly Smith of Charleville.

In Mallow, the centre of much of the enemy activity, the services of Cumann na mBan were, as elsewhere, invaluable to the cause. Lying as it did at the crossroads of the south and surrounded by the large garrison centres of Buttevant, Fermoy, Ballyvonaire and Kilworth, it provided many opportunities for the work of the keen women who were active as intelligence agents for the IRA.

Women like Miss Lil Jones, Miss May Hegarty, the Misses Julia and Nora Greaney, Miss Dolly Hayes, Miss Chris O'Connell, Miss Lizzie Willis, Miss Kitty Byrnes, Miss Josephine Daly, Miss Madge Daly, Miss Julia Callaghan, Miss Siobhán Gregan, Miss Noreen Creen, Mrs A. Barton and the Misses Polly and Atty Cunningham were all at work on missions of different kinds.

In Cork city there were the late Miss Mary MacSwiney, Miss

Nora O'Brien, Miss May Daly, Mrs Seán Hegarty, Miss Eileen Beery to mention only a few.

National organiser of Cumann na mBan was Miss Leslie Price, now Mrs Tom Barry, who toured the country from her headquarters in Dublin, moulding the movement into an effective auxiliary to the armed forces.

Almost everywhere the enemy went he encountered (unknown to him) the members of that dauntless body of women. In tobacconists and newsagents' shops, in hotel bars, in dining-rooms and in railway carriages, and even on his own telephone exchanges, his conversation was listened to, sifted, emulated and passed on. His movements were noted and reported, as were his numbers, arms and equipment.

Cycling along bad roads on rain-lashed nights or walking across mountain paths, the women of Cumann na mBan carried the important dispatches of the IRA. In their homes and in the homes of others they nursed and fed the men of the columns before and after engagements. Evading the enemy in the streets of town and city and outwitting his agents with many a ready ruse, it is only fair to say that they worked as an unseen army without glory or reward.

Index